Negro Poetry and Drama

AND

The Negro in American Fiction

Negro Poetry and Drama

AND

The Negro in American Fiction

STERLING BROWN

with a new preface by Robert Bone

STUDIES IN AMERICAN NEGRO LIFE
August Meier, General Editor

ATHENEUM 1972 New York

PUBLISHED BY ATHENEUM
COPYRIGHT 1937 BY THE ASSOCIATES IN NEGRO FOLK EDUCATION
PREFACE COPYRIGHT © 1968 BY ROBERT BONE
ALL RIGHTS RESERVED
LIBRARY OF CONGRESS CATALOG CARD NUMBER 69-15521
MANUFACTURED IN THE UNITED STATES OF AMERICA BY
HALLIDAY LITHOGRAPH CORPORATION
WEST HANOVER, MASSACHUSETTS
PUBLISHED IN CANADA BY MC CLELLAND & STEWART LTD.
FIRST ATHENEUM PRINTING JANUARY 1969
SECOND PRINTING NOVEMBER 1969
THIRD PRINTING OCTOBER 1972

PREFACE TO THE ATHENEUM EDITION

by Robert Bone

In one of his favorite anecdotes, Sterling Brown tells
the story of T. D. "Jim-Crow" Rice, a white minstrel of
the 1830's. One of his routines consisted of a shuffling
clog dance, in which he impersonated a Negro hostler.
"Legend has it that when he appeared in the sketch on
a Cincinnati stage he was insistently encored, until a
small voice from the wings whimpered, 'Gimme back
mah clothes.' "

That small voice, behind and beyond the joke, is the
authentic voice of the Negro critic Sterling Brown. To a
culture with a chronic itch to impersonate the Negro, he
has been saying for nearly forty years: Give us back our
clothes! Restore to us the meaning of our own experience! For our lives have been robbed of their significance
by malicious portrayals and slanderous misrepresenta-
tions called stereotypes. And not only on the minstrel
stage, but in fiction, poetry, and drama; in cinema, radio,
and advertising; wherever false images of us have been
projected by a hostile white society.

To grasp the thrust and direction of Sterling Brown's
career, it is essential to place it in a proper historical
perspective. *The Negro in American Fiction* and *Negro
Poetry and Drama* were published in 1937. At that time
Richard Wright was known, if at all, as the author of a
handful of poems and stories. Ralph Ellison had published not a word. James Baldwin and Lorraine Hans-
berry were schoolchildren, while LeRoi Jones was a boy
of three. The future of Negro literature, in short, remained to be invented.

To be sure, the 1920's had witnessed a flurry of activity known as the Negro Renaissance. But the depression had brought a premature end to many of these promising careers. In retrospect, it was clear that the white writers of the jazz age had once again usurped the Negro's clothes. Eugene O'Neill and DuBose Heyward, Sherwood Anderson and Carl Van Vechten, Marc Connelly and Roark Bradford had succeeded in tapping a vein of folk material that by rights belonged to the black writer. In so doing they unleashed an avalanche of stereotypes that threatened to entomb the real McCoy.

These stereotypes were inspired by a movement in the modern arts known as primitivism, which celebrated the exotic, the atavistic, and the sexually uninhibited. While not perhaps as denigrating as the stereotypes of a more benighted age, they represented nonetheless a serious distortion of Negro life. To reclaim his own experience from the white man's falsifications thus became the black writer's most imperative concern. These false images had to be discredited before a more authentic portrait could be drawn. It was Sterling Brown, in the works that you are about to read, who undertook the necessary labor of destruction.

These are not, by modern critical standards, penetrating essays. Rather they are comprehensive surveys in the field of iconography, tracing through American fiction, poetry, and drama the changing image of the Negro. Their real focus is the sociology of literature, the politics of culture. They are concerned with the uses and abuses of the image-making function in society. In a thoroughgoing and conclusive study, Sterling Brown demonstrates that the American literary imagination has been obsessed with the figure of the Negro, and that with honorable exceptions our literary heritage is racist to the core.

The first consequence of Sterling Brown's approach is a narrow and self-limiting esthetic. What he looks for above all in a literary work is the realistic portrayal of Negro character. But realism, however useful as a corrective to the white man's stereotypes, cannot finally cope with the ambiguities of Negro life. The second and happier consequence is a firm commitment to Negro folk material. For it is this material that is most vulnerable to raids and depredations by the whites. To guard and cherish and interpret his own folk tradition thus became the cornerstone of Brown's career.

As poet, for example, and author of *Southern Road* (1932), his work was chiefly an attempt at folk portraiture. As anthologist, and co-editor of *The Negro Caravan* (1941), his effort was to make available a rich selection of spirituals, blues, work songs, ballads, and folk tales. As critic, he has written widely and persuasively of folk materials, and as teacher, he has inspired generations of Negro students with a love and acceptance of their folk origins. And simply as a man, through his not inconsiderable gift as anecdotist and raconteur, humorist and mime, jazz buff and blues collector, he has borne a kind of living witness to his folk tradition.

Nor was this the customary outlook for a man of his complexion and social class. Sterling Brown was born in 1901 in the city of Washington, a child of the misnamed black bourgeoisie. Educated at Williams College and Harvard University, he had every opportunity to repudiate his Negro heritage, as so many members of the Negro middle class had done. During much of his tenure at Howard University, the concept of a black culture would have been greeted with derisive laughter. But Brown transcended the provincialism of his social class, persisted in his search for roots, and discovered in the Negro folk the sources of his own identity.

He also transcended black chauvinism in all its forms. A race man to the marrow of his bones, he was never a race patriot. Sterling Brown has always been an integrationist; all his work is based on the assumption that the mainstream is the place to swim. He has never confused, in his own superb phrase, a racial bunt with an Aryan homer. Rather he writes with honesty and balance: "It is not at all advanced that the contemporary poetry of the American Negro is to be ranked with the best of modern poetry." With such candor he earns our trust, displaying those qualities of fairness and objectivity that are the basis of humanistic learning.

Sterling Brown belongs to a generation of Negro literary scholars who must not be forgotten by the young. Together with such men as Alain Locke and Saunders Redding, he has been a faithful steward of the Negro literary past. Without such books as Locke's *The New Negro,* Brown's *The Negro in American Fiction,* and Redding's *To Make a Poet Black,* the continuity of the black man's literary heritage would not have been preserved. This generation of scholars kept the faith when blackness was unfashionable, and on their pioneering efforts all future scholarship in the field of Afro-American studies will be compelled to build.

Teachers College,
Columbia University

October, 1968

Negro Poetry and Drama

EDITORIAL FOREWORD

The author of this study of *Negro Poetry and Drama* is himself a poet of distinction and a successful dramatic director of the Howard Players in addition to his seasoned academic acquaintance with these fields as a college teacher of literature. Sterling A. Brown, now associate professor of English at Howard University, was born and educated in Washington, D. C., was graduated from Williams College in 1922 with Phi Beta Kappa honors and the Clark Fellowship to Harvard, received his master's degree at Harvard in 1923, and has since pursued graduate work in English literature at Harvard University. He has had wide experience teaching at Virginia Seminary and College, Lynchburg, 1923-26, at Lincoln University, Mo., 1926-28; Fisk University, 1928-29; and at Howard University from 1929 to date. His volume of verse, *Southern Road,* published in 1932, put him in the advance-guard of younger Negro poets and, as well, the then new school of American regionalist literature. In 1937, Professor Brown was awarded a Guggenheim Fellowship for creative writing and will, among other things, complete for publication his second volume of verse,—*"No Hiding Place."* Since 1936, he has been directing editor on Negro materials of the Federal Writer's Project at Washington headquarters. For the last five years, his literary book review comments in *Opportunity* under the caption:—*"The Literary Scene: Chronicle and Comment"* have revealed a critical talent of sane but progressive and unacademic tendencies,—a point of view that the reader will find characteristically carried through in this provocative survey of the Negro theme in American poetry and drama and critical commentary on the Negro's share in that creative expression.

Alain Locke.

CONTENTS

INTRODUCTORY

This Bronze Booklet aims at a survey of the Negro in American poetry and drama, both as author and character. In recent years, the emergence of the Negro into the cultural life of America has been noteworthy. Until discoveries by Arthur Schomburg, of the New York Public Library, and books by Vernon Loggins and Benjamin Brawley, the long career of the Negro author was not well known. Early historical figures such as Jupiter Hammon and Phillis Wheatley were known to interested research students, but between them and Paul Laurence Dunbar there was supposed to be a waste land with the possible exception of Frederick Douglass' oratory. Carefully considered, however, the career of the Negro author is seen to have no great gaps, but to be continuous, with one period of writing evolving from, and frequently reacting against the preceding period.

The plan of our survey is to cover in the first chapter the poets of eighteenth and nineteenth century America. Of the poets discussed, only one, Alberry Whitman, is post-Civil War, and his subject matter, aims and attainments seem closer to his antebellum fellows than to Dunbar. The second chapter is devoted to the rich field of folk-poetry. Chronology is violated here, in that the creation of spirituals certainly antedated Hammon, and the last examples of folk-poetry cited are of our own day. It was thought best, however, to group all the varieties of folk-poetry together. And coming as it does, between the self-conscious early poets and the writers of dialect, the chapter serves as contrast; first, to the extremely "literary" predecessors, and second, to the dialect writers who, while professing folk interpretation, wandered a far way from the true folk.

1

Of the third and fourth chapters Dunbar is the key poet, since he was not only the founder of the traditional dialect school, but certainly in his standard English poems the chief exponent of the minor romantic tendencies so favored by succeeding Negro poets. The fifth chapter is devoted to contemporary Negro poets, sometimes called the New Negro school. The sixth and seventh chapters deal with poetry of Negro life and character written by white poets. Since one of our purposes is to show how attitudes to Negro life have developed in American thinking, it is very important that this body of poetry, frequently by leading white poets, be reviewed. From the minstrel song-composers to Vachel Lindsay and DuBose Heyward, the influence of these writers upon the American public and even upon Negro poets has been great.

In drama, on the other hand, the Negro has been more important as created character than as creative playwright. Reasons for this will appear in the course of our discussion. We shall trace the Negro character from the earliest subsidiary roles in American drama to the present major ones. The grouping of the plays of over a century into one chapter, whereas two chapters are devoted to contemporary drama, is not merely the familiar practice of ignoring American drama before Eugene O'Neill, but is due to the recent rapid growth of interest in and intelligent comprehension of the Negro, so indicative of a great change in the social attitudes of American drama.

Again, it has been thought wisest to handle contemporary folk drama in one chapter, and realistic and problem drama in another, rather than to try to hew to the strictly chronological line. Thus Eugene O'Neill is discussed after Paul Green, although O'Neill's plays about Negroes belong to his past and Paul Green's Negro plays are recent. The chapter on the realistic and problem drama seems to be the logical conclusion, since the present trend is toward plays of social protest. It is obvious, however, that overlappings occur. Green's *In Abraham's Bosom* and *White Dresses* certainly deal with problems. They are grouped with the folk-plays, however, because their emphasis seems to be upon the folk-way of life. *Stevedore* and *A Mighty Wind A-Blowin'* do contain fine glimpses of the lives of the folk (if the word "folk" is broadly understood) but the impact is one of radical social drama rather than of folk-description.

And thus, we hope to pass in review an important segment of the Negro's literary life and of the influence of Negro life on American literature.

3

PART I
THE NEGRO
IN AMERICAN POETRY

I

EARLY AMERICAN NEGRO POETRY

THE PIONEERS: JUPITER HAMMON

In the late eighteenth century when few American colonists found the time, energy and inclination to turn from building homesteads and townships to creating poems, a Negro slave, Jupiter Hammon (c. 1730-1800), was publishing verse broadsides in Hartford. Judged by even the standards of the time, these were by no means good poems, but that a slave, getting along in years, should feel urged to express his religion in verse and have it printed in a colonial literary center, is noteworthy. Hammon's writings were largely exclamations of Methodist piety in the diction and rhythm of Wesley and Watts. It is probable that Hammon's masters had noticed and encouraged his gift for rhyming, and steeped as they were, most likely, in the hymnody of the time, they could be forgiven for believing it good. Such poems as "Salvation By Christ, with Penitential Cries" and "The Kind Master and The Dutiful Servant" show how a Negro slave had been won over to the passive resignation of Christianity. Without any changing to speak of, Hammon gave back what he had been taught by kindly disposed masters.

> Believe me now, my Christian friends,
> Believe your friend call'd Hammon:
> You cannot to your God attend,
> And serve the God of Mammon.

In contrast to Hammon's crude doggerel is the polished work of his contemporary, Phillis Wheatley (1753-1784). When about eight years old, Phillis was brought in a slave ship from Africa to Boston. Fortunately for her she was bought by John Wheatley, and though nominally a slave, served as a maid and companion in his religious and educated household. Her feat of learning the English language and reading the Bible in sixteen months after her arrival startled the Wheatley circle. Her education, something of an experiment, whetted her desire to write, and at the age of fourteen, having devoured such New England library favorites as Pope's Homer, Milton, and the numerous elegies of the time, she wrote her first poem, an exhortation in blank verse "To the University of Cambridge, in New England." In 1773 her *Poems on Various Subjects, Religious and Moral* were published in London. Many later poems have been collected in subsequent editions.

Except for her first poem, which was written in blank verse, Phillis Wheatley made use of the heroic couplet of Alexander Pope, whose influence upon the poetry of England and America was then dominant. She closely approached Pope and his school in diction and cadence, and her mastery of the difficult couplet form is surprisingly precocious. A native African girl chanting approved sentiments, elegantly phrased, in faultless measure must have been a cause for wonder in Boston and London drawing rooms. But where Pope was intellectual and satiric, Phillis Wheatley was sentimental and pious; and where he was bold, she was, as might have been expected, shyly imitative. She wrote moralizing elegies in the approved contemporary style, warned Harvard students to "improve your privileges while they stay," and praised George

Washington and "Columbia" in abstract language. Her ideas were poetic commonplaces of the period. In her poem "Liberty" she praises, as her New England preceptors would have done, freedom from "Albion's tyrants," but there is no mention of the enslavement of her own people. She speaks only guardedly if at all of her own interesting life, and in missionary terms writes:

> Twas not long since I left my native shore
> The land of errors and Egyptian gloom;
> Father of mercy! 'twas thy gracious hand
> Brought me in safety from those dark abodes.

Her phrases are those hallowed by correct drawing room usage: "Fair Flora", "Aurora hail", "mental optics", "nectar sparkle on the blooming rose." The distress of Niobe for her children slain by Apollo calls forth a literary exercise; but the real griefs she experienced herself or could have witnessed are missing. And although these limitations are not solely hers but of the period itself, they are cause for regret. Unfortunately, like Hammon, she gave back only what she had got from others. If she had given more of Phillis Wheatley, her position in American literature might have been greater than that of a curiosity.

SLAVE JANITOR AND RHYMER

George Moses Horton (1797-1883) was likewise looked upon as a curiosity in the hamlet of Chapel Hill, North Carolina: he was a slave who had published a book. His life was romantic. Working about the campus for the college president, he was besought by the students to write love-poems for them. His charges were twenty-five or fifty cents for a lyric, according to the warmth desired. His first volume (published in 1829), supposed to raise funds for his liberty, had not sold well enough, and it was not until the Union soldiers appeared that Horton was freed.

6

> Thou boasted land of liberty
> It is to thee I raise my song
> Thou land of blood, and crime, and wrong. . . .
>
> Here Christian writhes in Bondage still,
>   Beneath his brother Christian's rod,
> And pastors trample down at will
>   The image of the living God.

At times he cries "How Long" to the God of the Garrisonian non-resistant; at others he cries to the God of battles. Though he spoke of himself as uneducated, his poetry shows traces of Scott and Byron, "The Misanthropist" being too close to Byron for comfort. Whitfield is at his best in singing one song— that of antislavery protest—but he sings it with force that is his own.

VASHON

The Haitian struggle for liberation was one of the best exhibits for the abolitionist poets. Lamartine's drama, Wordsworth's sonnet, and Harriet Martineau's novel on Touissant L'Ouverture had an American counterpart in Whittier's poems. George Vashon, (1820-1878) well-educated and ambitious, turned to Haitian subject matter for the first narrative poem of any length by a Negro poet. He had visited the West Indies, and probably while there, learned of the Haitian mulatto, Vincent Ogé, one of their revolutionary heroes. *Vincent Ogé* appeared in *Autographs of Freedom* (1856). It is the work of a disciple of Byron and Scott, but it does move swiftly and interestingly. At times there is graceful description. "A Life Day" is a narrative of the South, dealing with what has since come to be conventional but was fairly novel then—the love affair of a master and his slave. The characters are idealized and the situation expected. The master dies, the slave-wife mother loses her children:

9

> Hundreds of maidens full as fair
> As she whose little life you gave,
> Know what a dowry of despair
> Is beauty in a female slave. . . .

The story is indirectly told, and not filled out; it succeeds in pathos where it could have touched tragedy. But these are weaknesses of the time and in spite of them Vashon's narratives belong with the most creditable antislavery poetry.

OTHER ANTISLAVERY POETS

Friend to John Brown and strong worker in the antislavery cause, James Madison Bell (1826-1902) devoted most of his poetry to celebrating freedom. "The Day and The War," dedicated to John Brown, is a prosaic account of the Civil War, with praise for the Black Brigade, and Lincoln's Proclamation. Bell must have felt deeply on these subjects, but his rendering is cold and lifeless because so conventional.

> And we today reiterate
> With warmth of heart and depth of soul
> God bless America's magistrate!

This needs only to be placed beside the folk lyric

> And before I'd be a slave
> I'd be buried in my grave
> And go home to my Lord and be free!

for telling contrast. Frances Ellen Harper (1825-1911), writing simply, succeeds better as antislavery poet. She was also active in the movement, and her poems and lectures were widely popular. Her models were the domestic sentimentalists Longfellow, Whittier and Mrs. Hemans. Poems like "The Slave Mother" and "Bury Me In A Free Land" gain from their simplicity:

> I could not rest if I heard the tread
> Of a coffle gang to the shambles led
> And the mother's shriek of wild despair
> Rise like a curse on the trembling air.

10

At times her emotion goes into sentimentality, her phrasing into the melodramatic, and too often she is banal and trite. Besides her antislavery poems she wrote feminist poetry such as "Vashti" and moralizing and biblical narratives such as "Truth" and "Moses." She was aware of the possibilities of Negro folk character in poetry; "Sketches of Southern Life" (1873) tell us of Aunt Chloe and Uncle Jakey, but these are merely suggestions. The colloquial language seldom rings true and her humor is frail. She remains, for all of her wide popularity, more interesting as a person than as a poet.

ALBERRY WHITMAN

Alberry Whitman (1851-1902) has been aptly grouped with Phillis Wheatley in the "mocking-bird school of poets." Born in slavery, inspired by Bishop Payne at Wilberforce to a literary career, he had read widely and remembered his reading. His first volume *Leelah Misled* (1873) is not racial in theme. His second *Not a Man and Yet a Man* (1877) the longest poem ever to be published by a Negro, is crammed with melodrama. A mulatto slave Rodney rescues his master's daughter from an Indian massacre, is sold South to check a budding love affair with her, meets a beautiful slave Leona, is separated from her, and finally meets up with her in Canada for a happy ending. Whitman experiments with the verse form and subject matter of poems as various as Goldsmith's *Deserted Village,* Longfellow's *Evangeline, Paul Revere's Ride,* and *Hiawatha,* Scott's *Lady of the Lake* and Whittier's *Snowbound.* Of the *Rape of Florida, or Twasintas Seminoles* (1844) an experiment in the " 'stately verse,' mastered only by Spenser, Byron, and a very few other great poets", Whitman writes: "Some Negro is sure to do everything

11

that any one else has ever done, and as none of the race have executed a poem in the 'stately verse,' I simply venture in." Such a motive alone could not bring success. The poem is diffuse, obscure, and pretentious. There is occasional fluency, but characterization and the story (of Indian removal from Florida) are sacrificed to description of a "literary" sort. Whitman's "The Octoroon" (1901), like Vashon's "A Life Day" deals with a love affair between idealized master and idealized slave. Since Whitman had written that all the " 'Uncle Toms' and 'Topsies' ought to die," his conciliatory praise of the antebellum South in "The Southland's Charm and Freedom's Magnitude" (1902) is surprising. Whitman seems inclined in this poem to accept certain conventional beliefs about Negro character, and his favoring mulattoes, quadroons and octoroons as his heroes and heroines seems to be in line with an underestimation of the pure-blood Negro. Whitman's shorter poems, while derivative, show talent. His few dialect poems, such as "Tobe's Dream," are the best dialect work by a Negro before Dunbar. In his ambitious work Whitman is often content to rely upon an undoubted facility and a memory too well stored with lines and images from famous poets. His love for these was genuine, but the poetry he wrote in their shadow was not.

SUMMARY

The record of the conscious literary artist among Negroes thus goes as far back as America's colonial period. Antebellum Negroes, both slave and free, wanted to be poets, read and studied as widely as circumstances permitted, and wrote down their thoughts in the forms approved by their times. There was earnest effort and sometimes surprising talent. Different traditions sired different poets. Phillis Wheatly

12

wrote as a cultured Bostonian whose chief interests were in the library. Jupiter Hammon, whose experience of poetry was confined to Wesleyan hymns, repeated what New England puritanism had dinned into his ears. George Horton was by chance a rhymer, using everything that came to him on a college campus as grist for his poetic mill. Whitfield and Vashon wrote according to the models that antislavery poets set up before them. Alberry Whitman wrote as a man whose boyhood had been starved for books, and whose manhood was overfond of the newly discovered fare. None of these poets had the strength to go beyond their models. Reviewing their lives, one does not wonder at this, but rather at the amount of creditable work done in spite of difficulties. But it remains true that the so-called "conscious" poets were frequently too self-conscious. While they were "poetizing", folk-Negroes were creating poetry of depth and originality. For the genuine poetry of the Negro of this period, for poetry that still has the power to portray and to move, one must go to the sly and sardonic folk-rhymes and the profoundly revealing spirituals.

DISCUSSION QUESTIONS

What is meant by the "Mocking-bird School of Poets"?

What are possible reasons for the failure of the first Negro poets to protest against slavery, or to portray the conditions of their people?

Why has Phillis Wheatley been called a poet of "the mocking-bird" school?

What is noteworthy about Horton's place of residence in comparison to the other poets?

Was the choice of a Haitian, Touissant, as a revolutionary Negro the only possible one?

List the English and American poets who served as models for early Negro poets.

What are the chief failings of early Negro poetry? How may these be accounted for?

READING REFERENCES

Brawley, Benjamin Griffith: *The Negro in Literature and Art*—Duffield & Co., New York—1929, revised and enlarged to *The Negro Genius*—Dodd, Mead & Co., New York—1937.

13

Brawley, Benjamin Griffith: *Early Negro American Writers*—The University of North Carolina Press, Chapel Hill, N. C.—1935.

Johnson, James Weldon: *The Book of American Negro Poetry*—Harcourt, Brace & Co., New York—1931.

Kerlin, Robert T.: *Negro Poets and Their Poems*—The Associated Publishers, Washington—1935.

Loggins, Vernon: *The Negro Author*—Columbia University Press, New York—1931.

White, Newman Ivey, and Jackson, Walter Clinton: *An Anthology of Verse By American Negroes*—Trinity College Press, Durham, N. C.—1924.

14

NEGRO FOLK POETRY

THE SPIRITUALS

When Thomas Wentworth Higginson, scholar, abolitionist, and army officer, first heard the soldiers of his black regiment sing around the evening campfires, he was startled by "the flower of poetry in that dark soil." Of the line "I'll lie in de grave and stretch out my arms" from the spiritual "I Know Moon-rise", he wrote: "Never, it seems to me, since man first lived and suffered, was his infinite longing for peace uttered more plaintively than in that line." Shortly after his fine appreciation, three other persons—likewise Northerners—published *Slave Songs of The United States* (1867). Then followed the Fisk Jubilee Singers, a group of trained young people who carried over America and Europe the songs their slave parents had sung. And then the spirituals came, deservedly, into their own.

AUTHORSHIP

The matter of authorship might be left in the words of a contemporary poet:

> We do not know who made them
> The lips that gave them birth
> Are dust in the slaves' burying ground,
> Anonymous as earth. . . .

James Weldon Johnson, who has had so much to do with stirring a twentieth century interest in the spirituals, speaks of their makers as "black and unknown bards of long ago." He is inclined to believe that many spring from highly gifted individuals, reasoning from the example of one "Singing" Johnson. Colonel Higginson reported that an oarsman boasted that he had made a song on an "ole nigger driver" by "just puttin' a word and den annuder word." The theory of composite or group authorship is held by another collector who heard this explanation: "Dey make 'em, sah . . . My master calls me up, and order me a short pack of corn and a hundred lash. My friends see it, and is sorry for me . . . Dat night dey sing about it. Some's very good singers and know how; and dey work it in—work it in, you know, till they git it right; and dats de way." It is likely that although lines, couplets, or even entire songs may have originated with individuals, the folk were the court of final resort. They approved or rejected, changed lines that they did not understand, inserted stanzas from many different sources wherever they pleased, sometimes sang a choral response unrelated to the leader's line, e.g.,

> Leader: You never can tell what a hypocrite will do
> Chorus: Way in de middle of de air. . . .

and kept them in the storehouse of their memory, for oral transmission to the next generation or for circulation in their wanderings to other, sometimes remote sections. The spirituals are folk products.

ORIGIN: AFRICAN, AMERICAN NEGRO, OR WHITE

Whether these songs are African or American Negro, influenced by whites, or copies of white camp-meeting "spirituals" is a subject into which scholars (many white, and a few Negro) are zealously delving. As far as the poetry of the spirituals is concerned, painstaking scholarship has revealed (what hardly needed such effort) that the Negro spiritual relies heavily upon biblical phraseology and ideas. Many similarities, some striking, to lines of evangelical

16

hymns in old white camp-meeting hymn-books have been established: the scholars have overthrown, sometimes by forcing parallels, the complete "originality" of Negro religious songs. What this proves is familiar enough to a student of Negro, or any folk music. The Negro singer took what he liked where he found it. And then he changed it, and, what is the important point, *made it his own.* Thus: "I'll safely ride on Jordan's wave" becomes "I'm a-goin' to wade cross Jordan's river"; "At his table we'll sit down, Christ will gird himself and serve us with sweet manna all around" becomes "Gwine to sit down at the welcome table, gwine to feast off milk and honey"; and (according to an *authority*) "To hide yourself in the mountain top, to hide yourself from God" becomes "Went down to the rocks to hide my face, the rocks cried out no hiding place." Even if these changes are not unanimously considered improvements, they are patently far from the originals.

In bringing forth proof that in words and melody many Negro spirituals are traceable to white songs, southern white scholars have succeeded in disproving the romantic theory of completely African origin for the spirituals. All of those who assiduously collect evidence grant, however, that now the Negro song is definitely the Negro's regardless of ultimate origin, and one of them writes as follows: "The words of the best White Spirituals cannot compare as poetry with the words of the best Negro spirituals." It remains to be said that for the best Negro spirituals, camp-meeting models remain to be discovered.

PHILOSOPHY

Many interpreters of the spirituals have stressed the note of resignation, of other-worldliness. Since the spirituals reflect Christianity with its creed of other-worldliness and turning the other cheek, there is some truth in this interpretation. But it is not the whole truth. It is also true that "the wild, sad strains tell, as the sufferers themselves could, of crushed hopes, keen sorrow and a dull, daily misery, which covered them as hopelessly as the fog from the rice swamps." This type of comment irritates certain southern white authorities on the spirituals, who cannot see what the slave had to grieve about. They therefore insist that references to hard trials here below are to be found in white "spirituals," and that the oppression lamented is the "oppression of sin." Since, according to these authorities, "the Negro slave seldom contemplated his low estate," when the Negro sang of freedom he meant "freedom from sin." This is ingenious, perhaps, but convincing only to those who must defend slavery at all costs.

OPPOSED TO PLANTATION TRADITION

Against the tradition of the plantation as a state of blessed happiness the spirituals speak out with power and tragic beauty. Too many rash critics have stated that the spirituals showed the slave turning his back on this world for the joys of the next. The truth is that he took a good look at this world and told what he saw. Sometimes he was forthright in denouncing slavery, as in "No Mo' Driver's Lash for Me" or in that trumpet call:

> Go down, Moses
> Way down in Egypt land
> Tell ole Pharaoh
> To let my people go!

It is not surprising that this class of songs is no larger: these songs were dangerous in a South on the fringe of hysteria. Often, as Frederick Douglass and Harriet Tubman tell us, the songs had double meanings, some not so hidden. Thus the Negro soon saw his plight as parallel to that of the Israelites, Canaan became Canada, and Pharaoh the master-class:

> Oh Mary doan you weep, doan you mourn
> Pharaoh's army got drownded. . . .

"Didn't My Lord Deliver Daniel" includes the line "and why not every man?" The word "free" occurs very often in the spirituals. If they did come from white hymns, it could hardly be accidental that so many were selected that could be taken as embodying the slaves' own hopes.

"SORROW SONGS"

But even greater witness is the main body of the spirituals. If the slaves were not "contemplating their low estate," they at least described it in terms of which history has proved the accuracy. The slave sang of an unhappy figure "rolling through an unfriendly world," "a motherless child," "rebuked and scorned," "whose way was cloudy" and who was like a blind man, standing in the middle of the road and crying. Or he sang in that couplet of tragic intensity:

> I don't know what my mother wants to stay here fuh
> Dis ole world ain't been no friend to huh. . . .

All too often he sang of the separation of families—mother, father, sister, brother gone. Frequently there was the quiet resignation of "Bye and bye, I'm gonna lay down dis heavy load," or of "Deep River, my home is over Jordan." But there was fortitude as well: "Oh stand the storm, it won't be long, we'll anchor by and by" and

> Done made my vow
> And I can't turn back
> Gonna see what de end will be.

19

It is fantastic to believe that the singing slave referred only to "freedom from sin," that his eyes were closed to his condition, that he was not singing of himself.

"WHEN I GET TO HEAVEN"

There are, of course, spirituals in which this heavy burden was lightened, jubilant announcings of heaven and its glories: "settin' down side of de Holy Lamb," "When I get to heaven gonna put on my shoes, walk over God's heaven," "I'm gonna feast at de welcome table"—"When I get to heaven I'm gonna ease, ease":

> Oh when de saints go marchin' in
> I wanna be one in dat number. . . .

But these are rejoicing at *escape*. Sometimes the joy is almost anguished because of the present contrast, and sometimes what should be a happy release is still in the mournful strain:

> Swing low, sweet chariot. . . .

BIBLICAL NARRATIVES

There are other spirituals narrating biblical episodes such as "Ezekiel Saw The Wheel," "Joshua Fit de Battle of Jericho," "Mary Had A Little Baby." Many of these are more than merely narrative: "He Never Said A Mumbling Word" and "Were You There", which tell of the suffering on the cross, are among the most moving lyrical cries of all literature. Simply phrased, these spirituals are all the more profound because they well from the hearts of people who were themselves deeply acquainted with grief.

PREACHING THE WORD

There is religious exhortation as well. Aphorisms and advice abound:

> I tell you once, I tell you twice
> There is sinners in hell from shootin' dice.

20

Joshua was the son of Nun,
He never would stop till de work was done.

Keep a inchin' along, lak a po' inch worm.

Better mind now, sister, how you walk on de cross
Yo' foot might slip an' yo' soul get lost. . . .

At times irony and satire crept in: "Live Humble"
was changed in transmission to "Live-a-Humbug," and
it is submitted that the slave who so altered the line
had his own arch wisdom.

THE SECULARS

Down in the slave-quarters there grew up, side by
side with the spirituals, secular folk-rhymes, which
were variously called "fiddle-sings," "corn-songs," and
"jig-tunes." Religious slaves were known to dislike
them, considering them "devil-tunes." At times this
hostility was deserved, for many of the seculars are
"upstart crows" and irreverently use biblical phrases
in a satirical, free-thinking way:

Our Fader, who art in heaven
White man owe me 'leven, pay me seven,
Thy kingdom come, they will be done
And ef I hadn't tuck that, I wouldn't git none.

I don't want to ride in no golden chariot,
I don't want to wear no golden crown,
I want to stay down here and be
Just as I am without one plea.

I seen Solomon and Moses
Playing ring around de roses. . . .
I seen King Pharaoh's daughter
Seeking Moses on de water. . . .
Seen ole Jonah swallowin' de whale
And I pulled de lion's tail;
I've sailed all over Canaan on a log.

21

The seculars were more favored by the masters and overseers who preferred their gay lightheartedness to the brooding of the spirituals. Some are nonsense songs: "Juba dis, Juba dat, Juba skin de yaller cat"; some show a mammy in her off moments: "Ole Aunt Dinah she got drunk, fell in de fire and kicked out a chunk." Some are dance songs such as "Gonna raise a ruckus tonight"; their syncopation demands the clapping of the hands, the patting of the feet:

> "Did you feed my cow?" "Yes, Maam!"
> "Will you tell-a me how?" "Yes, Maam!"
> "Oh, what did you give her?" "Cawn and hay!"
> "What did you give her?" "Cawn and hay!"

which anticipates the hey-hey of such a modern dance as the "Charleston." Many come back to the Negro folk from the borrowing minstrels, not too altered for recognition and welcome. Some, of course, are Negro versions of Anglo-Saxon play-songs.

REALISM OF THE FOLKRHYMES

The seculars contribute again to a realistic understanding of slavery. We hear that "master bought a yaller gal, He bought her from the south," we hear of short rations, patrollers, slave-dealers and "po' white crackers." There is clowning, but very little of the mutual love of master and slave as in Foster's "Massa's In The Cold, Cold Ground." Instead there is bitter humor. The ideas for some of the songs must have been smuggled in, and these had to be sung behind the master's back. The best is the cynical:

> My ole mistis promise me
> Befo' she died she'd set me free
> She lived so long dat her haid got bal'
> And she give out'n de notion of dyin' at all.

which closes with the sinister line about the master: "A dose of pisen helped him along. . . ." Some

22

are like the fables, shrewdly using Brer Rabbit and Brer Fox, telling of Brer Hog who decided "to die in de pig-pen fighting, die wid a bitin' jaw!" With emancipation there came scornful references to "mosser and missis," and shouts of jubilee. The seculars, like the spirituals, are of sturdy stock, and like them, are being improvised in our own day.

BALLADS: TRADITIONAL

Although it strikes some collectors as odd to find a Negro singing "In London-town where I was born" the fact remains that the Negro folk, like other southern folk groups, have kept alive traditional English and Scotch ballads learned in early days. "Barbara Allen," "The Briary Bush":

> "Hangman, hangman, slack the rope
> Slack the rope awhile. . . ."

and the broadside "Mistuh Frog Went A Courtin', He Did Ride" (first printed in 1580) are examples of these. The lifting of stanzas from one old ballad and singing them in another is frequent. Lines familiar to Negroes:

> Whose gonna shoe yo' little feet.
> Whose gonna glove yo' hand   ..

first belonged to an old ballad "The Lass of Roch Royal."

BALLADS: NEGRO HEROES

The Negro has not been content, however, just to sing ballads which, for all their charm, pertain but little to his life. He has created ballads of his own heroes. In the way of folk literature, he tells of his outlaws, "Stackolee," the river desperado; "Railroad Bill," who is only semi-legendary; and "Bad Man Lazarus" "who broke in de commissary" and "been paid off." "Frankie and Johnnie" with its countless blooms,

23

stems from the Negro folk, as did "Casey Jones" which, though about an engineer, has been claimed by them. These heroes sleep with "their hand cannon," get "blowed down wid a great big number forty-five," in bravado are going to "start a graveyard all their own," or in dismay run up against deputies, twelve big jurymen, and judges who say ninety-nine years as easily as they cough. They reveal that the folk are not such naïve happy children of the soil as they are often made out to be.

JOHN HENRY

Outstanding among the ballads is "John Henry." Here is an ideal epical figure whose story is well beloved in America, especially in railroad and mining sections. John Henry is one of America's finest folk creations. A giant steel driver, he pitted his strength against the new-fangled steam drill:

> John Henry started on the right-hand side,
> And the steam drill started on the lef'.
> He said, "Before I'd let that steam drill beat me down,
> I'd hammer my fool self to death,
> Hammer my fool self to death. . . .

Swinging a "ten pound hammer wid a whale bone handle" that causes a mighty rumbling wind, aided at one moment of sick dizziness by his little woman, Polly or Julie Ann (in some versions Mary Magdalene), cheered by his "shaker," his mates, and especially by the listeners to this stirring battle song, he defeats the machine, but is killed by the great strain. He dies a hero, remembered in railroad roundhouses, in shacks perched upon gray West Virginia hills, in cabins secreted in the foothills of Virginia. As a little fellow, "sitting on his pappy's knee," he had foreseen his own death. He went down unbroken in spirit. The folk love him for it:

> Great Gawd, he was a steel driving man. . . .

24

Other narrative ballads reflect a less heroic life but have the same gusto. "Old Dog Blue" tells of a first-rate treeing dog who, even in death, sustains his fame:

> Let him down with a golden chain
> Every link I called his name. . . .
> Go on Blue, you good dog you!
>
> When I hear old Blue bark
> He's treeing possums in Noah's ark,
> He's treeing possums in Noah's ark. . . .

The "Ballit of Boll Weevil" shows this ballad making in its contemporary form. This little bug came all the way from Mexico, into Texas and to wherever the singer is, "just looking for a home."

> Done et up all yo' cotton
> An' now I'm gonna start on yo' corn.
> I'll have a home, I'll have a home.

"De merchant got half de cotton, de boll-weevil got de rest." "Long Gone, Lost John" and "The Travelling Man" tell of far wanderers, travelling light and fast:

> He boarded de Titanic. . . .
> When he saw dat big iceberg
> Overboard he flew. . . .
> De white folks rushed on deck
> And dey said "Dat man's a fool."
> But when de ole Titanic ship went
> Down
> He was shooting crap in Liverpool.

Through the years the folk Negro has put into rhyme the current tragedies that he runs across: like the medieval jongleur he spreads the news: A big storm has swept over Charleston, a train is wrecked, the Titanic has gone down, Floyd Collins is entombed in Kentucky, the river is a-rising from Memphis down to New Orleans . . . .

WORK SONGS

Travellers in Africa from the earliest observed the

25

Africans singing in rhythm with their work. Col. Higginson recorded the songs that Negro oarsmen sang in time with their long sweeps. Hoeing songs and the "coon-jine"—the rhythmical song of roustabouts carrying cotton on a bucking gang-plank—were recorded even in slavery days. Today, in railroad gangs, in convict camps, the Negro sings at his laying of rails, at his "driving steel on down." He sings as he lifts his heavy hammer, and punctuates his song with the downswing and a grunt. He sings to his hammer—which killed John Henry (wasn't that a shame, baby, wasn't that a shame)—that if he could hammer like John Henry, he'd be a man. Or in irony:

> It won't kill me, baby, it won't kill me.
> Take dis hammer—hunh
> Carry it to de Captain
> Tell him I'm gone, baby,
> Tell him I'm gone.

He improvises: "Oh she asked me—wham—in de parlor—wham"; or "Says to my Captain—wham— My hands are cole—wham—" "Says to my Captain —wham—Ain't de pay check come?" Or he sings with bitter resignation:

> Done bust dis rock—boys—
> From here to Macon
> All de way to de jail, boys
> All de way to de jail.

These work songs are fluid, changing with the mood and the experiences of the singer-worker. They have the interest of life close to the soil. And they tell a very great deal.

THE BLUES

Probably the most popular of the seculars today are the blues. The parentage of these has been traced to W. C. Handy, author of the "Memphis Blues" and "St. Louis Blues," and to Ma Rainey, authoress of "Li'l Low Mamma Blues." Although these conscious artists have definitely influenced their spreading, it is likely that the blues go far back beyond their adaptation, even to slavery. In the most usual form a line is repeated (often with a slight variation) then coupled with a rhyming line. The fact that "priestesses of the blues" have been most potent in popularizing them has led to the misconception that they are a woman's longing cry for her "man." The subject matter is not so limited, however, and blues aplenty can be found bewailing tornadoes, high water, hard times in farming, or insisting upon the need for travelling, for leaving this cold-hearted town. As well as self-pity there is stoicism in the blues. In spite of much repetition of phrases there are flashes of fine imagery:

> My gal's got teeth like a lighthouse on the sea
> Every time she smiles she throws a light on me.

> De workhouse is down dat long old lonesome road.

> You been a good ole wagon, daddy, but you done broke down.

> The wind was howlin', buildin's begin to fall
> I seen dat mean ol' twister comin' jes' lak a cannon ball.

> I got de worl' in a jug, de stopper in my hand.

> A good-lookin' woman makes a bulldog gnaw his chain.

> Blues ain't nothin' but a po' man's heart-disease.

The blues tell a great deal about folk-life. The genteel turn away from them in distaste, but blues persist with their terse and tonic shrewdness about human nature. At times they belong with the best of folk-poetry, and the people who create them at their best cannot be dismissed as clowns.

27

Odum and Johnson, Carl Sandburg, and John and Alan Lomax in their collections of Negro songs include many that show awareness of the harsh side of life. The folk-songs of slavery had often been ironic, with double-meanings either lost upon or concealed from the collectors, but contemporary songs are more direct. Sometimes the songs turn the tables of mockery:

> When dey gits old and gray
> White folks looks like monkeys,
> When dey gits old and gray.
>
> * * *
>
> White man, white man, laying in de shade
> Laziest man that Gawd evah made.

"Cultivating and cementing confidences with individual Negroes without which an attempt to get to the core of the living folklore is foredoomed to failure," Lawrence Gellert railroaded and hitch-hiked the length and breadth of the deep South with a mechanical phonograph and a sawed-off megaphone. He found in living folklore an "otherwise inarticulate resentment against injustice, a part of the unrest stirring the South." Some of his findings have been published in magazines and in his *Negro Songs of Protest*. This newer folk Negro discovered by Gellert sings defiantly:

> Yo' head 't ain no apple fo' danglin' from a tree
> Yo' body no carcass for barbecuin' on a spree. . . .

Or he satirizes the preacher, "big and fat, sleek and shiny lak a beaver hat," who preaches to his restive flock the "Bible way, of getting one's dues on Jedgment day":

> Two prayin' Niggers ninety-nine years in jail
> Waitin' fo' Jesus to pay dere bail.

28

He reveals grim knowledge of the mean bosses such as Cap'n Bob Russell who shoots down the Negro worker impudent enough to ask for his pay, of Joe Brown's coal-mine, run on convict labor, "a sun-down job"; of the easy arrests of Negroes who—"standin' on the corner, weren't doin' no harm," are forced into peonage; of the tie-up of the bosses and sheriffs, who "take mah labor and steal mah time." He sees the bad man with some social understanding:

You put a mark on my people and it must be carried on . . .

He is tired of starving, of being poor and cheated all the time, of working so that someone else can be at ease, of being framed and lynched. He sings symbolically:

All ah wants is dese col' iron shackles off my leg.

Negro folk-songs, from the earliest down to those uncovered by Lawrence Gellert, are invaluable to anyone seeking to know the American Negro. They constitute a very adept self-portraiture. Rich in humor, equally convincing in lightheartedness and tragedy, they put to shame much of the interpretation of the Negro from without.

DISCUSSION QUESTIONS

Why were Northerners the first to collect and record the spirituals?
What are reasons why there are few collections of spirituals by Negroes before the present century?
Account for the unknown authorship of the spirituals.
What is meant by "The spirituals are folk products"?
Discuss the problem of origin.
Discuss the statement that "freedom" as used by the slave meant "freedom from sin."
Briefly, what is meant by the "plantation tradition"?
What types of spirituals are joyful?
What do the "upstart crows" tell about slave life?
Do the seculars show a careless acceptance of slavery?
Why do Scotch-English ballads survive among southern Negroes?
Who are some Negro folk-heroes?

What additions can you make to the material on John Henry?
What is the value of the work song to a gang of workers?
What is the difference between "folk-blues" and the Broadway type?
Why are songs of protest so difficult to find in collections?
Why are songs of protest more numerous today than in slavery?

READING REFERENCES

Allen, Wm. F., Ware, Charles P., and Garrison, Lucy McKim: *Slave Songs of the United States*—Peter Smith, New York—1929.

Ballanta, N. G. J.: *Saint Helena Island Spirituals*—C. Scribner, New York—1925.

Brown, Sterling A.: The Blues as Folk Poetry—*Folk Say,* 1930, University of Oklahoma Press, Norman, Oklahoma.

Dett, R. Nathaniel: *Religious Folk Songs of the Negro*—Hampton University Press, Hampton, Virginia—1927.

DuBois, W. E. B.: "The Sorrow Songs", in *Souls of Black Folk*—A. C. McClurg, Chicago—1903.

Gellert, Lawrence: *Negro Songs of Protest*—American Music League, New York—1936.

Grissom, Mary: *The Negro Sings A New Heaven*—University of North Carolina Press, Chapel Hill—1928.

Handy, W. C., and Niles, Abbe: *Blues*—Boni, New York—1926.

Higginson, T. W.: Chapter IX, *Army Life in a Black Regiment*—Fields, Osgood, Boston—1870.

Hurston, Zora Neale: "Spirituals and Neo-Spirituals" in *Negro Anthology*—edited by Nancy Cunard, Wishart & Co., London—1934.

Jackson, George Pullen: *White Spirituals From The Southern Uplands*—University of North Carolina Press, Chapel Hill, North Carolina—1933.

Jessye, Eva: *My Spirituals*—Robbins Engel, New York—1926.

Johnson, Guy: *Folk Culture on St. Helena Island*—University of North Carolina Press, Chapel Hill, North Carolina—1930.

Johnson, Guy: "Negro Folk-Songs" in *Culture In The South*—Edited by W. T. Couch, University of North Carolina Press, Chapel Hill, North Carolina—1935.

Johnson, Hall: Review of Lawrence Gellert's Songs of Protest—*Opportunity,* August, 1936.

Johnson, James Weldon, and Johnson, J. Rosamond, *The Book of American Negro Spirituals*—Viking Press, New York—1925.

Johnson, James Weldon, and Johnson, J. Rosamond, *The Second Book of Negro Spirituals*—Viking Press, New York—1926.

Kennedy, R. Emmett: *Mellows*—Boni, New York—1925.

Krehbiel, H. E., *Afro-American Folk-Songs*—Scribner, New York—1914.

Locke, Alain Leroy: "The Negro Spirituals," in *The New Negro*—Boni, New York—1925.

Lomax, John A., and Lomax, Alan: *American Ballads and Folk Songs*—The Macmillan Co., New York—1935.

Lomax, John A., and Lomax, Alan: *Negro Folk Songs As Sung By Lead Belly*—The Macmillan Co., New York—1936.

Niles, John: *Singing Soldiers*—Scribner, New York—1927.

Odum, Howard, and Johnson, Guy: *The Negro and His Songs*—University of North Carolina Press, Chapel Hill, North Carolina—1925.

Sandburg, Carl: *The American Songbag*—Harcourt, Brace & Co., New York—1927.

Scarborough, Dorothy: *On The Trail of Negro Folk Songs*—Harvard University Press, Cambridge—1928.

Talley, Thomas: *Negro Folk Rhymes*—The Macmillan Co., New York —1922.

White, Newman I.: *American Negro Folk- Songs*—Harvard University Press, Cambridge—1928.

Work, J. W.: *Folk Songs of The American Negro*—Fisk University Press, Nashville, Tenessee—1915.

Van Vechten: "The Blues" in *Vanity Fair,* August, 1925, and March, 1926.

III

DUNBAR AND TRADITIONAL DIALECT

EARLY DIALECT

As has been pointed out, Dunbar was not the first Negro poet to use dialect, although his predecessors had not realized the possibilities of the medium. The influential work of white authors in Negro dialect, from Stephen Foster and the minstrel song writers through local colorists such as Irwin Russell, J. A. Macon, Joel Chandler Harris and Thomas Nelson Page, will be our concern in the concluding chapters devoted to poetry. In spite of these forerunners, however, Dunbar was not only the first American Negro to "feel the Negro life aesthetically and express it lyrically," as William Dean Howells wrote, but also the first American poet to handle Negro folk-life with any degree of fullness. As a portrayal of Negro life, Dunbar's picture has undoubted limitations, but they are by no means so grave as those of Russell and Page.

DUNBAR: PLANTATION TRADITION

Writing in the heyday of the dialect vogue, Dunbar (1872-1906) could not completely escape the influences of these two writers, but the shadow of Page, much the lesser poet, fell more darkly upon him. Almost all of Dunbar's poetry about slavery is of the Page school, some of it directly copied. Old slaves grieve over the lost days, insisting upon the kindliness of old master and mistress, and the boundless mutual affection. Treated approvingly, they grieve that the

32

freedmen deserted the plantation, or wish to die so
that they can get to heaven to continue serving old
master, or faced by their master's poverty, indig-
nantly decide to

> "Tell Marse Linkum for to take his freedom back."

The master is generally pictured as "smiling on de
darkies from de hall," or listening to the corn-song
from his veranda with a tear in his eye. In *Parted,*
a slave, separated from his beloved, knows that he
will come back to her, since

> God knows ouah hea'ts, my little dove,
> He'll help us from his th'one above

—which seems to be a cruel misreading of history.
The very few other poems that admit the distresses
of slavery, forget them in memories of cabin dances.
"When Dey Listed Colored Soldiers" shows Negroes
fighting for their own freedom, but love for the gray-
clad masters is expressed as well.

FOLK LIFE IN DUNBAR

These unworthy perpetuations of plantation senti-
mentalities are fortunately not what Dunbar is known
by. He is at his best in his picture of the folk life
of his day. He did not know the deep South, but, a
willing listener to his mother, an ex-slave, he probably
got a good background of folk lore and speech, and
he knew small Negro communities of Ohio, Kentucky,
Eastern Shore Maryland and the District of Columbia. Influenced by the popular James Whitcomb
Riley, he wrote that the

> sandy roads is gleamin' wile de city ways is black
> Come back, honey, case yo' country home is best.

His fancy is caught by the parties, spelling bees,
church services, by nodding and drowsing in front of
the hickory fire, by ripened cider ready to be drunk

while the back log is slowly burning through. He deals
with charming rural love-affairs, from which the bitterness and disillusion of his personal love poetry are
noticeably lacking. Farmers brag of an old mare, or
welcome the rain so that they can tinker 'round mend-
ing harness, or, like Tam O'Shanter, return a bit
worse for drink to irate spouses, and lay the blame
for the slowness on old Suke, the nag. For these
people Dunbar conveys his friendship warmly. Like
Longfellow and Field he does many of his best poems
about children ("Candle-Lighting Time," "Little
Brown Baby," "Turning the Children in Bed"). The
slugabed scamp, Lias, is rightly popular with both
children and vexed parents.

THE HAPPY PEASANT

Though he has written that "it's mighty hard to gig-
gle when dey's nuffin' in de pot," he barely mentions
dire poverty, his world being one where

> De po'est ones kin live an' play and eat
> Whair we draws a simple livin' from de forest an' de tide.

He writes of the countryman's delight in good food,
of "wheat bread white ez cotton an' a egg pone jes'
like gol' "; of hog jowl, roasted shoat, and all the
partitions of the hog; of chickens, turkeys, sweet pota-
to stew, mince pies. One of his poems on possums is
a rhymed cooking recipe; one of his less worthy pieces
tells of a backwoods suitor winning a wife with a possum. He has a fondness for poetry about hunting
and fishing, and the festal seasons of Thanksgiving
and Christmas. He is definitely a poet of the happy
hearthside and pastoral contentment. Poems that do
not show the pleasant life are few. "Blue" suggests
a vaguely understood melancholy, poems like "Two
Little Boots," with the touching quality of Eugene

34

Field's "Little Boy Blue," express the grief of stricken parents, and "A Christmas Song" makes use of the folk-saying that a green Christmas means "a hongry churchyard." But explicit revelation of the folk Negro's hardships is absent.

Dunbar's best qualities are clear. Such early poems as "Accountability" and "An Antebellum Sermon" show flashes of the unforced gay humor that was to be with him even to the last. With a few well-turned folk phrases he calls up a scene as in "Song of Summer," or

> Tu'key gobbler gwine 'roun' blowin'
> Gwine 'roun' gibbin' sass an' slack
> Keep on talkin' Mistah Tu'key
> You ain't seed no almanac. (Signs of The Times)
>
> Tek a cool night, good an' cleah
> Skiff o' snow upon de groun' ("Hunting Song")

Except when unexplainably urged to write Irish dialect or imitate Riley's "Orphant Annie," or to cross misspelling with moralizing as in "Keep A Pluggin' Away," his grasp upon folk-speech is generally sure. His rhythms almost never stumble and are frequently catchy: at times as in "Itching Heels" he gets the syncopation of a folk dance. Most of all he took up the Negro peasant as a clown, and made him a likeable person.

PASTORAL PICTURE

Unlike Irwin Russell, whose views of Negro life and character are those of an outsider on a different plane, Dunbar, writing more from within, humanizes his characters and gets more of their true life. There is still, however, a great deal omitted. His picture

35

is undoubtedly idealized. Believing with the romanticists that "God made the country and man made the town," writing that

> "the folks I meet in any other spot,
> Ain't half so good as those I knowed back home in Possum Trot"

he left out many of the more unpleasant aspects of life. His backsliders are guilty only of such "sins" as dancing after joining church, or of comic fisticuffs. More serious is his omission of the hardships that the Negro folk met with as much in Dunbar's day as in ours. Reasons for such omission may have been Dunbar's own kindheartedness and forgivingness, or his lack of deep acquaintance with the South. Or it may have been the influence of his literary school, his audience and his publishers, or of the professional conciliators who in that day guided racial expression. Be the reason what it may, one of these or all, the fact of omission remains. Dunbar concentrated upon a pastoral picture. No picture of Negro life that is only pastoral can be fully true.

JAMES EDWIN CAMPBELL

Contemporary with Dunbar was James Edwin Campbell, whose book, *Echoes From The Cabin and Elsewhere,* contained many dialect poems, some of them earlier than Dunbar's. Campbell makes use of a dialect near to the Gullah speech of South Carolina handled today by such writers as Ambrose Gonzales and Julia Peterkin. Campbell has his own originality. "Ol' Doc Hyar" shows the folk-use of fabling to point satire upon human pretense: the figure of the Doctor Hare, who cares little for his patients but greatly for his pay and upper class status, is excellently observed.

He put on he specs an' he use beeg wu'ds,
He feel dee pu's den he look mighty wise;
He pull out he watch an' he shet bof eyes;
He grab up he hat an' grab up he cane,
Den "blam!"—go de do'—he gone lak de train
                Dis ol' Doc Hyar
                Whar lib up dar
En ur mighty fine house on ur mighty fine hill

"De Cunjah Man" is a good recording of superstitions, and "When Ol' Sis Judy Pray" is tender and reverential. Campbell was well acquainted with the currents of folk life, and at times gets something of the hard realism missing in Dunbar. He catches the apt phrase and the unrestrained rhyme, and his rhythms, whether slow-moving or syncopated, are well handled.

DANIEL WEBSTER DAVIS

One of the most popular of these dialect poets was Daniel Webster Davis, whose first volume, *Idle Moments,* was enlarged into *Weh Down Souf* (1897). Davis was a teacher and preacher in Richmond, Virginia. His tone is conciliatory. As a lecturer and reader he was careful not to give offense to his white audiences. "Stickin' To De Hoe" satirizes "edikashun" and praises the girl who can wash, iron and cook ham and greens, and the man who plows and sticks to the hoe; it is only by these that the Negro will "make his points." "Night On the Old Plantation" dismisses the hardships and flatters the joviality of slavery. "Ol' Mistus" celebrates the ministering angel of the quarters, with as great a worship as a white fellow Virginian, Thomas Nelson Page, gave to the black mammy. In many respects, Davis is merely a Negro Thomas Nelson Page. "Hog Meat" is a typical comment on the Negro whose happiness depends upon gluttony, and who forgives his enemies when he has hog's ears, souse, cracklings, spare-ribs, chine, or any of the other parts of the hog upon his plate. "De Nigger's Got to Go" humbly sets forth the Negro's services to America and ends with trust in God who "will fix things here below." So does the Atlanta Negro Congress poem, "The Negro Meets To Pray." Except for a few grudged admissions about slavery and church squabbles, Negro life in Davis' poems is oddly free of difficulties, and therefore unbelievable. The humor is of the joke-book sort, and the frequent philosophizing is empty. The writing is crude, and needless misspellings such as "plezzun mem'riz," "kan't," "teeched," "koats" and "roe" indicate that to this author the speech of the folk Negro was merely an excuse for fun-making. And so, to judge from *Weh Down Souf,* was the folk Negro's experience.

J. MORD ALLEN

Deserving to be better known than Davis is J. Mord Allen, who was both a writer for the stage and a boiler-maker. His *Rhymes, Tales and Rhymed Tales* appeared in 1906. His work is unpretentious, but contains good genre pictures and pleasant humor. Best of his poems is "The Devil and Sis Viney," a somewhat long poem in couplets recounting how a tempting widow, of rare prowess as a cook, overcame an elder who wanted to live like Saint Paul. The church life where "er elder draws de sisters lak er warm brick draws er kitten" is well shown, and the domestic pictures, done with relish, are like those of *The Biglow Papers.* "When the Fish Begin to Bite" catches the gusto of the folk Isaak Waltons, and "Shine On, Mr. Sun" has such good details of winter as:

Warm, inside hyeah, sence de ol' man
Chinked mah spring pants in de cracks,
En mah feet don't have ter suffer
Long ez I got gunny-sacks.

White folks trompin' th'ough dis weather
Blowin' steam er yard erhead. . . .
So, I'll jes' stay by dis fire
Out o' col' en snow en win's
Smokin' mah rich long-green 'backer
Toastin' mah rheumatic shins.

THE PREACHER POETS

Like Daniel Webster Davis, many Negro preachers turned to writing dialect poetry. James David Corrothers in "An Indignation Dinner" shows a typical dialect pattern. A meeting is held to protest abuses: "Ef you'd keep a mule a-wo'kin, don't you tamper wid his oats," but what promises to have something of social realism ends up with the usual joke-book stealing of turkeys and chickens. John Wesley Holloway's *From the Desert* contains "Discouraged" which is a good catalogue of a farmer's ills (bollworm eatin' up de cotton, mildew eatin' up de corn, colry killin' off de cattle). Though a slightly comic note intrudes, the poem is one of the nearest to actuality. "Plowin' Cane," "Calling The Doctor," "The Corn Song," "The Pop-Call," show definite knowledge of folk-life. Holloway is in Dunbar's tradition, but he has his own authenticity. Charles Bertram, another preacher, is the author of some well-turned gentle pastorals of Negro folk-life.

MINOR WRITERS OF DIALECT

Writing with quiet heroism from a sick-bed, Ray Garfield Dandridge, the author of *Zalka Petruzza, and Other Poems,* is chiefly in the Dunbar tradition. Although here and there he turns off an interesting

39

observation, his dialect poetry is conventional and crude, and his concern for misspelling is too great. Thus, for dialect's sake he writes *ruff, fashun, taik, campane* and forces into dialect words that are uncomfortably out of place. Alex Rogers, writer for the stage, turned out poems near to the minstrel tradition, catchy at times but of little lasting value. Other users of traditional dialect are Sterling Means, S. Tutt Whitney, and Waverly Carmichael. The dialect of Joseph Seamon Cotter, however, has both point and pith. "The Don't Care Negro" satirizes a type viewed sympathetically by other dialect poets. Though he has something of a schoolmaster's severity, Cotter does indicate bitter truths about Negro life:

> Neber min' what's true tomorrow
> So you· libs a dream today. . . .
> Neber min' yo' manhood's risin'
> So you hab a way to stay it.

In a much later poem, "The Tragedy of Pete," he writes in the realistic speech of "the bully of the bootleg-town," and he reveals a hard irony that would have shocked earlier exploiters of dialect.

JAMES WELDON JOHNSON

In James Weldon Johnson's *Fifty Years and Other Poems* there was a section of dialect poems called "Jingles and Croons." Many of these, written with the author's eye on Broadway, were set to music by his brother, J. Rosamond Johnson; "Since You Went Away," the best known, has become a concert success. Here again the influence of Dunbar is evident; there are lullabies to pickaninnies, rivalries between rustic swains, stealing of turkeys, and warnings to possums. Occasionally there are glints of humor as in "Explana-

40

tion" and "Answer to Prayer"; Tunk is advised to get education because educated white men

> jis does a little writin'; does dat by some easy means;
> Gals jis set an' play piannah on dem printin' press machines.

But there is little true folk life. The older days "were good times sho," sorrow is to be laid away "high upon de shelf" to the tune of banjo plunking; the life preferred for description is when

> we's eatin' watermelon, an' a layin' in de shade.

James Weldon Johnson admits the triteness of these early pieces, and later attacks them, together with all the conventionalized Negro dialect poetry, for "exaggerated genialty, childish optimism, forced comicality, and mawkish sentiment."

SUMMARY

From the above indictment which holds for almost all of the traditional dialect poetry, James Weldon Johnson does not completely absolve even Dunbar. Johnson blames a mold established on the minstrel stage; Louis Untermeyer calls traditional dialect "an affectation to please a white audience." It is true that too often there was an anxiety to agree with what one poet states: "Nowhere has the Negro better friends than among the white people of the Southland." Conciliatory tactics forbade the use of material that might have brought discomfort to southerners, or even white Americans in general. Thus anything terrible or tragic in Negro experience was to be glossed over: insults, inequities, peonage, lynching were to be as absent from the picture of Negro life as they were present in actuality. Forgetting and forgiving were the watchwords. It was a poetry of evasion, for all of its local color. Nor was there much

41

revelation of folk character. Instead there was mis-
understanding or misinterpretation that seconded the
attitude of white America. Many of the authors were
preachers and teachers, consciously literary, who
looked down with good humored condescension upon
a ridiculous way of life, or were shocked by the
departures of the folk from gentility. A few pat
phrases, a few stock situations and characteristics,
some misspelling: these were the chief things necessary. The wit and beauty possible to folk speech, the
folk-shrewdness, the humanity, the stoicism of these
people, they seldom saw.

But because conventionalized dialect poetry has
these faults, dialect does not have to be dismissed as
capable of only two stops, humor and pathos. If
Daniel Webster Davis saw his folk Negro only a huge
feeder on hogmeat, the fault is in Davis, not in the
medium of folk-speech. Let us look at the folk-
speech in the spirituals

> De ole sheep, dey knows de road
> Young lambs gotta find de way.

> Deep River, my home is over Jordan.

> My Lord, what a morning
> When de stars began to fall.

> Dey whupped him up de hill,
> And he never said a mumblin' word

Or in the folk-rhymes, which for all their lack of pretense have social value:

> My name's Ran, I wuks in de san
> I'd ruther be a nigger than a po' white man. . . .

Or in the novels of white observers:

> I told dem people right yonder at Heaven's Gate
> Church if you was to come home cold an' stiff in a
> box, I could look at you same as a stranger an' not
> a water wouldn' dream out my eye. I mean it, July.

42

An old grandmother speaks to the New York steamer hooting as it puts out to sea, headed for New York:

> Git along den. Git along. Ah ain't holdin'
> yo'. An' when yo' get whar yo' is goin'
> 'member what Ah tol' you an' gib my gal
> huddy fuh me.

In contrast to the Victorian gentility of the dialect love-poems might be placed:

> I heard my daddy call some other woman's name
> I know he don't mean me; but I'm gonna answer jes de same.

Dialect, or the speech of the people, is capable of expressing whatever the people are. And the folk Negro is a great deal more than a buffoon or a plaintive minstrel. Poets more intent upon learning the ways of the folk, their speech, and their character, that is to say better poets, could have smashed the mold. But first they would have had to believe in what they were doing. And this was difficult in a period of conciliation and middle class striving for recognition and respectability.

DISCUSSION QUESTIONS

What Negro poets attempted dialect before Dunbar?

Why was Dunbar influenced by Page and Russell?

What is meant by the pastoral version of Negro life? Is it representative?

What are some of the omissions from Dunbar's picture?

How is Campbell distinctive?

In what way do the other poets form a school of Dunbar?

Is dialect merely misspelling? Why are "kote", "snaik" and "ruff" bad dialect?

What made dialect writing popular?

Why was dialect unpopular to a large number of Negro readers?

Is dialect limited to two stops, pathos and humor?

What is your attitude to dialect?

Should modern poets shun dialect or merely break down its conventional limitations of social viewpoint?

READING REFERENCES

Brawley, Benjamin Griffith: *Paul Laurence Dunbar, Poet of His People*—University of North Carolina Press—1936.

Brown, Sterling A.: *Outline for the Study of the Poetry of American Negroes*—Harcourt, Brace & Co., New York—1931.

Gaines, Francis Pendleton: *The Southern Plantation*—Columbia University Press, New York—1925.

Green, Elizabeth Lay: *The Negro in Contemporary American Literature*—University of North Carolina Press—1928.

Johnson, James Weldon: *Along This Way*—Viking Press, New York—1933.

Wiggins, Lida Keck: *The Life and Works of Paul Laurence Dunbar*, with an introduction by William Dean Howells—Dodd, Mead & Co., New York—1907.

Wood, Clement: *Negro Songs, An Anthology*—Haldeman Julius Co., Girard, Kansas—1924.

Also books, already cited in Chapter I, by James Weldon Johnson, Kerlin, Loggins, and White and Jackson.

44

DUNBAR AND THE ROMANTIC TRADITION

ANTAGONISM TO DIALECT

Contemporary with the dialect poets were many poets generally antagonistic to dialect, and determined to write in the accepted romantic tradition. It would be inexact to consider them a school—the dialect poets were more that, in their resemblance to Dunbar—but they did manifest common tendencies. The most gifted proved that Negroes, as they became educated, could share in the legacy of culture and contribute respectably to it, even though in a minor way. In too many instances, however, these poets were more concerned with making copies of the "beauty" that was the stock-in-trade of a languishing tradition.

THE ROMANTIC TRADITION

The conscious reacting of these poets against dialect was good in so far as it meant a refusal to perpetuate stereotypes of Negro life and character. Too often, however, this reaction, in order to prove "cultural unity," seemed to mean something else. References to race were avoided or else couched in abstract, idealistic diction. Valuably insisting that Negro poets should not be confined to problems of race or pictures of Negro life, these poets too often committed a costlier error out of timidity at being Negroes: they refused to look into their own hearts and write. We have seen how the dialect poets furthered the traditional underestimation of Negro life and character. We shall see in this chapter, how many of the non-dialect poets accepted the same tradition at face value, by turning

45

away from their people and from themselves. The resulting verse, with exceptions to be noted, was escapist and derivative, and although accomplished at times, was too often without vitality.

DUNBAR: STANDARD ENGLISH

In "The Poet," Dunbar was regretful that the world had turned from his "deeper notes to praise a jingle in a broken tongue." Many critics have stated that he was dissatisfied with his dialect pieces, not because he felt that they stopped short in delineating the folk Negro, but simply because they were dialect. Other friends of Dunbar have stated that he was proud of his dialect, and recited it with gusto. Whatever the truth may be, many of his own people welcome the poems in standard (miscalled "literary") English and consider the dialect to be merely pot-boiling, or at least, the harmless straying of genius. This comes largely from what James Weldon Johnson calls "second-generation respectability," and is of a piece with photographing Dunbar in full dress for one of his collected editions. Needless to say it does Dunbar an injustice. Frequently his standard English becomes consciously "literary"; the full dress does not always wear well.

Dunbar's poems in standard English are of many sorts. There are many love-poems, some heavily sentimentalized like "Ione," which is certainly worse than any of his dialect; and echoes of belated romantic poets, conventional and undistinguished. At times, however, as in "The Debt," "Parted," and "Forever" he speaks simply and directly; sometimes the burden of his own unfortunate love affair breaks through and the result is rewarding.

> I had not known before
> Forever was so long a word.
> The slow stroke of the clock of time
> I had not heard. . . .

Dunbar's ability to write poems that sing themselves has attracted composers; one of his last poems, "Who Knows?" is one of the most popular of American love-ballads. His nature poems frequently have a delicate charm.

MORALIZING AND PHILOSOPHICAL POEMS

In the manner of his time, Dunbar wrote many moralizing and philosophizing poems. One of the most quoted of these is "Life," which summarizes life as "a pint of joy to a peck of trouble" but finds compensations:

> Joy seems sweeter when cares come after
> And a moan is the finest of foils for laughter.

This alternating of melancholy and optimism runs through many poems. He at times is aware that "the waking world is full of lies most palpable, uncouth, forlorn," but finds refuges in love and dreams. If any poet needed escapes Dunbar was that poet; unhappy in love, stricken with tuberculosis early and aware of his doom, ambitious and frustrated, he had to believe, and the attempt to do so is sadly like whistling in the dark. Friendly with Robert Ingersoll, he at times expressed mild religious scepticism; just as often, however, he praised true Christianity. These are the poems considered Dunbar's deeper notes. They express no consistent philosophy and are merely phrasings, sometimes felicitous, of contrasting moods. The prevailing tone is that of romantic poetry, a vague melancholy, a dissatisfaction with the "waking world," and a yearning for a world remade by desires.

RACE CONSCIOUS POETRY

Dunbar likewise wrote race-conscious poetry. This varies in quality from the school-boy recitation pieces

47

like "The Colored Soldiers" and "Black Sampson of Brandywine,"

an ebony giant
Black as the pinions of night—

to more dignified sonnets to Harriet Beecher Stowe, Robert Gould Shaw, the militant Douglass and the unmilitant Booker T. Washington. Only occasionally does he speak out. "The New South" can still refer, in the accents of Gray's "Elegy" to the slave "jocund as the day," can contrast the abuses of the present with the "glory of the South's ancient days:"

And thou [the South] wilt take, e'en with thy spear in rest
Thy dusky children to thy saving breast.

"We Wear The Mask" is probably a poem about the race; but it is generalized protest, still masked. "The Haunted Oak" is a specific poem upon lynching in the ballad form; the spokesman is the oak tree. When Dunbar dealt with the harsher aspects of Negro life, he discarded not only dialect, but also directness and simplicity. Such a poem as "Ode to Ethiopia" is popular with Negro audiences, probably because of its propaganda of aspiration. Like so much of Negro expression of the period, it praises the nobility of forgetting and forgiving.

DUNBAR: SUMMARY

Many of Dunbar's standard English poems are deservedly among his best known. His mastery of rhythm and of the poetic vocabulary of romantic poetry is superior to that of any preceding Negro poet. Being too facile, however, and having little chance for thorough grounding in his craft and in thinking, he could not rival his poetic masters, Shelley and Tennyson, but neither did the school of American Tennysonians to which he belonged. Although his

48

standard English poems lack the freshness, humor, and life of his dialect, their imitativeness is to be expected from a poet of his time and upbringing, and their achievement in many instances is high. The wonder is that this poet, who died so tragically young and belonged to a generally denied and despised race, should have written so well.

BRAITHWAITE

In 1904, while Dunbar was alive, there appeared a volume of poems, *Lyrics of Life and Love,* and in 1907 another, *The House of Falling Leaves,* which equalled Dunbar's best work in finished artistry. These were the work of William Stanley Braithwaite who, through his criticisms and anthologies, was to become one of the pioneers in the poetry revival in America. Braithwaite was on terms of friendly intimacy with such important modern poets as Edwin Arlington Robinson and Amy Lowell, but the poetic qualities they sponsored or exemplified are not his. A widely read man, his poetry is derivative of the romantic tradition, the Pre-Raphaelites, and such poets of the end of the century as Swinburne and Ernest Dowson. It resembles what the French call "crepusculaire": poetry of the twilight. Favorite words are "dream" and "trance":

> Turn me to my yellow leaves,
> I am better satisfied. . . .
> Let me dream my dream entire
> Withered as an autumn leaf. . . .

Although he has written that the world to him is "a place of wonder" "just a will of God's to prove beauty" he reveals more of its wistful regret. "Death is life's best, truthful friend." An earlier mystical note

> This life we live so sensible and warm
> Is but a dreaming in a sleep that stays
> About us from the cradle to the grave—

becomes in later poems extremely obscure.

Braithwaite objected to his poems being classed indiscriminately as "Negro" poetry. A sensitive man of the library, he is concerned nowhere in his poems with race but wishes them to be "art for art's sake." The result is the usual one: the lines are graceful; at their best, exquisite, and not at their best, secondhand; but the substance is thin. Even the fugitive poetry of some of Braithwaite's masters had greater human sympathies.

JAMES WELDON JOHNSON

According to William Stanley Braithwaite, *Fifty Years* and *Other Poems* by James Weldon Johnson "brought the first intellectual substance to the content of our poetry, and a craftsmanship . . . . less spontaneous than Dunbar's, but more balanced and precise." Although containing lyrics of quiet sincerity such as "Beauty That Is Never Old," "The Glory of The Day Was In Her Face" and "Mother Night," this volume will probably be remembered longest for its poems of race-consciousness. "Fifty Years," grouped by Brander Matthews with the noblest American commemorative poems, celebrates the fiftieth anniversary of freedom, praising the Negro for his part as laborer and patriot in building up America, protesting the lack of justice with more militancy than Dunbar, but closing like Dunbar with religious trust. "O Southland!", like Dunbar's "The New Slavery", pleads for help to the weak; "To America" poses the challenging question: shall Negroes be

> Strong, willing sinews in your wings?
> Or tightening chains about your feet?

Less rhetorical than these, and the most vigorous poem of protest from any Negro poet up to his time is "Brothers." Reminiscent of Markham's "The Man With The Hoe," this poem describes with grim detail a lynching, refusing to urge the innocence of the victim, but attempting to explain how he had become brutalized:

> Lessons in degradation, taught and learned,
> The memories of cruel sights and deeds,
> The pent-up bitterness, the unspent hate. . . .
> Sprung up and found in me sporadic life.
> In me the muttered curse of dying men,
> On me the stain of conquered women, and
> Consuming me the fearful fires of lust
> Lit long ago, by other hands than mine. . . .

And the last muttered words of the brute to the lynchers stated what the America of his day had not often heard:

> Brothers in spirit, brothers in deed are we . . . .

Where the southern tradition could see only the sentimental side, Johnson points out in "The Black Mammy" what was really a tragic experience. In "Black and Unknown Bards" he gives very high praise to the slave-creators of the spirituals. One of Johnson's earlier poems is "Lift Every Voice And Sing"; set to music by his brother, J. Rosamond Johnson, this has been accepted as the Negro National Anthem. Johnson's poems of this period were largely expressions of race pride or defense, protesting with vigor, but trusting unfailingly in God and the future.

ROMANTIC LYRICISTS

Shortly after Dunbar, poems of James David Corrothers appeared in *The Century*. "At The Closed Gate of Justice" is a plea written with dignity, slightly rhetorical:

> Still must one succor those who brought one low,
> To be a Negro in a day like this.

Corrothers wrote poems of fine appreciation for Dunbar and for the goodly estate of poetry. "The Negro Singer" is one of the earliest expressions of pride in Africa. Though written in the romantic vocabulary, Corrothers' poetry does have some personal distinction; poetry was obviously a deeply felt joy to this man who was in turn bootblack, janitor, lumberjack and finally a well known minister. Charles R. Dinkins, another preacher, writes in a poem echoing Kipling's "Recessional," an attack upon democracy's inconsistencies:

> Forgive thine erring people, Lord,
> Who lynch at home and love abroad.

Thomas Fortune, a journalist of note, wrote many poems, some upon literary subjects, and some in praise of liberty, all conventional.

Although born in the South and educated there, George Marion McClellan refused to write dialect poetry: "Dialectic verse is too much like the 'ragtime' music, considered quite the proper dressing for Negro distinction in the poetic art." McClellan's few pictures of Negro life nevertheless are of

> joyous shouts
> Of Negro songs and mirth awake hard by
> The cabin dance.

Most numerous in his *The Path of Dreams* are his poems of nature worship and description. At times there are poetic rubberstamp figures such as "Zephyr scatters as she goes Sweet attars everywhere," but generally there is a simply phrased rendering, in melancholy mood, of landscapes, or flowers, insects, and birds. "The Feet of Judas" teaches the lesson that

> no wrong this side the gate of heaven
> Was ever too great to wholly be effaced. . . .
> Christ washed the feet of Judas.

52

Eloquent and militant are the words most descriptive of the poems appearing in W. E. B. DuBois' *Darkwater*. Although considered by their author as "unworthy to stand alone", these convey something of the passion and force of their author who was the leading intellectual influence of his generation. "A Litany At Atlanta" is a bitter indictment of the Atlanta riot from whose loins "sprang twin Murder and Black Hate." Booker T. Washington's maxim of "Work and Rise" is attacked in passing: optimism is checked by terrible reality. "The Riddle of The Sphinx" is a cry of hatred for oppression of black men by the "white world's vermin and filth," who bear "the white man's burden of liquor and lust and lies," and it hopes for a black Christ to introduce democracy. "The Prayers of God" is a prayer for humanity to leave its cruelty and come to the aid of God. "A Hymn To The People" closes with a prayer to make Humanity divine. DuBois' thought at times is emotionally socialistic, at times arrogantly racial. His hatred for the abuses of civilization at times becomes anguished and his expression suffers:

> I hate them, Oh!
> I hate them well
> I hate them, Christ!
> As I hate hell!

"All the long aisles of Thy Great Temples, God, stink with the entrails of our souls. . . ." He often affects alliteration to the extreme: "mad with the madness of a mobbed and mocked and murdered people"; his style favors the highflown, which at times becomes bombastic:

> Thou art not dead, but flown afar up hills of endless light,
> Through blazing corridors of sun. . . .
> Where endless time doth moan,
> Where endless light doth pour
> Through the black kingdoms of eternal death.

53

but the eloquence does not always overreach itself, and at times there is such irony as "Men may be brothers in Christ, even though they be not brothers-in-law." What gives these poems distinction is the phrasing of protest and bitterness, of an understanding and consequent hatred of exploitation. Unlike the Negro poets of his time, DuBois generally uses a rhapsodic free verse, more akin to the Bible than to Whitman. For all of DuBois' desperation, he generally closes his poems with religious confidence:

> Finally I believe in Patience . . . . with the tardy triumph of joy and the mad chastening of Sorrow: Patience with God!

KELLY MILLER

Mathematician, sociologist, and publicist, Kelly Miller has likewise turned his hand to poetry. In the chant form used by DuBois, Miller's poem "I See And Am Satisfied" catalogues the historic wrongs of the Negro: "the ocean basin whitened with his bones, the ocean current running red with his blood, amidst the hellish horrors of the middle passage," slavery with its lashings, slave hunts, and concubinage, "the sinister silence and acquiescent guilt" of reconstruction, the persecution and lynching of the present. Nevertheless Miller still holds out hope: "the path of progress . . . has always been a zig-zag course amid justice and injustice, cruelty and mercy . . ." "the great generous American heart will finally beat true to the higher human impulse . . ." and awaiting the Negro's universal welcome into the patrimony of mankind:

> I look calmly upon the centuries of blood and tears and travail of soul, and am satisfied.

Miller takes the long view; one must say that it is very long.

Leslie Pinckney Hill is author of some quietly moving poems of life, and many not so moving that come more from the library than life. "Christmas at Melrose" celebrates domestic comfort around the hearth; Burns, Whittier and Longfellow are pleasantly echoed but Milton is directly copied at the close. "Summer Magic" is similarly pastoral. "To The Smartweed" makes incongruous use of literary diction ("rustic deem, swain, scion of thy stock, regal will and martial quality") in a way condemned by Wordsworth, one of Hill's masters. "The Teacher," frequently quoted, and "Self Determination" are of ethical purpose; the second urges forgivingness, laughter (philosophic mirth), idealism, and loyalty as racial blessings. "Freedom" and "The Wings of Oppression" confront race difficulties with faith that tomorrow "right will rise and mercy shine." "Tuskegee" combines hope and doubt. "So Quietly" is a calm rebuke of lynching, "soul-blight of a nation." Hill's most ambitious work is "Touissant L'Ouverture," a closet drama in five parts and thirty-five scenes, Shakespearean in derivation and intent.

Even more heavily reliant upon books is the poetry of Benjamin Brawley. Though Brawley praises Chaucer (for "writing in a book of dreams, telling tales of lovers for the years") his models are Victorian, both in style and content. Robert Gould Shaw, who fell in battle leading Negro troops, is spoken of in terms of Lancelot, Bedivere, and Galahad. Similarly Tennysonian is the idealistic optimism that in all "the strife and striving"

> I can see the great contriving
> Of a more than human plan.

Brawley's greatest effort is "The Seven Sleepers of

Ephesus," the presentation of religious belief in smoothly flowing ballad stanzas.

ROMANTIC MISCELLANY

Of the four volumes of poetry by George Reginald Margetson, the last, "The Fledgling Bard and The Poetry Society," is the most original. This is a satire, done in colloquial language. It is garrulous and consequently prosey, a hodge-podge of things to be scorned or ridiculed, but the satirical approach is new, and a few hits on "professional race men" and American democracy are scored. Joshua Henry Jones in *The Heart of the World* gives little besides banal jingling. Edward Smythe Jones' *The Sylvan Cabin* is pompously literary, none of his verses being as poetic as his biography. Looking upon education at Harvard as the greatest thing to be desired in all the world, he tramped to Harvard Square and there was arrested as a vagrant. The poem making use of this experience is so sentimental that the reader is not shocked at his being jailed. "O God Wilt Thou Help Me In School" expresses a commendable prayer in uncommendable rhyme. Other minor lyricists are Lucian Watkins, William H. A. Moore, and Otto Bohanan. R. Nathaniel Dett is another of the examples of a musician seeking to weld music and poetry.

SUMMARY

We have thus seen how in the first years of this century, many poets came along the literary trails where Dunbar had pioneered. With varying degrees of talent, almost all relied upon models, as young poets will do, and since most of them confined their expression to a single volume, there was little chance for them to reveal any matured style of their own.

56

At its worst their imitation was almost undraped plagiarism:

> How sad to my thoughts are the scenes of my childhood
> As recalled to my mind now at three-score and five. . . .

Pompous literary diction prevailed. One of the many *Odes To Ethiopia* begins:

> Thou Sovran Queen of Afric's sunny strands
> I smite my lyre to sing thy praise unsung. . . .

Another poem refers to Egypt as follows:

> For, as fled on the flight of years,
> The unrelenting Hand of time
> Wiped her sweet visage off the globe. . . .

This appeared in a poem thus praised by a noted Negro critic: "With its fine imaginative sweep, it is as good as any poem I have seen which that occasion [Lincoln's birthday] called forth." Gems such as the following were all too frequent:

> Alas! thou lovely floweret wee
> Fate blew a blighting breath
> Upon the delicate form of thee,—
> Thou'st met untimely death.

Or,

> 'Mong the stately larches, larches
> Where the willow arches, arches,
>   And the lilies bow;
> In the meadows yonder, yonder,
> Little Sue would wander, wander,
>   Looking for the cow.

Such an early stanza as this, written in all seriousness by a "gentleman of culture and a natural poet", is a type of crime which the more polished versifiers following Dunbar did not commit, but the same impulse to the pretty, decked out in literary finery, was too often theirs.

Noticeable in these poets is their disposition to melancholy. This might be attributed to the examples of their masters whose works were steeped in wishful thinking and regret, or to the pathos of the Negro "talented tenth" which found the doors of opportunity double-barred. Their poetry seeks escape from a burdensome reality, but almost never is the burden explicitly stated, or the protest more than a vague dissatisfaction. DuBois and Johnson, occasionally Dunbar, challenge the existing order; most of the others are decorous, restrained, evasive. Perhaps they believed what Dunbar stated: "We must write like the white man. . . . Our life is now the same."

The lives of many of these poets were exciting; the difficulties met and surmounted would have been fine material for poetry. Many of them had seen all kinds and conditions of men. They chose to write conventionally about the peace of nature. Walt Whitman had heard America singing, had included in his vast panoramas people like these poets. They probably did not read him; if they did, they preferred Thomas Bailey Aldrich and Bayard Taylor. They chose to follow the current of American poetry of the time, but it was a current that led wearily to a lost bayou.

Among their adventures, that which meant most to them, apparently, was their obtaining an education. This, in their generation, was the distinguishing thing. Some received academic training, in spite of hardships; others burned the midnight oil after menial occupations. Their struggling was not seldom heroic. But worship of education meant a worship of the traditional and bookish. Some became pedantic in the way of the culturally retarded; others, more educated, believed that poetry was the monopoly of the academies, divorced from life. The pressure of their times inclined them to stifle originality: the Negro leader or spokesman excelled in proportion to his resembling the favored white élite. They became timorous of any reminder of a wretched past or

58

present. They wanted to get away from it all, into a secure gentility. The religious instruction they received in the missionary schools made them believe in the Christian virtue of noble forgiving. And, it is worth remarking that although as members of the "talented tenth" they were frustrated, still in comparison to the Negro masses they did not have so very much to forgive.

With few exceptions these poets turned away from their people and from their own interesting personalities. Poetry was a romantic escape for many of them, not a perception of reality; for others it was a hallmark of "cultural" distinction. Their work as poets paid a penalty.

DISCUSSION QUESTIONS

Compare Dunbar's poetry in dialect and standard English.
Summarize Dunbar's achievement in standard English.
What are the merits of Braithwaite's achievement?
What types of poetry were written by James Weldon Johnson?
What distinguishes the poetry of W. E. B. DuBois?
What is the relationship of the literary poets to the poets of Chapter I?
What are the weaknesses of the romantic attitude? What factors partly explain them?

READING REFERENCES

Braithwaite, William Stanley: "The Negro In American Literature" in *The New Negro*—edited by Alain Locke, New York, Boni—1925.
Alain Locke: "The Negro's Contribution to American Art and Literature," in *The American Negro, The Annals of the American Academy of Political and Social Science*—Philadelphia—1928.
Also books already cited by Brawley, Brown, Green, Johnson, Kerlin, White and Jackson.

V

CONTEMPORARY NEGRO POETRY
(1914–1936)

The extensive migrations from the South, quickened by the devastations of the boll-weevil, the growing resentment at injustice, and the demand of northern industries; the advance of the Negro in labor, wealth, and education; the World War with its new experiences in camp and battle; the Garvey movement with its exploitation of "race", all of these contributed to the growth of the "New Negro." In 1935, Alain Locke, editor of *The New Negro* wrote:

> The intelligent Negro of today is resolved not to make discrimination an extenuation for his shortcomings in performance, individual or collective; he is trying to hold himself at par, neither inflated by sentimental allowances nor depreciated by current social discounts. For this he must know himself and be known for precisely what he is, and for that reason he welcomes the new scientific rather than the old sentimental interest . . . . Now we rejoice and pray to be delivered both from self pity and condescension.

The New Negro was marked by self-respect (which, admittedly at times, became self-preening) and by self reliance. He asked for less charity and more justice. Negro poetry reflected all of this. Coincidentally in the post-war years the "new poetry" appeared in American literature, and New Negro poets naturally shared in this movement's reaction against sentimentality, didacticism, optimism, and romantic escape. They learned to shun stilted "poetic diction," to use fresher, more original language and to humanize poetry. Race was no longer to be caricatured or neglected; they did not plead "for a race" but attempted

60

to express it. At their best they belonged with the renascent American poets who "in the tones of ordinary speech rediscovered the strength, the dignity, the vital core of the commonplace."

The resulting poetry had five major concerns: (1) a discovery of Africa as a source for race pride (2) a use of Negro heroes and heroic episodes from American history (3) propaganda of protest (4) a treatment of the Negro masses (frequently of the folk, less often of the workers) with more understanding and less apology and (5) franker and deeper self revelation. Some of this subject matter called for a romantic approach, some for a realistic. It must be added that much of the poetry written in the period of the "New Negro Renaissance," belongs, in subject matter and treatment, with the poetry already discussed.

FENTON JOHNSON

Fenton Johnson's works show the two extremes of Negro poetry after 1914. Some of his poems are conventional in form and substance; others, patterned upon his fellow Chicagoan, Sandburg, are striking departures in Negro poetry. With Sandburg's technique and Edgar Lee Masters' outlook, Johnson included in *African Nights* snapshots of bitter experience such as "Aunt Hanna Jackson", "The Banjo-Player", "The Minister", "The Scarlet Woman" and "Tired." Unfortunately Johnson, like so many of his Negro contemporaries, fell silent shortly after these poems. Perhaps there was little audience for their pessimism, either within a race whose optimism is proverbial, or without, where the Negro's brooding over his lot is generally unwelcome. "The Scarlet Woman", educated for more than a white man's kitchen, is driven by poverty to street-walking, and gin is her only way of forgetfulness. "Tired" indicts civilization:

61

> I am tired of building up somebody else's civilization . . . .
> let the old shanty go to rot, the white people's clothes turn
> to dust, and the Calvary Baptist Church sink to the bottom-
> less pit. . . .
>   Throw the children into the river; civilization has given
> us too many.

Negro "leaders" who direct the race into optimism,
condemned this view of life, but it is tonic after such
frequent insistence on "a good time coming bye and
bye." Like so many modern poets, Fenton Johnson
held to the words of Thomas Hardy that

> If way to the better there be, it exacts a full look at the worst.

WOMEN POETS

Georgia Douglas Johnson continues in the main the
tradition discussed in the last chapter. According to
a sponsoring critic, Mrs. Johnson has "set herself the
task of documenting the feminine heart . . . and
in a simple declarative style engages with ingenuous
directness the moods and emotions of her themes."
The poems in *The Heart of A Woman* (1918),
Bronze (1922), and *An Autumn Love Cycle* (1928)
are written to appeal to the heart, and are generally
autumnal in tone. *Bronze* contains "Hegira," "The
Octoroon" and "Aliens" upon race themes; one section
"Motherhood" at times goes deeply into the tragic
problems of Negro mothers aware of what faces their
children. Though conventional in phrase and meter,
her poems are skillful and fluent. Angelina Weld
Grimké is the author of many musical lyrics, frequently
in a carefully worded and cadenced free verse. Intellectual and sensitive to injustice, she has written poems
of irony and quiet despair: a puppet player twitches
"the strings with slow sardonic grin."

> Let us forget the past unrest
> We ask for peace.

She is influenced by imagism, but her images are of the twilight, or of winter.

Alice Dunbar Nelson, wife of Paul Laurence Dunbar, in addition to her better known sketches of Creole life, wrote many poems. These echo the romantic themes, some being concerned with descriptions of Nature "the perfect loveliness that God has made" in contrast with man-made imperfections. "I Sit and Sew" laments a woman's enforced inactivity in time of war.

VOICES OF PROTEST

More forthright, but done with less artistic care, are the poems of Walter Everette Hawkins. His book is called *Chords and Discords;* the "chords" are conventional lyrics about love or duty, but the "discords" foreshadow new Negro poetry. "The Iconoclast" and "To Prometheus" are self-consciously radical, but the theme was new for Negro poets. "A Festival in Christendom" describes a lynching, but since literary diction is used for lurid details, it does not succeed as poetry:

> Then from his side they tore his heart
> And watched its quivering fibres start.

In "Thus Speaks Africa" Hawkins combines race-pride and race-history in a manner favored by many contemporary Negro poets.

> I am Africa:
> Wild is the wail of my waters,
> Deep is the cry of my Congo.
> I laid down my life at Fort Pillow. . . .
> I died on the flag at Fort Wagner
> My bones lie bleaching in Flanders.
> I was burned at the stake down in Georgia,
> I was fuel for the mob in Texas. . . .

After such a catalogue, he states less convincingly:

> And then like the Phoenix of Egypt,
> I rose from the ashes immortal. . . .

63

Carrie W. Clifford in *The Widening Light* likewise looks forward anxiously to the bursting "full-flowered into life" of black folk choked into a death stupor. Many of her sonnets are race-conscious like "The Black Draftee From Dixie," which tells of one of the many soldiers who were lynched upon their return from overseas.

One of the many Negro poets who died young, Roscoe Jamison is best known for his poem "Negro Soldiers," beginning

> These truly are the Brave,
> These men who cast aside,
> Old memories, to walk the blood-stained pave
> Of Sacrifice, joining the solemn tide
> That moves away, to suffer and to die
> For Freedom—when their own is yet denied!

Similarly cut off at the outset of his career, Joseph Seamon Cotter, gifted son of a gifted father, left behind him a sheaf of poem *The Band of Gideon And Other Poems*. Cotter had a definite lyrical facility, seen in the title poem, "Supplication," and "Rain Music." Closer to the New Negro concern for social themes, done with quiet persuasiveness is

> Brothers, come!
> And let us go unto our God
> And when we stand before him
> I shall say—
> Lord, I do not hate,
> I am hated.
> I scourge no one,
> I am scourged.
> I covet no lands,
> My lands are coveted.
> I mock no peoples,
> My people are mocked.
> And brother, what shall you say?

CLAUDE MC KAY

Claude McKay's voice was the strongest in the immediate post-war years. Born in the West Indies,

McKay soon after his arrival in America discovered the shams of "democracy." With Floyd Dell and Max Eastman he became one of the editors of *The Liberator,* a magazine dedicated to social justice. In the epidemic of race-riots occurring shortly after the war, a much quoted cry of defiance was McKay's

> If we must die, let it not be like hogs,
> Hunted and penned in an inglorious spot. . . .
> Like men we'll face the murderous, cowardly pack
> Pressed to the wall, dying, but fighting back.

"The Lynching" with its crowd where men were jostled by steely-eyed women and "little lads, lynchers that were to be," and "America," "which feeds me bread of bitterness" contain desperate truth. Africa is called, with point and power

> The harlot, now thy time is done
> Of all the mighty nations of the sun.

Street-walkers of Harlem, cabaret dancers, and urban workers are treated with understanding. McKay looks searchingly at reality and reveals its harshness. But there is a McKay other than the hater, the rebel, and the realist,—there is the dreamer, nostalgic for the sights and sounds of his native West Indies. "The Tropics in New York" is a poem of memory stirred by the sight of West Indian fruits in a store window. "My Mother" is a simply, tenderly phrased reminiscence. "Flame-Heart," a listing of the delights of youth in Jamaica, is one of the best lyrics in Negro poetry. "Two an' Six" is a charming pastoral of Jamaican life, closer to Burns than to Dunbar. When McKay turned almost completely to prose fiction, Negro poetry suffered a real loss.

ANNE SPENCER

Anne Spencer is the most original of all Negro women poets. Her devotion to Browning, attested by

65

one of her best poems "Life-Long, Poor Browning",
results in a closely woven style that is at times cryptic,
but even more often richly rewarding. She makes use
of poetic tradition without being conventional, and of
new styles with a regard for form; her vision and
expression are those of a wise, ironic but gentle woman
of her times. She is sensitive to natural beauty, praising her home-state Virginia :

> Here canopied reaches of dogwood and hazel
> Beech tree and redbud fine-laced in vines
> Fleet clapping rills by lush fern and basil
> Drain blue hills to lowlands scented with pines

"Neighbors," "I have a Friend," and "Innocence,"
convey a great deal, in the deceptively simple manner
of Emily Dickinson. "Before The Feast of Shushan"
is a poem of vivid sensuous beauty, telling an old story
in modern terms. "At The Carnival" has a bitter
wisdom; Mrs. Spencer sets before us graphically the
drab cheapness: the blind crowd, the sausage and garlic
booth, the dancing tent where "a quivering female-thing
gestured assignations," the "Limousine Lady" and the
"bull-necked man" in contrast to the gleaming beauty
of the "Girl of The Tank." But

> Little Diver, Destiny for you
> Like as for me, is shod in silence;
> Years may seep into your soul
> The bacilli of the usual and the expedient;
> I implore Neptune to claim his child today!

Original, sensitive, and keenly observant, the poems
of Anne Spencer should be collected for a wider
audience.

JESSIE FAUSET

Though better known as a novelist, Jessie Fauset is
likewise a poet. Her interest in French literature is
apparent in many titles of her poems, and in her trans-

lations of poets of the French West Indies, who should be better known. Most of Miss Fauset's personal poems are about love, written with a care for form, and an ironic disillusionment. "La Vie C'est La Vie", the best of these, sets forth a triangle of lovers, loving and unbeloved:

> But he will none of me. Nor I
> Of you. Nor you of her. 'Tis said
> The world is full of jests like these—
> I wish that I were dead.

"Oriflamme" celebrates Sojourner Truth, making her symbolic of the Negro mother, bereft of her children, "still visioning the stars."

JEAN TOOMER

Jean Toomer is best as a poet in the beautiful prose of *Cane* (1923). His few poems in the same volume, however, are original and striking. Jean Toomer has written that Georgia opened him up; "Reapers" and "Cotton Song," show this awaking to folk material. In "Georgia Dusk" there is a sense of the ominous mystery of the Southland:

> The sawmill blows its whistle, buzz-saws stop,
> And silence breaks the bud of knoll and hill. . . ,
> Smoke from the pyramidal sawdust pile
> Curls up, blue ghosts of trees. . . .
> . . . . the chorus of the cane
> Is caroling a vesper to the stars. . . .

With a mastery of the best rhythmical devices of Negro folk-music, "Song of the Son" expresses the return of the younger Negro to a consciousness of identity with his own, a return to folk sources, to the "caroling softly souls of slavery"—

> O land and soil, red soil and sweet-gum tree,
> So scant of grass, so profligate of pines,
> Now just before an epoch's sun declines,
> Thy son, in time, I have returned to thee,
> Thy son, I have in time returned to thee.
>
> In time, for though the sun is setting on
> A song-lit race of slaves, it has not set. . . .

67

In spite of the small number of his poems, Toomer remains one of the finest and most influential of Negro poets. His long silence has been broken with the publication of "Blue Meridian," a rather long poem calling for a "new America, to be spiritualized by each new American." In it there are only occasional references to Negro life:

> The great African races sent a single wave
> And singing riplets to sorrow in red fields
> Sing a swan song, to break rocks
> And immortalize a hiding water-boy . . . .

JAMES WELDON JOHNSON

James Weldon Johnson has also felt the need of recording the lives and thoughts of those "leaving, soon gone." After collecting and editing two volumes of spirituals, he turned to the task, attempted in an earlier poem,—"The Creation", of fixing something of the rapidly-passing old-time Negro preacher. *God's Trombones, Seven Negro Sermons In Verse* (1927), was widely acclaimed. Material which is usually made ludicrous, is here invested with dignity, power and beauty. Convinced that dialect smacks too much of the minstrel stage, Johnson attempts to give truth to folk idiom rather than mere misspellings. The rhythms of these chants have true poetic quality. The advance from his earlier dialect "Jingles and Croons" is a great one; *God's Trombones* are truthful and sincere renditions of a belief and a way of life. There is the occasional grotesqueness of the folk preacher:

> Wash him with hyssop inside and out
> Hang him up and drain him dry of sin.

but there is the tenderness of the reference to Sister Caroline, down in Yamacraw, who had borne the burden of the heat of the day and to whom Death "looked like a welcome friend," and the intimacy of telling a novice in the mad, bad Babylon of scarlet women, dancing and drinking

> Young man, young man,
> Your arm's too short to box with God.

If the hell-border city of Babylon recalls Memphis, New Orleans, and Harlem, "The Crucifixion" and "Let My People Go" recall other Negro experiences:

> Listen! — Listen!
> All you sons of Pharaoh
> Who do you think can hold God's people
> When the Lord God himself has said,
> Let my people go?

The visionary qualities of the spirituals are seen throughout, especially in "The Judgment Day".

> The sun will go out like a candle in the wind,
> The moon will turn to dripping blood,
> The stars will fall like cinders,
> And the sea will burn like tar. . . .

The same visionary type of imagination is to be seen in *Saint Peter Relates an Incident of the Resurrection Day* (1930), a caustic satire of the treatment accorded Negro Gold Star Mothers. The Unknown Soldier, arriving in heaven, is discovered to be a Negro; the G.A.R., the D.A.R., the Legion, the Klan, the trustees of the patriotism of the nation are astounded and want him buried again. In these later poems, both the interpretation and the protest are less rhetorical and more dramatic than in *Fifty Years,* and consequently more persuasive.

COUNTEE CULLEN

Most precocious of contemporary Negro poets is Countee Cullen, who was winner of many nation-wide poetry contests in high school and college, and who published his first volume when he was only twenty-two. This volume, *Color* (1925), is by many critics considered Cullen's best. Like Dunbar's standard English poems, and Braithwaite's, Cullen's work is marked by technical skill; it is the most polished lyricism of modern Negro poetry. Cullen is a follower of tradition in English verse, of what he calls "the measured line and the skillful rhyme." His chief models are Keats and Edna St. Vincent Millay. But he has poured new wine into the old bottles. His gifts are fluency and brilliant imagery; he can convey deep emotion and concise irony. He writes of the gay abandon of lovely brown girls in Harlem "whose walk is like the replica of some barbaric dance" but he is impressed with the transiency of happiness, "the winter of sure defeat." He is capable of the tenderness of "A Brown Girl Dead":

> Her mother pawned her wedding ring
> To lay her out in white;
> She'd be so proud she'd dance and sing
> To see herself tonight. . . .

and of the epigrammatic:

> She even thinks that up in heaven
> Her class lies late and snores
> While poor black cherubs rise at seven
> To do celestial chores.

Cullen insists, as any poet should, that he wants "no racial consideration to bolster up" his reputation, and (a different thing, this) does not wish to be confined to "racial" themes:

> What shepherd heart would keep its fill
> For only the darker lamb?

It is nevertheless true, as James Weldon Johnson points out, that his best poems are those motivated by race. "The Shroud of Color" celebrates a mystical experience in which the poet turns from despair to identity with his people:

70

> Lord, I will live persuaded by mine own.
> I cannot play the recreant to these;
> My spirit has come home, that sailed the doubtful seas.

"Heritage" is a statement of the atavism that was a cardinal creed of New Negro poetry, of "old remembered ways" from Africa persisting in civilization:

> I can never rest at all
> When the rain begins to fall
> Like a man gone mad with pain
> I must match its weird refrain. . . .

But the Africa is "literary", and romanticized, and the theme is too close to Lindsay's "Congo, creeping through the black." "Heritage", for all of its color and facility, does not quite convince. Cullen has also written sonnets of protest. *The Black Christ* (1929) is a narrative poem about lynching, but like others of his late poems, relies more upon literature than life.

LANGSTON HUGHES

Langston Hughes is like Cullen in productivity and wide popularity. These two poets are about the same age; Hughes' *The Weary Blues* (1926) appeared the year after *Color*. Where Cullen is traditional in form, Hughes is experimental, substituting Sandburg for Keats, and going as far in metrical revolt as "The Cat and The Saxaphone, 2 A. M." Cullen is subjective whereas Hughes is frequently objective and dramatic, concerned with the Negro masses. Cullen has most recently translated the *Medea* of Euripides; Hughes' most recent work is communist propaganda. Both poets have strains of pessimism, at times met stoically, but Hughes has now turned to a cause that he believes will usher in social justice.

In *The Weary Blues* Hughes helped to celebrate jazz-mad Harlem, but a note of sadness intrudes as in

71

"To Midnight Nan at Leroy's" and "Song For A Banjo Dance." He believes that

> We should have a land of sun. . . .
> And not this land where life is cold.

He, too, sings atavistically of Africa, of the boy in whose blood "all the tom-toms of the jungle beat." But, aware that the dark peoples are caged in "the circus of civilization," he turns realistically to description of his people. His folk portraits are good in "The Weary Blues", "Aunt Sue's Stories", and the tender, stoical "Mother to Son", one of the best Negro poems:

> Well, son, I'll tell you:
> Life for me ain't been no crystal stair. . . .

This interest is continued in *Fine Clothes To The Jew* (1927) in which he combines the melancholy and irony of the folk-blues. An abandoned woman sings

> Don't know's I'd mind his goin'
> But he left me when de coal was low. . . .

He gives dramatic sketches of city workers—elevator boys and porters "climbing up a great big mountain of yes, sirs!" "Ruby Brown", like Fenton Johnson's acid sketches, and "A Ruined Gal" have shocked those who wish poetry to be confined to the pretty and sweet, but they ring true and sympathetic. Another side of Negro experience is made real in "Feet o' Jesus", "Prayer", and "Angel's Wings." "Cross" is a quizzical, and "Mulatto" a direct commentary upon the bitter social fruit of race mixture.

Generalized interpretation of the race appears in "I, Too Sing America" and in "A Negro Speaks of Rivers," one of his finest poems. He calls his people "loud-mouthed laughers in the hands of fate," but is convinced that "their soul has grown deep like the

72

rivers." "Minstrel Man" takes an old concept and reveals a new truth:

> Because my mouth
> Is wide with laughter
> And my throat
> Is deep with song,
> You do not think
> I suffer after
> I have held my pain
> So long.

Hughes' awakened interest in communism has resulted in such poems as "Good-Bye, Christ", "Letter to the Academy", "Elderly Race Leaders" (which closes with twenty-four dollar signs), the "Ballad of Lenin", "Ballad of Ozzie Powell" and the better "To The Kids Who Die", "America", and "The Ballad of Roosevelt";

> The pot was empty
> The cupboard was bare.
> I said, Papa
> What's the matter here?
> I'm waitin' on Roosevelt, son,
> Roosevelt, Roosevelt,
> Waitin' on Roosevelt, son.

OTHER NEW NEGRO POETS

Waring Cuney likewise absorbed something of the spirit of the blues and spirituals, and his poems, like those of Hughes, have a deceptive simplicity. "I Think I See Him There", "Troubled Jesus", "Crucifixion" and "Wake Cry" deal gently and truthfully with folk religion. "Burial of The Young Love", "The Death Bed", "Threnody" and "Finis" attain a true melancholy with economy of phrase. "No Images" tells of the girl who thinks "her brown body has no glory."

73

If she could dance
Naked,
Under palm trees
And see her image in the river
She would know.

But there are no palm trees
On the street,
And dish water gives back no images.

Helene Johnson also writes with pride of race. Her "Sonnet to a Negro in Harlem" praises him for his magnificent disdain, his arrogant and bold laughter. Like Hughes, she believes his setting should be palm trees and mangoes. She writes in Harlemese a sketch of a jazz prince, with his shoulders "jerking the jig-wa." "Bottled" is a semi-humorous lament for a Negro "in trick clothes . . . . yaller shoes and yaller gloves and swallow-tail coat", who would be beautiful back in pagan Africa. Gwendolyn Bennett's poems are generally race conscious; like most of the New Negro school, she writes in "To A Dark Girl":

Something of old forgotten queens
Lurks in the lithe abandon of your walk. . . .

Gladys May Casely Hayford, a native African, writes with a conscious desire to imbue her own people "with the idea of their own beauty, superiority and individuality, with a love and admiration for our own country which has been systematically suppressed." Her "Rainy Season Love Song" is colorful and warm, but the verse form is traditional in cadence and phrasing.

One of the best Negro novelists, Arna Bontemps, is likewise a poet of distinction. His work is meditative, couched in fluent but subdued rhythms. It is poetry of the twilight, of reverie, as so much of Negro poetry, but the artistry is of high order. "Nocturne," "Nocturne at Bethesda," "Gethsemane," "Golgotha Is A Mountain" and "Return" are his best

74

works, and their titles are indicative. Whether writing in the traditional forms or in free verse, Bontemps' concern seems to be music above all else. The symbolism is at times successful; "Nocturne at Bethesda" has racial import:

> .... and why
> Do our black faces search the empty sky?
> Is there something we have forgotten? Some precious thing
> We have lost, wandering in strange lands?

One of the New Negro poets, Bontemps makes frequent reference to Africa, now grieving over the lost glory, now insisting upon his heritage, and now writing

> Those mountains should be ours.

Something of the attitude of the Garvey movement is to be seen in Lewis Alexander's poems to Africa: there is the allegiance to the "motherland," and a romantic faith in her resurgence.

> Rise from out thy charnel house to be
> Thine own immortal, brilliant self again.

This type of idealization of Africa was an attempted corrective to the typical undervaluation, but was more poetic dreaming than understanding. "The Dark Brother" pleads rhetorically for brotherhood. Lewis Alexander has also experimented with all types of poetry from the Japanese Tanka and Hokku to the Blues. Intellectual irony is in the free verse poetry of Frank Horne. "To A Persistent Phantom" and "More Letters Found Near A Suicide" are modern portraiture, vivid, racy and unhackneyed. "Nigger, A Chant For Children" is a recital of Negro heroism with the race-pride of the New Negro movement. One of the finest poetic re-creations of slavery days and characters was "Dead and Gone" by Allison Davis. This dramatic narrative (appearing in the only issue

75

of the magazine *Harlem*) showed understanding and power.

Clarissa Scott Delaney wrote poems that bore witness to a spirit sensitive and in love with life. "The Mask" is a well done portrait. Sensitivity likewise marks the poems of Esther Popel Shaw. "Salute To The Flag" departs from her usual nature description; it attacks the shams of democracy by placing the patriotic teachings of the schools side by side with the newspaper report of a lynching. George Leonard Allen, a poet-musician of North Carolina, was awarded a prize for the best sonnet in a state-wide contest conducted by the United Daughters of the Confederacy. He wrote fluently of nature and music; before his untimely death he was attempting as well to deal with folk-experiences. Another southern poet, Jonathan Brooks, writes with quiet surety. His poems, generally religious in nature or in imagery, are thoughtful and moving. Simple in phrasing and rhythm, they are unobstrusively symbolic. A collection of them would reveal that Brooks has a talent of distinction. *Negrito* (1933) by J. Mason Brewer is commendable in its purpose of recording Negro experience in the southwest, but the shadow of Dunbar lies heavy and there is little reference to anything but the happier side of life.

STERLING BROWN

Southern Road by Sterling A. Brown (1932) is chiefly an attempt at folk portraiture of southern characters. Brown sought to convey the tragedy of the southern Negro, in poems like the title poem, "Children of The Mississippi," "King Cotton" and "Sam Smiley," and the comedy in the Slim Greer series and "Sporting Beasley." The wandering roustabout is recorded in "Long Gone" and "Odyssey of Big Boy." The irony to be found in Negro folk-song appears in "Mr. Samuel and Sam." "Strong Man," making use of a refrain found in Sandburg—"The strong men keep coming on"—is an expression of the dogged stoicism Brown has found in Negro experience. He has made a fairly close study of folk-ways and folk-songs, and has used this in interpreting folk-experience and character which he considers one of the important tasks of Negro poetry. He is not afraid of using folk-speech, refusing to believe dialect to be "an instrument of only two stops—pathos and humor." He uses free verse and the traditional forms as well as folk-forms, and many of his poems are subjective. His second volume, to be called "No Hiding Place," re-explores the southern scene with more emphasis on social themes.

REALISM AND PROTEST

Trumpet in The New Moon by Welborn Victor Jenkins (1934) is a panoramic picture of the Negro in American life. It recalls Whitman in its patriotism (and its cataloguing) and Sandburg, but has an original place in Negro poetry:

Remember the service:

Come Susie, rock the baby—Go Hannah, get the dinner—
Uncle Jim, go plough the new ground—
Here Sambo, grab my satchel and get to hell—

Remember the sweat, the cotton fields, the lumber
logs, the brick yards, the sawmills and turpentine
plantation—all black labor.

Realistic and novel in detail, the poem repeats a pattern dear to Negro poets from Whitfield through Dunbar and James Weldon Johnson: the recording of Negro service will effect

the joys of Rebirth and Regeneration
At the solemn Love-Feast of Brotherhood and Democracy.

Frank Marshall Davis is likewise panoramic in

77

Black Man's Verse (1935). "What Do You Want, America" like "Trumpets in the New Moon" lists the services of Negroes, but comments more sardonically on the abuses of democracy. Davis is at times a mystic escapist, but at his best he is bitterly realistic. "Chicago's Congo," "Jazz Band," "Mojo Mike's Beer Garden" "Cabaret" and "Georgia's Atlanta" are forthright transcripts of reality. "Lynched" is a powerful protest. Davis is satiric about Negro "society": Robert Whitmore, ruler of the local Elks,

> died of apoplexy
> when a stranger from Georgia
> mistook him
> for a former Macon waiter.

Davis at times leans heavily upon Masters and Sandburg, but his gift of realistic portraiture, his irony, and his knowledge of Negro life should stand him in very good stead. Richard Wright, likewise of Chicago, is not content with either listing Negro achievement or registering the abuses of American life. He believes in poetry as a weapon, and in his driving rhythms urges Negro workers to rise up like men, side by side with white workers, to establish communism in America:

> I am black and I have seen black hands
> Raised in fists of revolt, side by side with the
>   white fists of white workers,
>   And some day—and it is only this which sustains me—
> Someday, there will be millions and millions of them
> On some red day in a burst of fists on a new horizon!

ROMANTIC ESCAPES

Quite a few books of verse have been produced by Negro poets within recent years, which are romantic escapes for the sensitive authors from depressing actualities. *Make Way For Happiness* (1932) by Alpheus Butler promises "I will bring you pretty things

78

measure for measure" and the resulting "prettiness" is trite. J. Harvey L. Baxter bewails the fallen estate of noble poetry which will still be sung

As long as stars, or waves of sea.

That Which Concerneth Me (1934) is unconcerned with race experience or the revelation of a personality; what concerns the poet, according to Baxter, is "the song of rose and bee." "Eve Lynn's" *No Alabaster Box* is praised by her sponsor because "not once does she refer to the peculiar problem of her own group." Marion Cuthbert's *April Grasses* is generally escapist; the interesting subject matter Miss Cuthbert is acquainted with she seems to consider unfit for poetic expression. Mae Cowdery's *Lift Our Voices* contains too often vague yearning and the romantic worship of nature, but at times has poetic drive. These poets by denying racial, or even personal experience pretend to touch "universality," which according to one Negro critic, means a concern with the universe.

SUMMARY

Contemporary Negro poets are too diverse to be grouped into schools. Certain chief tendencies, however, are apparent. More than Alberry Whitman, Dunbar, and Braithwaite, the contemporary poets, even when writing subjective lyrics, are more frankly personal, less restrained, and as a general rule, less conventional. They have been influenced by modern American poetry, of course, as their elders were by post-Victorian, but one of the cardinal lessons of modern poetry is that the poet should express his own view of life in his own way. It has been pointed out, however, that "bookishness" still prevails, that the so-called new poetry revival has left many versifiers untouched. Secondly, more than the older poets who

79

hesitantly advanced defenses of the Negro, the contemporary Negro poet is more assured, more self-reliant. He seems less taken in by American hypocrisy and expresses his protest now with irony, now with anger, seldom with humility. The poets who have taken folk-types and folk-life for their province no longer accept the stereotyped view of the traditional dialect writers, nor, lapsing into gentility, do they flinch from an honest portrayal of folk-life. Their laughter has more irony in it than buffoonery. They are ready to see the tragic as well as the pitiful. They are much closer to the true folk product than to the minstrel song.

It is not at all advanced that the contemporary poetry of the American Negro is to be ranked with the best of modern poetry. Too many talented writers have stopped suddenly after their first, sometimes successful gropings. The Negro audience is naturally small, and that part devoted to poetry, much smaller. Few Negro poets have the requisite time for maturing, for mastering technique, for observation of the world and themselves. Negro poets have left uncultivated many fields opened by modern poetry. Many still confine their models to the masters they learned about in school, to the Victorians, and the pre-Raphaelites. Almost as frequently they have been unaware of the finer uses of tradition. The reading world seems to be ready for a true interpretation of Negro life from within, and poets with a dramatic ability have before them an important task. And the world has always been ready for the poet who in his own manner reveals his deepest thoughts and feelings. What it means to be a Negro in the modern world is a revelation much needed in poetry. But the Negro poet must write so that whosoever touches his book touches a man. Too often, like other minor poets, he has written so that

80

whosoever touches his book touches the books of other
and greater poets.

DISCUSSION QUESTIONS

What are characteristics of "The New Negro"? Are all of these
absent from earlier Negro history?

What are chief characteristics of "New Negro" poetry?

Why is Fenton Johnson's "pessimism" a new note?

Distinguish between optimism and stoicism, between pessimism and
stoicism.

What are two types of poetry written by McKay?

What is significant in the work of Jean Toomer?

Contrast James Weldon Johnson's earlier poetry discussed in Chapter IV with his recent poetry.

Compare Cullen and Hughes.

In what respects are Jenkins and Frank M. Davis similar?

What are some forces opposed to modern Negro poetry? What are
some forces favoring it?

READING REFERENCES

Calverton, V. F.: "The Growth of Negro Literature" in *Anthology
of American Negro Literature*—edited by V. F. Calverton, Modern Library, New York—1929.

Chamberlain, John: "The Negro As Writer" in The Bookman LXX,
pp. 603-611, February—1930.

Clay, Eugene: "The Negro in Recent American Literature" in *American Writers' Congress*—International Publishers Co., New York
1935.

Cullen, Countee: *Caroling Dusk, An Anthology of Verse By Negro
Poets*—Harper & Brothers, New York—1927.

Johnson, Charles S., editor—*Ebony and Topaz*—National Urban
League, New York—1927.

Johnson, Charles S.: "The Negro Enters Literature" in The *Carolina
Magazine*, Negro Number—University of North Carolina Press
—May, 1927.

Johnson, James Weldon: *Black Manhattan*—Alfred Knopf, New York
—1930.

Locke, Alain: *Four Negro Poets*, The Pamphlet Poets Series—Simon
and Schuster, New York—1927.

Locke, Alain: "The Negro In American Culture" in *Anthology of
American Negro Literature*—edited by V. F. Calverton, the Modern Library, New York—1929.

Locke, Alain: "Propaganda or Poetry" in *Race, A Quarterly*—Sumner
—1936.

Locke, Alain: "The New Negro" and "Negro Youth Speaks" in *The
New Negro*—A. and C. Boni, New York—1927.

Also works already cited by Braithwaite, Brawley, Brown, Green
Johnson, and Kerlin.

Files of *The Crisis*, and *Opportunity, A Journal of Negro Life*.

81

WHITE POETS ON NEGRO LIFE (TO 1914)

EARLY ANTI-SLAVERY POETRY

At the founding of the republic when the watchwords were liberty, equality and fraternity, the poets joined the antislavery protest. Philip Freneau's "The Beauties of Santa Cruz" and "To Sir Toby," denounced conditions in the West Indies. Sir Toby's slaves were in a veritable hell of which Freneau forcibly delineates the separate tortures.

> O'er yond' rough hills a tribe of females go
> Each with her gourd, her infant, and her hoe
> Scorched by a sun that has no mercy here,
> Driven by a devil whom men call overseer. . . .

Freneau's invective is partly anti-British; in less partisan times it could have been directed against plantations nearer home, in his own "free asylum" for the enslaved. Timothy Dwight in *Greenfield Hill* (1794) describes the Connecticut slave, whose status was nearer that of the hired man, as one

> Of care oblivious . . . [of a] laughing mind . . .

But he considers the typical American slave to be suffering the chief curse of mankind,

> Conditioned as a brute, tho' formed a man.

For the freed Negro who sank to thieving and drunkenness, Dwight offers the sensible defense that America denied him opportunity to do otherwise. In Joel Barlow's epic *The Columbiad* (1807) the evil and danger of slavery are pointed out.

In this earlier period Thomas Branagan wrote two long antislavery poems, "The Penitential Tyrant" and

82

"Avenia" (1810). The first expressed the repentance of a slave-trader and overseer after seeing a vision of the victims of the system. The second is a sentimental and melodramatic narrative of an African heroine who commits suicide rather than be enslaved. Branagan's heart is right but the poetry is bad. Like the magazine heroines of the time, Avenia is hopelessly sentimentalized, and unbelievable as an African, or for that matter, as any human being. And so are the victimized heroes and heroines in *The Anti-Slavery Harp* and *Songs of Freedom*. The sympathies of these minor poets and poetesses could not make up for inadequate knowledge of Negro life.

NINETEENTH CENTURY HUMANITARIANISM

This same charge could well be levelled against some better-known poets of the nineteenth century. Bryant's "The African Chief" (1825) tells of a noble savage who died of grief when he could not buy his freedom to return to his wife and young children. Longfellow's *Poems on Slavery,* written on a return voyage from Germany, are labors of duty more than of love; his "Slave's Dream" (1842) shows another noble savage, an African king, who dies heartbroken because of his fate. Longfellow's descriptions of Africa and of domestic slavery are confusing, both being derived from hearsay. But there is no doubt that the simpler pathos of poems like "The Slave In The Dismal Swamp" and "Quadroon Girl" stirred Longfellow's wide audience against what he called the "feudal curse," the ruinous "blind Samson in the vast temple of our liberties."

Whittier was much more powerfully "the balladist of abolitionism." Strong in praise of men like Garrison and Seward, or in blame of pro-slavery forces, northern and southern, he wrote many poems dealing with the hardships of slavery. "The Slave Ships", "Hunters of Men", "Farewell of a Virginia Slave Mother" deal with the callousness of the slave traffic. "Slaves of Martinque" is a story of exceptional slaves, both "noble savages," told in a Tennysonian manner. Whittier attempts dialect in "The Song of the Negro Boatmen" but can hardly be said to succeed:

> Ole Massa on he trabbles gone;
> He leaf de land behind:
> De Lord's breff blow him furder on,
> Like corn-shuck in de wind. . . .

Barrett Wendell accused the abolitionist poets of misinterpreting the Negro "by the simple process of daubing their faces with burnt cork." There is point to his criticism. But if Whittier's speech and occasionally his characterizing are not convincing, there is still realistic truth in his slave-auctions, slave-treks, Negro driving bullies, and unsubmissive Negroes. "The Panorama" portraying

> A slave plantation's slovenly repose
> Where, in rude cabins rotting midst their weeds,
> The human chattel eats, and sleeps, and breeds

cannot be thrown aside as unrealistic.

PRO-SLAVERY

It is certainly more realistic than William Grayson's *The Hireling and The Slave* (1856) a southern counterblast to the abolitionists. This long poem contrasts the hard lot of New England laborers with the ease and comfort of South Carolina slaves. According to Grayson, life for the slave, chiefly hunting and fishing, was

So unassailed by care
So blessed with moderate work, with ample fare,
With all the good the starving pauper needs,
The happier slave on each plantation leads. . . .
And Christian slaves may challenge as their own
The blessings claimed in fabled states alone—
The cabin home, not comfortless, though rude,
Light daily labor, and abundant food,
The sturdy health that temperate habits yield
The cheerful song that rings in every field
The long, loud laugh, that freemen seldom share,
Heaven's boon to bosoms unapproached by care. . . .

When the slaves were freed by unwise masters they became drunken, debauched and criminal. Slavery was the Negro's suitable condition, and the kindness of masters made it paradise. So says South Carolina's poet-laureate.

MINSTRELSY

The minstrel song-writers, thriving during the period of the abolitionist poets, did more toward fixing popular conceptions of the Negro. They, too, could be badly artificial in such faked phrases and foreign experiences as "ten days upon the ocean wave, brought feelings quite cathartic", "like Massa Shakespeare's Hamlet", and "Come, darkies, come, 'tis the hour for pleasure, Let mirth prevail then, without measure", or in descriptions like that of Sam Johnson's daughter Rose:

Fair as darkey's child could be
Luscious lips and raven hair
Pearly teeth and step so free,

whose elopement with her beloved is written thus:

And then, I ween, two forms were seen
And swiftly from the shore they fly. . . .

These songs are likewise unconvincing in their picturing an abject Negro who ridicules himself, with no sense of shame, just to make the white folks laugh. This is

85

understandable when we consider that these songs were almost entirely by white writers for white audiences and sung by white minstrel troupes.

Playing to audiences on both sides of the Ohio, the minstrel songs show conflicting tendencies. The majority praise slavery. Slaves hymn "old Massa":

> Long live old Massa, from him ne'er we'll part. . . .
> Hither we go, his wish to fulfill. . . .

Or they frolic at "blackberryings", "darkey weddings" or cabin breakdowns: where "Lemuel makes the fiddle hum, the banjo tum", "happy are we, darkies so gay", "tripping lightly the old Virginia reel." Dandy Jim of Caroline, dressed up and proud, is cock of the walk; and lovely Lucindys, Dinahs, and Lucys wait in the canebreak down by the mill in the cool of the evening for their dusky lovers: "O, Virginny Nebber Tire!" Some songs, however, sound the mournful note: selling slaves down the river and separation of loved ones are mentioned, as in Hanby's "Darling Nellie Gray" which has survived. But these are less numerous, and none really rise to the tragic bitterness of the truth, which the audience could hardly have been expected to appreciate.

Some of the minstrel writers did study Negroes realistically for purposes of better mimicry. Such songs as "Zip Coon", "Dan Tucker", "Clar de Kitchen" and "That Long-Tailed Blue" caught something of the flavor of folk speech and psychology. Others make use of phrases from the spirituals, and in spite of the irreverence sometimes draw close to reality:

> He done seed ole Peter and he ain't a-gwine to wait
> You'd better be dar 'fore it gets too late,
> Kase dar ain't a-gwine to be no scrougin' round de gate
> He's a-gwine to meet you early in de mornin'.

Stephen Foster sought fidelity in both words and music.

Some of his early pieces show a happy-go-lucky slave existence: "The Camp Town Races", "Away Down South" (father of a brood), and "Oh, Susanna", a nonsense song dear to the forty-niners. "Massa's In The Cold, Cold Ground" is the conventional song of mutual affection, but in later songs, although the full truth is not spoken out, the sadness of being sold deeper south from gentler Kentucky, or of the separation from the old folks at home, is implied. Henry C. Work, officer in the union army, wrote with more direct partisanship. His songs satirize the master, give rallying tunes and catchwords to the contrabands, and cheer the day of jubilee. Nicodemus, of African birth, prophesies freedom in "Wake Nicodemus"; "Kingdom Coming" tells of a plantation abandoned by a cowardly master, where the slaves "confiscate" the wine and cider and sing:

> De overseer, he make us trouble
> An' he dribe us round a spell
> We lock him up in de smokehouse cellar
> Wid de key trown in de well.
> De whip is lost, de han' cuff broken. . . .

"Babylon is Fallen" tells of the "black clouds" of Negro soldiers rising from the plantations "to fight for Uncle Sam." Though mixed with comic nonsense, the song still shows the slaves to be jubilant at freedom, ironic, and spirited. The minstrel song was getting to reality in more than dialect.

CIVIL WAR POETRY

The Negro's striking a blow for his own freedom caught the attention of George Boker, who among his *Poems of the War* included "The Black Regiment", a stirring ode. Equally sympathetic, Herman Melville was moved by a portrait to write of an old slave-woman whose face, now that "too late deliverance

87

dawns" shows the sufferance of her race, and yet is lit with "sibylline prophecy." This poem should be compared with Walt Whitman's "Ethiopia Saluting The Colors", in which an old crone, dehumanized by slavery, greeting Sherman's army of liberation, is made into a figure of tragedy and prophecy. Although Whitman, in his prose, wrote of the Negro with surprising and undue severity, his poetic references are humanitarian. His "sympathetic identification" with the runaway slave "limpsy and weak . . . with galls on his neck and shoulders" revealing much in a few words, is continued in:

> I am the hounded slave, I wince at the bite of the dogs,
> Hell and despair are upon me. . . .
> I clutch the rails of the fence. . . .

Being a "caresser of life", a lover of the vigorous, out-of-doors self-contained man, Whitman praises a picturesque giant Negro who

> holds firmly the rein of his four horses. . . .
> steady and tall he stands poised on one leg on
> the string-piece
> His blue shirt is calm and commanding, he tosses the
> slouch of his hat from his forehead,
> The sun falls on his crispy hair and mustache, falls
> on the black of his polished and perfect
> limbs. . . . .

LOCAL COLOR: IRWIN RUSSELL

But the lead towards realism in Whitman was not continued in the post-war poets. Sidney and Clifford Lanier lightheartedly tossed off a few poems in dialect about the southern Negro. "The Power of Prayer" or "The First Steamboat Up The Alabama" is a rhymed version of an amusing anecdote used by Mark Twain. Though preceded by the Lanier brothers, Irwin Russell went at the job more seriously, and is therefore considered the first American poet to portray the Negro in dialect with any degree of success. Russell, a Mississippian, is an able local colorist. Some of his poems are about antebellum life: the title poem of his volume *Christmas In the Quarters* is a pastoral poem picturing the slave in his festivities. It definitely influenced Dunbar, and the part of it telling how Ham, lonely on the ark for music, invented the banjo and strung it with hairs from the tail of the possum (since then hairless) is rich humor. This tale has gone back into American folklore; Roark Bradford's biblical re-creations are like it in approach. "Mahsr John" shows an old slave regretting freedom since it removed a master from his blessed state of

> settin' on de galry, lookin' awful big an' wise,
> Wid little niggers fannin' him to keep away de flies.

"Business in Mississippi" and "Selling A Dog" are good-humored sketches of folk cunning. "Nebuchadnezzar" is the farce of a mule kicking a farm hand. Joel Chandler Harris praises Russell for his perfect grasp of Negro character and experience. This is overpraise. Russell was a good humorist who knew Negro speech, and something about Negro life in the delta. But his poems treat only those aspects of Negro life and character agreeable to a white Mississippian in reconstruction days. His characters exist mainly to be laughed at, or patted on the back when they speak of their love for fine white folks.

THOMAS NELSON PAGE, JOEL CHANDLER HARRIS

Thomas Nelson Page and A. C. Gordon in *Befo' De War* wrote dialect poetry to prove that slavery was a blessed state. Uncle Gabe dreamed of the vanished glory of his family. Uncle Jack, unwillingly set free, commands his son to give his hard-earned money to his white master, since:

89

> He ain' been use ter diggin'
> His livin' out de dirt;
> He carn't drink out a piggin,
> Like you; and it ud' hurt
> Old Marster's pride, and make him swar,
>   In glory dyar!

Having thus won Page's approval, Uncle Jack dies and is rushed to heaven to be his master's servant "in glory dyar." Joel Chandler Harris was too sensible for this sort of thing. His poems are either recombinations of folk-rhymes he had garnered, or creations that catch the syncopation and the idiom of Negro speech, but they are a bit too mechanically fluent for complete resemblance. They generally celebrate the good times of rural life, or express the slave's religion.

> Nigger mighty happy w'en he layin' by co'n
>   Dat sun's a slantin';
> Nigger mighty happy w'en he year de dinner horn
>   Dat sun's a slantin'. . . .

But Harris omits any other side of Negro life: getting close to it only in lines like

> De ole bee make de honey-comb
>   De young bee make de honey,
> De niggers make de cotton en co'n
>   En de w'ite folks gits the money. . . .

But these Harris did not write: he only recorded them.

LATER LOCAL COLOR

J. A. Macon's *Uncle Gabe Tucker,* not known so well as the works mentioned, contains verses which are intimate pictures of Negro life in the quarters. If the main tone is pastoral, still the poems do not exist merely to please a southern white audience as do Page's. Macon sees Negro life as worthy of interest in its own right. Later imitators of Russell, like Belle Harrison, write either amusing or sentimental anecdotes. Frank Stanton turned from dialect of the

90

Georgia whites to write a few poems on the Negro; but he largely confined himself to the Negro and possum and watermelon, an eternal triangle.

John Charles McNeill in *Lyrics From Cotton Land* (1907) is a local color realist. Conventionally jocular in poems like "The Coon From The College Town", "Ligion" and "A Soft Nap", he is at times a shrewd witness, as in "August Meeting", which is a Tarheel variant of Burn's "Holy Fair":

> Dar wus razors, knives en wrenches;
> Planks fum offen busted benches. . . .
> En I seed one fool er-fightin' wid his han's.

"Protest" and "The Red Shirts" are a folk Negro's grumbling at the chain gang and the night riders, but too humorous to be completely truthful. "Mr. Nigger" states how necessary the Negro is to America (to rag-time composers, planters, politicians whose stock-in-trade is Negro abuse, lynchers "who burn to excite the North);" it concludes: "Don't you fear expatriation, Mr. Nigger." If McNeill had not been so hot on the trail of jokes, he might have said something about his native South worth listening to.

SENTIMENTALITY

Side by side with the poems gibing at the Negro's clownishness or approving his quaint philosophizing were many stressing his sentimentality (or at least the sentimentality of the white authors). Many of these were lullabies. Hattie Starr's "Little Coon" is both lullaby and baby's prophecy:

> When I's big, I's gwine to wed a yellow gal:
> Den we'll hab pickaninnies of our own

and is artificial in both instances. "Go Sleep My Honey", by Edward D. Barker, is better; so is "Kentucky Babe", though the point of view is one of amused and consciously tolerant "white folks":

> Lay yo' kinky, wooly head on yo' mammy's breast.

91

Stanton's "Mighty Lak A Rose" is probably the best known of this type, still very dear to those who believe that the relationship between black nurse and white charge is the Negro's supreme experience. There were so many of these songs written by white versifiers in the first years of this century that one correspondent from Georgia to the *Ladies Home Journal* insisted that Cole and Johnson, who were doing similar songs, must therefore be white.

DISCUSSION QUESTIONS

What are the weaknesses of antislavery poetry? What are its strong points?

What different types of songs were sung by black-face minstrels?

In what respects are minstrel songs artificial? Are they completely unrealistic?

Compare the Civil War poets with the local colorists.

How does the sentimentalizing of a Negro mammy differ from humanitarianism?

READING REFERENCES

Standard histories of American literature such as *The Cambridge History of American Literature*, Barrett Wendell's *A Literary History of The American People*, V. L. Parrington's *Main Currents In American Thought*, and Percy Boynton's *Literature and American Life*.

Christy's Minstrel Songs, title page missing.

Fulton, Maurice Garland: *Southern Life in Southern Literature*—Ginn and Co., New York—1917.

Gaines, Francis Pendleton: *The Southern Plantation*—Columbia University Press—1924.

Hibbard, Addison: *The Lyric South*—Macmillan Co., New York—1929.

Minstrel Songs, Old and New—Oliver Ditson and Co., Boston—1882.

Nelson John Herbert: *The Negro Character In American Literature*—Department of Journalism Press, Lawrence, Kansas—1926.

Parks, Edd Winfield: *Southern Poets*—American Book Co., New York—1936.

Paskman, Dailey and Spaeth, Sigmund: *"Gentlemen, Be Seated!"*—Doubleday, Doran and Co., New York—1928.

Stedman, Edmund Clarence: *An American Anthology*, 1787-1899—Houghton, Mifflin and Co., Boston—1900.

Trent, W. P.: *Southern Writers*—The Macmillan Co., New York—1905.

Turner, Lorenzo D.: *Antislavery Sentiment in American Literature*—Association For The Study of Negro Life and History, Washington—1929.

Wynn, William T.: *Southern Literature*—Prentice-Hall, New York—1932.

VII

WHITE POETRY OF NEGRO LIFE (CONTEMPORARY)

THE REALISTIC MOVEMENT

With the ushering in of the realistic movement in the second decade of this century, poets turned to the Negro with less sentimentality, less condescension, and greater truth. Most of the major figures of the American poetic renaissance have written of him. Edwin Arlington Robinson in a dramatic portrait has recreated Touissant L'Ouverture. Alfred Kreymborg has written lilting dramatic monologues of Harlem. Ridgely Torrence's "Blackbird" is an indirect account of a lynching: the pity and terror of this poem make it one of the most memorable of the century. William Ellery Leonard's fine human sympathies appear in "The Lynching Bee", a fierce attack upon mob violence.

Here and there in his panorama of America, Carl Sandburg has included snapshots of Negroes caught at work or play: "Jazbo, the dockwolloper":

> I listened to the five of you harmonizing
> six ways to sing 'Way Down Yonder in the Cornfield!

Sandburg's *American Song Bag* bears witness to his great interest in Negro folk music. Unconventional in picture and idea are Maxwell Bodenheim's early poems "An Old Negro Asleep" and "The Cotton Pickers":

> the pent satin of her face was always cut by a smile
> As she hummed of a joyous Christ.

93

His "Jazz Kaleidoscope" sets in contrast the high-hearted jazz of Harlem with the bitterness of lynching. John Gould Fletcher in "Down The Mississippi" uses for decorative purposes Negro stevedores:

> Frieze of warm bronze that glides with catlike movements
> Over the gang-plank poised and yet awaiting,
> The sinewy thudding rhythm of forty shuffling feet. . . .

William Rose Benét's "Harlem" is one of the liveliest poems of discovery of the music and abandon in Negro cabarets and dancehalls. Jazz rhythm is used:

> Drug-store, pool-room, turn them loose
> On the Ringtail, Florida and Beale Street Blues;
> Antillian flats take up the dance
> In a crack-a-knuckle, crack-a-knuckle shuffling trance,
> They reel,
> They roll,
> They sway across my soul. . . .

VACHEL LINDSAY

Vachel Lindsay has been most influential upon poetry about Negro life. "The Congo" (1914) was a successful experiment in jazz rhythms, although it hardly accomplished its boast of being "A Study of The Negro Race." But Lindsay, attempting to sing America, saw that the Negro could not be left out of the song. He was caught by the picturesque, spectacular, uninhibited aspects of his life. "The Congo" renders the abandon of Negroes in barrel-houses, gambling halls, and churches. Their "basic savagery", irrepressible high spirits" are traced to

> The Congo, creeping through the black
> Cutting through the jungle with a golden track. . . .

a metaphor that, for all of its influence upon both Negro and white poets, remains dubious. The hope of Negro religion is to throw off mumbo-jumbo and to bring about an Africa "transfigured for the Negro nation":

> For a Congo paradise, for babes at play,
> For sacred capitals, for temples clean. . . .
> A million boats of the angels sailed
> With oars of silver, and prows of blue
> And silken pennants that the sun shone through. . .

(All of which sounds more like Vachel Lindsay's dream of America than the hope of Negro religion.) The central ideas of "The Congo" are debatable, but there is no gainsaying its mastery of rhythm and phrase. These evoke definite scenes, which though often on the exotically romantic side, have counterparts in Negro experience:

> Fat black bucks in a wine-barrel room
> Barrel-house kings, with feet unstable
> Sagged and reeled and pounded on the table. . . .
> Beat an empty barrel with the handle of a broom,
> Hard as they were able,
> Boom, boom, BOOM,
> With a silk umbrella and the handle of a broom,
> Boomlay, boomlay, boomlay, BOOM.

Or, a second example:

> A good old Negro in the slums of the town
> Preached at a sister for her velvet gown.
> Howled at a brother for his lowdown ways,
> His prowling, guzzling, sneak-thief days,
> Beat on the Bible till he wore it out. . . .

Without using dialect Lindsay attempts to get the qualities of Negro sermons in "Simon Legree" and "John Brown." Thus he preceded James Weldon Johnson's *God's Trombones* without equalling them: the short rhymed lines are not so near the mark as Johnson's chanting free verse. But they are interesting explorations of Negro character and idioms, and with "The Congo" deserve to be known as informed and sympathetic treatments of Negro life.

EDGAR LEE MASTERS

Although sharply critical of typical American attitudes, Edgar Lee Masters himself furthers one of these, when, in a poem dedicated to Vachel Lindsay, he has a character say (apparently with the poet's approval) :

> You know I love a nigger
> And I love this nigger. . . .
> Now to think! here's a human who has no other cares
> Except to please the white man, serve him when he's starving. . . .
>
> Just think for a minute, how the Negroes excell
> Can you beat them with a banjo or a broiling pan?

He praises the Negro as one of two things really American, not hybrid; Christian Science is the other. The Negro is "elemental hope, heartiness, mirth." This is hardly worthy of the poet of Spoon River.

JOHN BROWN'S BODY

John Brown's Body, by Stephen Vincent Benét, celebrating the epical Civil War, includes, inevitably, Negro characters. Though they approximate familiar types, Benét makes them live, and comments upon them thoughtfully. As should be expected, we have the mammy Aunt Bess, "the family despot, and the slave,"

> They have made you a shrine and a humorous fable,
> But they kept you a slave while they were able. . . .

and Cudjo, the loyal pantryman, proud of his quality whitefolks, though never completely understood by them :

> But there was a bond, and the bond would hold,
> On either side until both were cold.

As foils to these are Tarbarrel, the African king, viewing his captors with steady hate; and Dangerfield Newby, freed Negro, the first of John Brown's raiders to fall. Although slavery is treated with something too much of tolerance, Benét does mention in passing the fact of miscegenation, and does show the jubilee

96

of the slaves at freedom. Spade, the runaway, is most fully characterized. Wanting freedom far above a good cabin and good victuals and a kind mistress, he is not afraid of "paterollers" or of a "pizen-mean" master. He runs away, finds the North coldly indifferent to him, fights for his own freedom and is wounded in the crater before Petersburg, and ends up as a farm-hand, working for a fellow veteran. He stands up, four-square, a man. Benét is aware of the beauty and power of the Negro's story in America, writing:

> I cannot sing you, having too white a heart,
> And yet, some day, a poet will rise to sing you
> And sing you with such truth and mellowness—
> That you will be a match for any song. . . .

THE SET-UP

The *Set-up* by Joseph Moncure March tells of a Negro prizefighter, Pansy Jones, dodged by the white champion because he is too good. After years have broken him, he is signed to a bout. Not knowing that his managers have sold the fight he knocks out his white opponent, a rising hope. He is then ganged and killed for "double-crossing." The poem is a harshly realistic exposé of the fight racket. Pansy Jones is convincing:

> Pansy had the stuff, but his skin was brown
> And he never got a chance at the middleweight crown
> Mean as a panther
> Crafty as a fox:
> He could hit like a mule
> And he knew how to box. . . .
> In the ring he had the general habits
> Of a blacksnake after a couple of rabbits.

The syncopated verse form is suited for brisk story-telling and especially for the fight scenes.

Many southern white poets have continued to write of Negro in preference to white characters. Some write like minstrels: "She can vocalate de music of a operatic song": some, in the sentimental tradition, glorify the black mammy fluently but inconsequentially; others, like Roselle Montgomery, are local colorists. Virginia Lyne Tunstall's "Brother" is a pathetic story a notch above the average. Donald Davidson, a twentieth century Confederate, urges the Negro who is "perhaps unfortunately no longer a child" to remember the wall anciently erected between white and black:

> But now I cannot
> Forget that I was master, and you can hardly
> Forget that you were slave. . . .
> Let us not bruise our foreheads on the wall.

Robert Penn Warren, a Confederate brother-in-arms, writes a poem in which a buzzard declares to Big Jim Todd in terror of a posse: "Nigger, your breed ain't metaphysical." The poem is, however.

CLEMENT WOOD

Before his important novel *Nigger* Clement Wood had written poems of the Negro folk in *The Earth Turns South* (1919). "Debbil Foot" is a version of superstition, and "Nigger Hebb'n" of folk religion. Mastery of folklore, dialect, and rhythm are apparent in these, but "De Glory Road" is even better. In a swinging rhythm this poem is one of the best recreations of Negro folk-beliefs, closer to the actual southern Negro than Lindsay's better known "The Congo".

> O Lawdy, it's de Debbil, comin' straight from Hell!
> I kin tell him by his roarin' and de brimstone smell! . . .
> An' I cried "Law'd sabe me!" "An' de Law'd cry "Sho!"
> An' hyah it was Heben, an' we shet de do!

Oh Glory, Glory, how de angels sang!
Oh Glory, Glory, how de rafters rang!
An' Moses 'n' Aron, an' Methusalum,
Dey shout and dey holler, an' dey beat de drum.
King Solomon kissed me un' his thousan' wives,
Jes, like dey knowed me, during all dey lives. . . .
An' de ravens fed me, an' Elijah prayed,
An' de Sabed Ones gathered, while de organ played.
An' dey cry, "O Sinnah, come and lose yuh load
On de Glory Road, on de Glory Road."

In "Birmingham" (1930) Clement Wood portrays the great industrial city of the South. He naturally includes sketches of Negroes, since these make up half the population. His account is convincing: "thirty-seven niggers jugged at a chitterling party" for which "the officers earn thirty-seven convictions; thirty-seven sets of costs"; good Negroes and bad, ("every third one a preacher") :

You hear them loud together,
Crunching barbecue pork at Baptist sociables,
Eating cold fish sandwiches at furnace noon-hours,
Driving picks like the pulse of God into a roadbed
With "Nobody Knows de Trouble I's Seen,"
"You May Bury Me In de East," "Go, Down Moses"—
The moan of a race awaking,
The mutter of a storm far away. . . .

DUBOSE HEYWARD

An outstanding novelist of Negro life, DuBose Heyward has written his best poetry about the southern roustabouts he knows so well. In "Gamesters All" a stevedore runs from a Marshal rather than face "degrading slavery upon the gang":

I saw Joe's eyes, and knew he'd never go.
Not Joe, the swiftest hand in River Row!
Springing from where he sat, straight, cleanly made,
He soared, a leaping shadow from the shade
With fifty feet to go.

The Marshal, "an honest sportsman, as they go," coolly shoots him down

And down the heat, I heard a woman moaning.

99

This is one of the most sympathetic tragedies by a southern poet. "Jasbo Brown" is a similarly sympathetic portrait of a vagabond piano player who must always be moving and for whom

> Life is jus' hello
> An' so-long.

There is no gainsaying Heyward's power in the handling of Negro speech, setting and character.

E. C. L. ADAMS

Another South Carolinian, E. C. L. Adams, has written transcriptions of Negro sermons and prayers in eloquent poetic form. "The Slave Barn" and "Old Man Hildebrand" in *Nigger To Nigger* are bitter indictments of slavery:

> Ole man Hildebran' was a bad ole man,
> He live in slavery time.
> He heart been iron and he head been stone,
> An' he pleasure been a nigger's groan.
> He eye been yellow, an' he soul been dead,
> An' he live in slavery time.
> Ole man Hildebran'! Ole man Hildebran'! Ole man Hildebran'!

Being a realist, Adams is willing to admit in his pictures the darker shades that are undoubtedly there. Far more important than his knowledge of folk-speech and the Congaree section is his grasp of the irony and bitterness of folk Negroes *when talking to each other*. It is clear that he has overheard, or been allowed to hear, a great deal. And that is why his work is so superior to local color.

RADICAL PROTEST

The twentieth century defense of the under-dog resulted in poems of protest; soon this humanitarianism deepened into socialism. The *Masses* and *Liberator,* besides publishing the Negro's own protests in McKay's poems, published such poems as Rolfe

Humphries' "To An Unhappy Negro" and E. Merrill Root's "A Southern Holiday", a ballad of a lynching. Present-day liberal and radical periodicals frequently contain poems attacking the exploitation of the Negro worker. Keene Wallis in "Coal Black Jesus" catches the misery and hopelessness of Negro criminals on their way to jail, and "Up and Down and Out" tells of a friendship between two youths, one white, the other Negro, who in revolt against society take to the road. Sarah Cleghorn, hearing the cry of "Negroes humiliated, cheated, driven, terrified, shot, hung and burnt, or in the chain-gang, in terror of the stretch and the sweatbox, or the sweltering roads of Georgia," wrote poems of protest, but believed them not to be half burning enough. There is fine sympathy in her "Lionel Licorish" (the chief hero of the Vestris wreck) and in the "Ballad of Glorious Harriet Tubman" (the Maryland underground agent who rescued so many of her people):

> She went again, she went again,
> She carried their slaves away. . . .

Maxwell Bodenheim, changing from the involved style of his earlier poetry, is now writing poems to serve as weapons in the class struggle. Some concern the organizing of Negro and white sharecroppers; "Gray Rivers" is one of the most striking of these. H. H. Lewis sketches Negro farmers side by side with the other Missourians whom he knows so well, and adds sharp criticism to his sketches. In the sardonic "Clean Fields", a Negro farmer, whose industry and planning irritate his white neighbors, is framed as an insulter of white womanhood:

> Rockyby, rockyby, rockyby, son
> Blackes' yit bawn. . . .
> Rockyby, rocky—ouah Joe's dead'n gawn. . . .

The authors of *Stevedore*, Paul Peters and George Sklar, have written "Lynchtown—A Mass Chant"

101

which pictures unforgettably the burning of twelve
Negroes who banded together in a cabin to defy a mob:

> Here twelve people lived and breathed and stood their ground
>   and fought to live
> And were consumed by fire.

SUMMARY

American white poets have thus been as attentive
to the Negro character as the fiction writers and
dramatists. Their work has reflected the poetic standards of their periods. Abolitionary humanitarianism,
idealization of the "Noble Savage", minstrel buffoonery, proslavery argument, local-color, realism,
social protest, and radical propaganda, have been suc-
cessively their concerns. Although some of the poets
have been hostile, or short-sighted, or condescending,
many others have tried honestly to set down what they
saw. A great deal of this portraiture is valuable
socially, and some is poetically outstanding. Taken
with the poetry of Negro life written from within,
this poetry from without constitutes an important
approach to understanding; increasing in truthfulness
and power as we approach our own time.

DISCUSSION QUESTIONS

Why would realism improve poetry about Negro life?
What poets used the "exotic" elements of Negro experience? Why
did this appeal to them?
What new types are in *John Brown's Body?*
Is *The Set-Up* about an unusual situation?
What do Wood, Heyward, and Adams add to local color?
What differentiates "humanitarianism" from "socialism"?
What types of poetry have white authors written about Negro life
and character?

READING REFERENCES

Kreymborg, Alfred: *A History of American Poetry: Our Singing
    Strength*—Tudor Publishing Co., New York—1935.
Kreymborg, Alfred: *Lyric America*—Tudor Publishing Co., New
    York—1935.
Untermeyer, Louis: *Modern American Poetry*—Harcourt, Brace &
    Co., New York—1930.
Untermeyer, Louis, *American Poetry Since 1900*—Harcourt, Brace &
    Co., New York—1923.
Also works, cited in Chapter VI, by Hibbard and Parks.

PART II
THE NEGRO IN DRAMA

VIII
EARLY DRAMA OF NEGRO LIFE (TO 1916)

EARLY APPEARANCES

The Negro entered American drama in a walk-on role, as self-effacing as he was supposed to be in real life. Today, instead of coming downstage to deliver or to be a joke and then retiring to upstage, or hovering in the wings with a letter or a glass, he is often found center-stage full in the limelight. Pulitzer prize winning plays and other plays of very long runs have been concerned with Negro life and character. At first, like the Irish in English drama, because of a roughly similar social position, the Negro seemed doomed to be the comic relief of plays sadly in need of comedy. Out of this grew black-face ministrelsy, a truly American product. But as the Negro became more and more an integral part of American life, and a disturbing problem, dramatists who wished to create a truthful national drama, were unwilling to leave him in the plainly artificial blackface roles. A roster of those who have dealt with Negro life includes Edward Christy, Harriet Beecher Stowe, Dion Boucicault, Edward Sheldon, William Vaughn Moody, Eugene O'Neill, Paul Green, Ridgely Torrence, Marc Connelly, John Wexley, Paul Peters and George Sklar. These are significant figures in the history of American drama; and in many cases, their reputation depends in great part upon their plays of Negro life.

103

Whereas in 1823 Edwin Forrest had to hire an old Negro crone because no actress would demean herself to play the role of a Negro woman, today a revival of *Uncle Tom's Cabin* sees a white star in the role of Liza, and one of the leading ladies of the American stage elected to play Scarlet Sister Mary. This is indicative, although in the main as Negro roles have become more realistic they have been played by Negro actors.

The earliest plays, as the earliest novels, show the Negro character chiefly as comic servant and contented slave. Two plays differ: *The Fall of British Tyranny* (1776) dramatizes a concern of the revolutionary period when slaves promise the British who have released them to kill their masters, and *Yorker's Stratagem* (1792) shows a New Yorker, disguised as a comic Yankee, marrying Priscilla, a West Indian mulatto. But Murdock's *The Triumph of Love* (1795) is in the main line of development: Sambo the servant is introduced for dialect and comic antics. Dunlap's *A Trip to Niagara* (1830) ridicules the appearance, dress, mannerisms and speech of Job Jerryson and Cato. The most easily accessible of the plays showing the comic servant is Anna Cora Mowatt's *Fashion* (1845); the treatment of Zeke is representative:

> I tell 'ee what, Missy, I'm 'st'ordinary glad to find dis a bery 'spectabul like situation! . . . . You've had a super-numerary advantage of me—seeing dat I only receibed my appointment dis morning. What I wants to know is your publicated opinion, privately expressed, ob de domestic circle . . . . Bery lucifer expressed. . . .

BLACK-FACE MINSTRELSY

The above bit of dialogue shows the influence of the minstrel vogue which was at its peak in the eighteen forties. In the twenties Edwin Forrest had strolled

104

through the streets dressed up for a blackface role; mistaken by an old Negro woman for a Negro she knew, he persuaded her to join him in a skit upon the stage. T. D. Rice, nicknamed Daddy and Jim Crow Rice, followed Forrest in the thirties, impersonating in a shuffling clog dance a Negro hostler, whose clothes he borrowed. Legend has it that when he appeared in this sketch on a Cincinnati stage, he was insistently encored until a small voice from the wings whimpered "Gimme back mah clothes." Rice followed up his success with many other Negroid songs and acts called "Ethiopian opera"; in one sketch he opened a valise and dragged out a tiny boy, and the two danced Jim Crow. The boy was Joseph Jefferson. An early impersonator was Andrew Leavitt who was called "The Hamfat Man," because hamfat was used as a base for burnt cork before the introduction of grease paint. In 1842, four men led by Dan Emmett, a Yankee who was to write Dixie, founded Negro minstrelsy. Probably the greatest early figure in this field was Edwin P. Christy, for whose troupe Stephen Foster wrote his best songs. Famous companies were The Virginia Minstrels, The Congo Melodists, The Ethiopian Serenaders, and The Famous Georgia Minstrels. Their popularity at home and abroad was amazing in the nineteenth century, and to judge from the catalogues of dramatic publishing houses, is by no means in a decline today. Indeed, most of the male stars of modern musical comedy and vaudeville as well as many of the straight character actors of the legitimate stage started in minstrelsy. P. T. Barnum, Lew Dockstader, Harrigan and Hart, Al Jolson and Eddie Cantor are among the famous who have appeared in black face.

The early minstrel performers studied Negro types and songs and dances, aiming at comic realism, but the

105

minstrel shows soon became ritualized. There was a fixed pattern: the semi-circle of grinning entertainers in flashy costumes, flanked by Mr. Tambo and Mr. Bones who waged a warfare of wit against the Interlocutor, then the "olio," a hodgepodge, frequently in the early days showing the carefree life of the plantation; then an afterpiece, and finally the grand walk-around. Produced by whites for whites the minstrel show soon lost its rudimentary realism: the dialect became gibberish and the caricature a cartoon. Any joke, whether antique wheeze or topical allusion, was forced into atrocious English, however foreign to Negro experience.

> "Why is your wife like a baseball umpire?"
> "Because she *never* thinks I'm safe when I'm out."

> Interlocutor: "Not a slambulnalist, a somnambulist, one who walks in his sleep."
> "Oh, you mean a policeman."

> "Listen! Penelope Ann and me squirreled . . . . I was a bustin wid indignation and I frew it at her in big chunks. . . ."

> "What time is it?"
> "It on'y wants a quarter of an inch ob ten now."

The minstrel show had a great deal to do with setting up the American stereotype of the comic Negro, addicted to the use of big words, to gaudy finery, to brawling with the razor, and to raiding chicken roosts. That is what has come down to the present; in the early years the emphasis was pro-slavery as well, although here and there minstrel balladists, who were fond of a good cry, included a slave's sentimental plaint.

EARLY NEGRO ACTORS

While white actors were bedaubing their faces with burnt cork to mimic Negroes, Negroes themselves were acting in the classic plays of the English stage. Most

106

famous of these was Ira Aldridge, who rose from a carpenter's bench in Maryland to become one of the greatest actors of the early nineteenth century. Having attracted the notice of Edmund Kean, he accompanied him throughout England and the continent. His best liked role was that of Othello to Kean's Iago, but a Russian critic preferred his Shylock. Aldridge played before crowned heads, the King of Prussia conferred upon him the title of chevalier, and the French romantics received him with open arms. Alexander Dumas spoke of him as *"Mon confrère."* Aldridge was well called the "African Roscius"; six feet in height with heavy, well proportioned frame, pleasing in manner, a master of the declamatory style of acting, he was received enthusiastically by audiences and critics. Dating from 1821, the African Company presented plays, notably Shakespeare's, in the African Grove, New York City. James Hewlett, their leader, was most famous for his impersonations of great actors in which critics saw a 'nice discrimination,' and for his performance as Richard III. The African Company was popular to its audiences, but not to the civic authorities and the mob "out for a lark," and the theatre was not long-lived. For these early actors there were no plays yet written seriously interpreting the life of their people in America, and they were too able and ambitious for the minstrel stage.

ANTI-SLAVERY PROPAGANDA: HARRIET BEECHER STOWE

The cruelties of slavery were used with some power as melodramatic material in *The Branded Hand* (1845), but it was not until *Uncle Tom's Cabin* was dramatized in 1852 that abolitionists made full use of the stage. Nineteenth century playwrights, as alert then as now to the possibilities of a best selling novel, rushed to put Tom, Eva, Topsy, Liza and the bloodhounds upon the boards. The success of the many stage versions was enormous: a decade ago it was estimated that *Uncle Tom's Cabin* had been presented 225,000 times. In 1878, five London theatres presented the play concurrently without the box-offices suffering. Acted more often than any other play in English, *Uncle Tom's Cabin* is still dear to the provinces (especially when heavily overlaid with melodrama and minstrel comedy). Even sophisticated Broadway has seen recent revivals and a very free adaptation by George Abbott called *Sweet River.* Many of the prominent actors of the older generation, and figures as diverse as David Belasco and the Negro prizefighter Peter Jackson, have been cast as Uncle Tom. Aiken's version, more a succession of exciting scenes than a play, has probably been more influential than the novel in fixing in the popular consciousness the figures of impish Topsy, pathetic Liza, and Uncle Tom, ideally forgiving and submissive, tender of his master's feelings and rights, the "perfect slave." "If sellin' me can get mas'r outer trouble, why den let me be sold . . . . Mas'r always found me on the spot . . . . he always will . . . . Mas'r ain't to blame, and he'll take care of my wife and little uns."

Harriet Beecher Stowe softened her attack upon the cruelties of slavery by making Legree a Yankee and the two Southern masters gentle and sweet. Though *Dred* (dramatized by J. Brougham in 1856) takes its title from an insurrectionary Negro (modelled upon Nat Turner), it continues, in the main, the earlier approach. Tiff and Old Hundred are the essence of loyalty to kindly masters; the mulattoes Harry and Lisette Gordon are counterparts to George and Liza. Harry is idealized, reciting:

108

> Freedom!—with what a greedy hungering of the soul I
> yearn to call thee mine . . . . how many amongst those who
> shout out thy sacred name in crowded assemblies . . . . care
> one jot beyond the grateful plaudits that accompany their
> labored oratory—no, it is a convenient rocking horse whereon
> to canter easily into present celebrity.

Though great antislavery influences, plays derived from Harriet Beecher Stowe's novels performed at least two disservices: they glorified the Negro's submissiveness and they fostered the error that the mixed blood characters, merely because they were nearer white, were more intelligent and militant, and therefore more tragic in their enslavement.

OTHER PROPAGANDISTS

The octoroon heroine, dear to so many audiences then and since, is the chief interest of J. T. Trowbridge's dramatization (1857) of his novel *Neighbor Jackwood*. The play attacks the fugitive slave law. Camille, a ravishing Creole beauty, escapes to New England from New Orleans. Captured by the slave-hunters she is in the nick of time rescued, purchased, and married by the Yankee hero. The play has its merits in dialogue and characterization but the outcome would hardly make for popularity. It seems that the octoroon must die when in such straits, as James Fenimore Cooper's Cora Munro and Boucicault's Zoe obligingly do. William Wells Brown's dramatic venture, *The Escape,* or *A Leap For Freedom* (1858), the first play by a Negro author, is not known ever to have been presented. It is a hodge-podge with some humor and satire and much melodrama. *Ossawatomie Brown* (1859) by Mrs. J. C. Swayze, the first dramatization of the Harper's Ferry Raid, portrayed Brown's comrade Negro insurrectionists.

Dion Boucicault was one of the canniest artificers of nineteenth century thrillers. In *The Octoroon* (1859) he was careful not to give offense to either North or South; the play was a box-office success. Although a tragedy, *The Octoroon* pictures slavery in a kindly light. There is warmth of affection between the owners and the owned. Slave buyers will not separate families. As the play's spokesman puts it:

> Nature has said that where the white man set his foot, the red man and the black man shall up sticks and stand around. But what do we pay. . . .? In protection, forbearance, gentleness in all that show the critters the difference between the Christian and the savage.

This must have been a "spot" for applause. The slaves, shown as sleepy-heads and happy-go-lucky domestics, are duly grateful. The villain, McCloskey, is a Yankee; this pleased the South; but one of the heroes, Scudder, is a Yankee too—this pleased the North. Zoe, the octoroon, is loved by and loves the hero, George; forbidden by law and "the fitness of things" to marry him, sold to the villain, she has no recourse but to take poison. She is a strange mixture of abjectness (likening herself to a poisoned thing) and pride, of forgivingness equal to Uncle Tom's and of devotion to her dead white father. "I can never repay him the love he bore his poor octoroon child on whose breast his last sigh was drawn." He had failed to guarantee her freedom. But she held no rancor: one-eighth of her blood was unclean, and her "race" knew "how to suffer." Though unmarried, Zoe is the mother of a numerous brood (in drama and fiction).

In the many plays celebrating the Civil War, the beautiful Southern belle, and the courtly planter, there was of course a swarm of Negro house-servants who could easily jump from one play to the other. *The Moctroon* by W. H. Peck followed and satirized Boucicault's play. Many novels of the old Confederate regime were dramatized: among these were Augustus Thomas' *Colonel Carter of Cartersville,* and the less worshipful Mark Twain's *Pudd'nhead Wilson.* Steele Mackaye's adaptation of *A Fool's Errand* (1881) presented Southerners as something other than Knights of the Round Table, Northerners "without suspenders and catarrh", and Negroes more recognizably human. Continuing the minstrel and vaudeville traditions, but novel in its concern with metropolitan Negroes was Edward Harrigan's Mulligan cycle of plays. In these appeared Rebecca Allup, the Reverend Palestine Puter, treasurer of the Full Moon lodge, and Captain Primrose, Negro characters designed for laughter but living a life other than that of happy servitors. Harrigan helped to fix the comic Negro with the Irish and German types in the vaudeville gallery.

NEGROES IN BLACK-FACE; THE NEGRO SHOW

The Negro himself did not appear in the minstrel show for a quarter century after the beginnings. Then there sprang up such troupes as Lew Johnson's Plantation Minstrel Company, Callender's Minstrels, and the Georgia Minstrels, with Billy Kersands of the enormous mouth. Negro performers, however dark they might be naturally, applied blacking to their faces as well: the artificial ritual had to be kept up.

111

In these companies were trained many Negroes who were to make their names on Broadway. In 1890, *The Creole Show,* first to glorify the colored girl, emerged from the minstrel pattern, and *The Octoroons* followed in 1895. A greater step from the minstrel show was taken by Bob Cole's *A Trip To Coontown,* the first show to be organized, produced and managed by Negroes. In 1898 two highly gifted collaborators, Will Marion Cook and Paul Laurence Dunbar, presented *Clorindy—The Origin of the Cakewalk,* a highly popular novelty of Broadway. By 1909 *Jes Lak White Folks, The Policy Players, The Sons of Ham, In Dahomey, Bandana Land, A Lode of Kole, The Shoofly Regiment,* and *Rufus Rastus* had appeared, making use of such talented theatrical people as Ernest Hogan, Bert Williams and George Walker, Alex Rogers, Jesse Shipp, S. H. Dudley, Bob Cole and J. Rosamond Johnson. These plays were fresher and less artificial than the minstrel shows. Bert Williams, as the Elder Eatmore sermons indicate, could get across folk-satire near to the real thing. But the blackface tradition was too fixed in the American theatre, and blackface meant chicken stealing and the rest of the clowning and such dialect as this from no less a writer than Dunbar: "Don't you know dere's no sich word in the dictionnumgary as perskivered . . . . I's got de best edjumingation."

APPROACHES TO PROBLEM DRAMA

But the comedy of Negro life did not monopolize the stage. A dramatic version of *The Clansman* followed the success of that sensational novel by Thomas Dixon before the movies were chosen as the best vehicle for the classic of Negrophobia. A Negro playwright, Joseph S. Cotter, Sr., turned to the problems of his people in *Caleb, The Degenerate* (1906).

112

William Vaughn Moody caught a great deal of Negro superstition and religious fervor and something of folk eloquence in the character of Uncle Abe, who adds interest to *The Faith Healer* (1909). The most ambitious problem drama was Edward Sheldon's *The Nigger* (1910) which has a hero of political ambitions who does not know that he is a Negro. When he learns this, he keeps silent, but after advancing to the governorship and finding himself unable to help Negroes, he confesses his race and pledges himself to his people. In 1916 Robert Hilliard presented *Pride of Race,* another play, unconvincing to the point of absurdity, on the problem of miscegenation.

THE PROBLEM OF MISCEGENATION

This problem, generally stated romantically, was stressed above all other problems which were of graver moment to the Negro. The chief reasons for this should be fairly obvious. The audience was readier to sympathize with heroes and heroines nearer to themselves in appearance. The superiority wished upon the octoroons was easily attributed to the white blood coursing in their veins, and the white audience was thereby flattered. On the other hand, the unfailingly tragic outcomes supported the belief that mixture of the races was a curse. Problems such as segregation, exploitation and the other denials of democracy, all uncomfortable theatre fare, were shelved, whereas the perplexities of a handful of fair mulattoes were misconceived, and exaggerated beyond recognition.

SUMMARY

We have seen, therefore, how from the beginnings of the American drama through the minstrels and the abolitionist plays down to the first feeble stirrings of

113

the problem play, the Negro was given scant justice. Serious comprehensive treatment, the important revelation of Negro life and character were left waiting for the advent of realism. Two new streams were to contribute:—the treatment of folk life with sympathy and understanding, influenced by the Irish Theatre, and the careful study of the Negro's social experience.

DISCUSSION QUESTIONS

What were the first roles of Negroes?
What stereotypes did the minstrel show develop?
How did the antislavery plays attack slavery?
What stereotype did the antislavery plays develop?
Why did Negroes participate in minstrelsy?
Compare the Negro song-and-drama show with minstrelsy.
What was the favorite problem for white playwrights?
What problems were left unmentioned?

READING REFERENCES

Goldberg, Isaac: *Tin Pan Alley*—The John Day Co., New York—1930.

Johnson, James Weldon: *Black Manhattan*—Alfred A. Knopf, New York—1930.

Moses, Montrose J.: *Representative Plays by American Dramatists, 1765-1819*—E. P. Dutton & Co., New York—1918.

Quinn, Arthur Hobson: *A History of the American Drama from the Beginning to the Civil War*—Harper & Brothers, New York—1923.

Quinn, Arthur Hobson: *A History of the American Drama from the Civil War to the Present Day*—F. S. Crofts & Co., New York—1936.

Rourke, Constance: *American Humor*—Harcourt, Brace & Co., New York—1931.

Wittke, Carl: *Tambo and Bones*—Duke University Press, Durham, North Carolina—1930.

Also works, already cited, by Gaines, Nelson, Paskman and Spaeth.

FOLK-DRAMA OF THE NEGRO

RIDGELY TORRENCE

William Butler Yeats, one of the founders of the Irish Theatre, believed that its purpose was "the making articulate of all the dumb classes, each with its own knowledge of the world, its own dignity." He urged that the movement be a return to the people; the reality of the true Irish peasant would drive off the artificial stage Irishman. The work of Yeats, Synge and Lady Gregory found American counterparts. Ridgely Torrence concerned himself with the hitherto dramatically inarticulate Negro folk, whose real qualities had been camouflaged by minstrel treatment, and pioneered with *Three Plays For A Negro Theatre* (1917). To the casual reader his guitar player and his superstitious Granny were mere continuations of stage familiars. But both *Granny Maumee* and *The Rider of Dreams* go deeper. *Granny Maumee* is the first Negro folk-tragedy. In it we get a sympathetic portrait of an old woman who nurses her hatred against white people because a mob had burned her son, and who is proud of her untainted "royal black" line. Although coincidence is stretched a bit too far, the play is impressive. *The Rider of Dreams* is a poetic folk-comedy of Madison, a dreamer and wastrel, and his religious hard-working wife. The lines, whether humorous or pathetic, ring true, and a fine folk eloquence is heard in Madison's speeches and his chanted dream:

115

Yassuh, I did, and Gawd he up an' gimme de go-by too.
What He bin doin' fo' me? Nuthin'. Now I goin' spit on my
han's and whu'l in an' trus' myse'f. An' I feel lots betteh.
I can feel conference wukin' all oveh me. I casts 'em all
off. I'm lookin' out fo' myself. M-m-m—It took me long time
to git heah but now I'm heah let 'em look out for me. . . .

Torrence obviously knew a great deal about folk life
and cared deeply for his characters. *The Rider of
Dreams* is one of the best American one-act plays.

PAUL GREEN

Paul Green's *No 'Count Boy* likewise was a gentle
portrait of a musical dreamer who longs for the far-
off places and is brought down from his dreaming
abruptly by the real world. Green's other one-act
plays, even the farcical happily ending *The Man Who
Died at Twelve O'Clock,* are harsher. *In Aunt
Mahaly's Cabin* is concerned with criminals in a house
of terrifying spooks. *The Prayer Meeting* shows an
old grandmother trying futilely to keep her grandchildren in the ways of respectability. *The Hot Iron*
is the tragedy of a washerwoman and farmhand who
in desperation kills her worthless husband. *White
Dresses* sardonically reveals what is generally tabu in
southern literature: a handsome mulatto girl, loving
the young master of the plantation, will only give him
up when she hears that he is her half-brother. Her
mother in youth had likewise "received a white dress."
The End of The Row is similar; a young landlord
becomes enamored of a good-looking farmhand and
persuades her to give up her ambition for schooling.
Poverty, loneliness, and her discontent with the field
hand Negroes bring about her surrender.

In Abraham's Bosom, Green's Pulitzer Prize winning play (1924), chronicles the heartbreaking struggle
of Abraham McCranie to educate himself and his
community. The hostility of his own people and of
the southern whites, and the failure of his home life,

116

work upon him so that in a pitch of frenzy he kills his white half-brother and is lynched. *In Abraham's Bosom* shows, as did the earlier Negro plays, a thorough grasp of folkways, folksong, and folkspeech. It required courage for a southern college professor to show how race hatred confounds the attempts of ambitious Negroes to better the conditions of their people. Abraham is not faultless, but he is revealed as a man, four-square, and his tragedy is somberly moving. *The House of Connelly,* an attack upon the plantation tradition, contains two Negro crones who are southern mammies with a difference, cackling their scorn of the follies of whites instead of singing their praises. In this play a favorite situation of Green's is repeated—the illicit affair of the master and a good-looking servant girl. It might be said in passing that Paul Green's treatment of the mulatto seems closer to the southern creed than his treatment of other types.

Paul Green deals with Negro life as the stuff of drama, objectively. And as he himself says:—

> The Negro has borne the brunt of the brutal dirty work . . . living in the vilest of huts, the prey of his own superstitions, suspicions and practices—he has struggled helplessly in the clutch of affliction and pain. Doubtless, readers of these plays will object that they are not generally representative of the Negro race. They are not meant to be . . . . the chief concern here is with the more tragic and uneasy side of Negro life as it has exhibited itself to my notice. . . . Those in search of happier and more cheerful records may find them elsewhere.

Roll Sweet Chariot (1935) is "a symphonic play of the Negro people," according to the author, but this claim seems to be over ambitious. It is experimental in nature, the actors passing from plain speech to speech-with-music, from that to song and back again without a break. The play aims at profound statement, but only succeeds in giving vividly and fluently a cross section of a southern shantytown. The thread of the

117

story is slight, the characterization is meager, but the impression of the forces of poverty, ignorance, superstition, and fear in the lives of "Potter's Field" Negroes is definite. Paul Green has little to say of the oppression that Potter's Field Negroes know; the chain-gang scene is brutal, but *Roll Sweet Chariot* registers little social protest. Paul Green's realism is generally hopeless and depressing, but it is convincingly rendered. A southerner born and bred, he is a powerful witness to the truth that shadows lie heavily over what has too often been called the "sunny South."

PORGY AND PLAYS OF SOUTHERN LIFE

In 1927 The Theatre Guild brought to New York an adaptation of *Porgy* by DuBose and Dorothy Heyward. A striking set of Catfish Row, the waterside slum of Charleston, was background for this story of primitive passion, hatred, humor, superstition, faith and sorrow. The central character, the crippled Porgy, and his girl Bess are sympathetically made real and the group scenes at the wake and in the storm brought a new quality to the theatre. Directed by Rouben Mamoulian, whose flair for picturesqueness and a type of emotional acting has been widely influential in Negro plays and movies, *Porgy* goes over into colorful romantic spectacle. Something of the grimness of southern life, whether caused by man or nature, is present, but *Porgy* is only incidentally realistic. Julia Peterkin's *Scarlet Sister Mary* was likewise dramatized, but even the presence of Ethel Barrymore as the errant sister of the plantation quarters, could not make this episodic story into a good play. *Roseanne* by Nan Bagby Stephens, author of the novel *Glory*, is a sympathetic treatment of folk religion in the South; less spectacular than *Porgy,*

118

it has its own quiet and at times stirring realism. One of the most trenchant writers about southern Negroes, E. C. L. Adams attempted in *Potee's Gal* a drama about the primitive life of the Congaree swamps. Though convincing in dialect, songs, the dance, and the church service, *Potee's Gal* is more of a series of interesting scenes than a play, the last act with its double murder being particularly weak.

THE GREEN PASTURES

The Green Pastures (1930) was a miracle in the medieval sense of a biblical story presented upon the stage, and in several more important ways. It was a miracle in the length of its run, in the tenderness and reverence that Marc Connelly was able to infuse into Roark Bradford's farces, in the beautifully compelling acting of Richard Harrison, and in the perfect appropriateness of the sonorous Hall Johnson spirituals to the narrative. Although it was called "an attempt to present certain aspects of a living religion in the terms of its believers," discerning critics have seen in *The Green Pastures* a statement in simple terms of the relationship of anyone and his God. George Jean Nathan wrote: "Most believers, black or white, ignorant or relatively intelligent, poor or rich . . . view the Almighty in much the same way." The frock-coat, fedora, and ten cent cigar are probably Marc Connelly's version of what Roark Bradford said was a Negro preacher's version of God, but the kindly, perplexed father of his people is like the God of the spirituals. If the play is not accurate truth about the religion of the folk-Negro, it is movingly true to folk life. Reverend Mr. Deshee's Sunday school; the fishfry (which, though placed in heaven, is delightfully true to the delta country) Noah's wish for the

119

second "kag"; young gamblers starting with "frozen" dice; honkey-tonk cabarets, magicians, country folk, city scoffers, the pure in heart, and the sinful; all of these make *The Green Pastures* a vivid resumé of folk types and folk experience. Most majestic of the folk scenes is the exodus: here in these marching people with their faces turned toward hope is a spectacle symbolic and moving. *The Green Pastures* is fantasy, but it is likewise simple profound reality.

FANTASY AND FOLK

Earth by Em Jo Basshe, a production in 1927 of the New Playwright Theatre, sacrificed plot and characterization for a lyrical expression of religious ecstasy in conflict with voodooism. Even though laid in 1880, the primitive cult is not convincing, but the play has exciting moments. Six years later, Hall Johnson, who had composed the weird spirituals for *Earth,* repeated the same theme with greater power and truth, in *Run Little Chillun.* This play was not a complete success. The introduction of a fantastic pagan band of pilgrims, although making for sensual spectacle, strains credence. In striking contrast, however, is the faithfully rendered revival meeting which was one of the truest bits of sympathetic realism ever produced in the drama of Negro life. The plot is melodramatic, but the picture of small-town religious life in the black belt is rewarding. *Run Little Chillun,* like *The Green Pastures* fuses music and drama; the music of the pagan sect was startling, if not convincing in the particular frame work, but the spirituals gave grandeur to the play. In addition to being one of the finest composers, arrangers and directors of music among Negroes, Hall Johnson revealed himself as a dramatist of high promise. With all of the weaknesses of

120

Run Little Chillun, it is still the most ambitious and accomplished drama by an American Negro.

NEGRO PLAYWRIGHTS ABOUT THE FOLK

Other Negro playwrights have attempted to present the folk-life of their people in one-act plays. Jean Toomer's *Balo* is more incident than play but shows early promise of the powers uncovered in *Kabnis,* which is a short story partly in dramatic form. Frank Wilson, an actor of talent, wrote *Sugar Cane,* which, for all of its melodrama and forced happy ending, has good observation of folk types. Wilson is likewise author of *Meek Mose* and *Walk Together Chillen.* C. D. Lipscomb's *Frances* and *Compromise* are bitterly realistic. John Matheus' *'Cruiter* dramatizes the conflict between an old mammy rooted in the South and the younger generation which was recruited for industry in the North. His *Ti Yette* is the tragedy of an octoroon girl who conventionally speaks of her "mind's equipment, the heritage of my father's people," and loathes Negroes. Her brother, extremely race-conscious, worshipful of the vengeful Haitian Dessalines, kills her rather than see her the wife of a white lawyer. *Black Damp,* a more original study of coal miners trapped in the mines, is sketchy rather than developed.

Langston Hughes, after success in poetry, the short story, and the problem play *Mulatto,* turned to comedies of the folk in *When The Jack Hollers* and *Little Ham.* The humor is swift and racy and the handling of the social setting is realistic. Randolph Edmonds, from his directing collegiate dramatics, has brought a knowledge of the Negro audience to bear upon his playwriting. He is convinced that this audience resents the fatalistically resigned character,

121

and, like all audiences without great experience in playgoing, cares most for sentimentality and melodrama. Edmonds' *Six Plays For A Negro Theatre* (1934) are sentimental and melodramatic, but they show knowledge of folk-life, and definitely take with Negro audiences. *Nat Turner,* dealing with the famous insurrection, is one of the few plays to tap historic sources. *The Bad Man* shows the reformation of a lumbercamp killer through the love of a good woman; *Breeders* deals with the tragedy of a slave girl forced to marry against her will. If the structure of George A. Towns' *The Sharecropper* had been equal to the grasp of dialect and local color, the play would have been a striking treatment of southern injustice. Ira D. Reid's *John Henry* has a first scene, laid in a camp shack, of great gusto. The second, which deals with the contest between hero and steam drill, suffers because of stage limitations. J. W. Butcher's *The Seer* is a hilarious farce, and his *Milk and Honey* combines whimsical fantasy and humor.

Zora Neale Hurston, a fiction writer of note, has turned her hand to plays. *Great Day* (1927), presented in New York, is more a series of folk scenes than a play, but it contained good raw dramatic material. Countee Cullen and Arna Bontemps, two poets and novelists, have collaborated on *St. Louis Woman* and *One Way to Heaven,* the second of which ran successfully at Jasper Deeter's Hedgerow Theatre.

SUMMARY

None of the Negro folk-playwrights show the structural skill of white dramatists like Marc Connelly, or the power and scope of Paul Green. This is to be expected, since these playwrights are still in their learning years. Their work, developed to its best, should

122

have greater intimacy, and a different point of view from that of even the most sympathetic white dramatist. But the Negro audience frequently wants flattery instead of representation, plaster saints instead of human beings, drawing rooms instead of the homes of the people. And the typical white audience wants stereotypes. Furthermore, the necessary apprenticeship of the playwright *in the theatre,* beyond the footlights, is still too rare, and college dramatics cannot sufficiently offset this. It is certain that if Negro playwrights could devote themselves to the observation of the lives of their people, as well as to the more arduous business of learning technique, their work would be of the greatest importance. The way is hard, and calls for diligence, integrity, and courage. But the rewards will be correspondingly high.

DISCUSSION QUESTIONS

What is the influence of The Abbey Theatre upon Negro Drama?
What are the contributions of Ridgely Torrence?
What distinguishes Paul Green from most southern authors?
What were the qualities of *Porgy?*
What differentiates *The Green Pastures* from Bradford's *Ol' Man Adam and His Chillun?*
What is the contribution of Hall Johnson to drama?
Account for the fact that few Negro playwrights have dealt with folk material.

READING REFERENCES

Clark, Barrett: *The Writings of Paul Green*—Robert McBride, New York—1928.
Locke, Alain and Gregory, Montgomery: *Plays of Negro Life*—Harper & Brothers, New York—1927.
Locke, Alain: "The Negro and The American Theatre" in *Theatre: Essays on The Arts of The Theatre*—Edited by R. Isaacs—Little, Brown, and Co., Boston—1927.
Also works, already cited in Chapter VIII, by Brawley, James Weldon Johnson, Nelson and Quinn.

REALISTIC AND PROBLEM DRAMA

EUGENE O'NEILL: THE EMPEROR JONES

When Charles Gilpin, in blue and red uniform, strode across the stage to a "dazzling eye-smiting scarlet" throne, dramatic history was made. The occasion was the opening of *The Emperor Jones,* the year 1920, and the place the Macdougal Street Theatre converted by the Provincetown Players from a stable. Eugene O'Neill had already shown a slight interest in West Indian Negroes in *The Moon of the Caribees* (1918), and in *The Dreamy Kid* had written with suspense and power of a young Negro gangster in New York, whose escape from the police was prevented by his superstitious fear of and love for his dying grandmother. *The Emperor Jones* was striking on two counts: it was a departure from the old rules of playwriting, and it introduced a memorable Negro figure on the stage. Brutus Jones, crafty, bold, arrogant, had learned in a hard American school the grasping ruthlessness of a dictator. His flight from the uprising of the natives, his reduction from a swaggering tyrant to a creature caught by panic fear, his circuitous return after many hours in the jungle to death by a silver bullet, these are done with mastery. The flashbacks to the chain-gang are grim realism. The play has nothing of social protest, but the American pressure upon Negro life is clearly portrayed. The Emperor, though not flattered, is far different from the comic servant or the naïve folk type. He is a twentieth century Negro; his "Talk polite, white man, talk polite, is you forgetting?", shows a truculence that no other playwright had ventured. The play has an exotic setting, shows a relapse into primitive fear at the incessant throbbing of the tom-tom (a relapse shared, according to report, by the "Aryan" audiences), and is symbolic rather than representative. It marks a historic step, however, in the treatment of Negro character in drama. This Negro is no longer comic relief, or a pathetic victim; he is a man, presented as of powerful dramatic interest in his own right.

ALL GOD'S CHILLUN GOT WINGS

All God's Chillun Got Wings (1923) is probably a closer approach to a consideration of a Negro problem, that of intermarriage. Jim Harris, a young law student, is filled with protective ardor for a white girl Ella Downey, who had been his childhood admiration. After she has been seduced by her gangster lover, he marries her. Ella, torn between gratitude and race prejudice intensified by society, goes mad. Jim promises in his "exalted" devotion to care for her, now a broken child, as her "old kind Uncle Jim." He is unfortunately more like old Uncle Tom. The contrast between the cheap, vicious whites and Jim is all in Jim's favor, but he remains too selfless for belief. Although, as in all of O'Neill's plays, there are moments of power, the general effect is painful. O'Neill shows some knowledge of self respecting, ambitious Negroes in the pictures of Jim's family, and a consciousness of the tragic effects of prejudice. But if this is a study of intermarriage, the central situation is too strained for a good test-case. Protests from North and South were plentiful, even though the boldest action on the stage was when the white girl kissed Jim's hand. *All God's Chillun Got Wings* did

125

not do a great deal towards presenting the life and serious problems of Negro life.

Eugene O'Neill did not write as a champion of the Negro, but on the other hand he did not write, as many critics intimate, out of hostility. Many have considered Brutus Jones and Jim Harris to stand for the entire Negro race, but unless the Cockney Smithers and Ella Downey stand for the entire white race, this seems more ingenious than tenable. If O'Neill does mean two Negroes in such exceptional situations to represent millions of Negroes he lessens his stature as dramatist. There is much in Negro experience and character that these plays do not, and could not hope to explore. Their achievement is to show that Negro characters can be interesting and colorful material for drama, worthy of tragic respect from dramatists and audience.

NATURALISM

Ernest H. Culbertson's one-act *Rackey* (1919) dealing with a reformed bad-man, is unconvincing, but *Goat Alley* (1922) gets something of the drab misery of Negro slum life. Lucy Belle, too handsome for Goat Alley and therefore pursued by many men, fights valiantly against loneliness and poverty, but when her lover Sam Reed is sent to prison, she can no longer hold out. When Sam returns and learns of her infidelity he chokes her to death. Lucy Belle is hard-pressed as much by chance as by environment, but her fate is truly pathetic, and *Goat Alley* marks a step in the serious treatment of Negro life.

Black Boy by Jim Tully and Frank Dazey (1926) chronicles the rise and fall of a Negro prize-fighter. As climax, after his dissipation of wealth and power, the fighter discovers that the woman he loved was not white as he had supposed, but a Negro. Realistic in setting and language and its showing of humanity in the raw, *Black Boy* is still remote from typical Negro experience and spectacular rather than interpretative. Another play dealing with the meaner aspects of life is *Lulu Belle* (1926) by Edward Sheldon and Charles MacArthur. This is the melodrama of a Harlem harlot's progress, sensational and in places powerful, popular largely because Lenore Ulric played the title role, but it remains exotic theatre only. Ransom Rideout's *Going Home* (1927) is unusual in dealing with Negro troops in the A. E. F., but like the two preceding plays makes concessions to conventions about Negro character. Israel, a Negro ex-soldier, enraged at Powell, a white major, who has just had an affair with his French wife, kills a friendly Senegalese soldier to save Powell's life. Powell, whom Israel had served in America as "Mr. Eddie", saves Israel from the French military police, and the two go out with Powell's arm around Israel's shoulder. The play is incredible; Israel's affection for the major is maudlin, and the propaganda for Negro submissiveness is poorly concealed.

URBAN "REALISM"

Like Culbertson, Willis Richardson deals with the life of urban Negroes. His *House of Sham* (1929) is partly concerned with the false front put on by upper class strivers, but most of his plays are like *The Broken Banjo* and *The Idle Head,* harsh transcripts of poverty and joblessness. Richardson's central figures are often driven to petty crime by circumstances; but since they seldom win the respect and liking of the reader, their mishaps are not tragically moving. May Miller's one-act plays show Washington and Baltimore life;

Riding The Goat is a comedy about a lodge parade, and *Scratches* deals with poolroom loungers and gamblers, turning harshness into sentimentality at the end. Georgia Douglas Johnson's *Blue Blood* is a somewhat far-fetched treatment of the results of miscegenation, but her *Plumes* is closer to reality, illustrating superstition and love of grand funerals among poor Negroes. Harlem life is dealt with by Eulalie Spence in many one-act plays such as *The Starter* and *Undertow*. Miss Spence is aware of the serious aspects of Harlem and writes a fluent and credible dialogue. The one-act plays of all of these authors, however, are chiefly significant as the Negro's effort to create a drama from within; they must be considered apprentice work even though they have frequently been awarded prizes in contests. Both the humor and tragedy are seldom memorable, and the playwrights are undoubtedly disadvantaged by having no theatre for laboratory experiments.

One distinctive play of urban Negro life is *Harlem* (1929) by Wallace Thurman, a Negro writer, in collaboration with William Rapp. The success of this play was due in part to the literary discovery of Harlem, but it is a swiftly paced melodrama of interesting, if seamy, aspects of the life of the Negro city within a city. It included such dramatic favorites as racketeers (number-barons and runners), hi-jackers, gamblers, and Harlem wantons, a murder solved interestingly, and a rent party with exaggerated dancing and hilarity. The Harlem depicted was "stagey" of course, but the scenes could be matched in life. *Singing The Blues* (1931) continues the exploitation of the gaudier Harlem: it is a thriller, a murder story, a romance, a tour of cabarets all rolled into one. *Savage Rhythm* (1932) though placed in Mississippi swamplands seemed nevertheless to be of Harlem—

128

the sinister voodooism and the sensuous dancing belonging more to cabarets than to cabins. The *Conjure Man Dies* (1936) is a dramatic version of Rudolph Fisher's clever mystery melodrama of a Harlem murder. These plays may have been a "discovery" of Harlem, but they can hardly be considered exploration.

PROBLEM PLAYS: THE UPPER TENTH

Problem plays with propaganda implied or stated, have continued in popularity. *Rachel* by Angelina Grimke (1920), tells of a sensitive, sentimental heroine whose grief at hearing of her father's lynching and of insults to little Negro school children makes her renounce marriage. There is no conflict and little characterization; the propaganda depresses rather than stirs. Annie Nathan Meyer's *Black Souls* (1932), like *Rachel,* deals with educated Negroes for propaganda purposes. While a new building is being dedicated in a southern Negro college, a lynching of one of the college teachers takes place in the neighborhood. A Southern Senator's lusting for the Negro president's wife whom he had seduced as a young girl, is balanced by his daughter's desire for David, a young Negro professor. Caught in a cabin in the woods near the campus, David pretends to assault the girl to save her fair name. The plot remains unconvincing, and the dialogue is too often stilted and heavy with direct propaganda, especially when the sentimental poet David speaks. The play does have a striking situation and much understanding of the truckling that Negro educators are forced to do.

DuBose Heyward's problem play *Brass Ankle* (1931) is akin to Sheldon's *The Nigger.* In a South Carolina town, a young mother who does not know

129

that she is a "brass ankle", that is, of Negro-Indian-white stock, bears a son who is a "throw-back" to some distant Negro ancestor. Rather than disgrace her little daughter and husband she announces that the child's father was a Negro hired man. The infuriated husband kills her. A small town's hatred of Negroes is realistically shown, but the use of the literary stand-by, the "throw-back", keeps the play in the ranks of the romantic anecdote. *Mulatto* (1935), by Langston Hughes and Martin Jones enjoyed a long Broadway run. Taken from a story by Langston Hughes, it has elements of both mordant realism and sensationalism in its account of an illicit relationship in the South, and the hatred of the mulatto son for his white father. It is at times more theatrical than plausible; Hughes has not brought to this play the powers of which he is capable. Samuel Raphaelson's *White Man* (1936) revives the age-old tragedy of the near-white in an unconvincing manner.

BEGINNINGS OF SOCIAL REALISM

A group known as The New Players attempted to freshen American drama with plays experimental in structure and radical in ideas. Michael Gold's *Hoboken Blues* (1927) was one of their most striking innovations. Subtitled *The Black Rip Van Winkle*, it shows Harlem at the turn of the century, an interlude in Hoboken, and Harlem twenty-five years later in the gaudy boom period. Crowded with spectacle and to the reader slightly confusing, this play succeeds in its early snapshots of church, saloon, and street scenes in Harlem. There is much hilarious comedy. But Sam Pickens, another "Rider of Dreams", who wants music, happiness and brotherhood, and his mother who, remembering a southern mob which burned her Jim-boy, has a mania against whites, are tragic figures done with fine sympathy. Sam's wanderings from one menial job to another, his final joblessness because he cannot surrender his manhood are shown with sharp protest. At the end Sam, who in Hoboken has dreamt of socialistic justice and brotherhood, is ridiculed by jazz-mad, money-mad Harlem. The play combines realism and fantasy; much of the characterization is first-rate and the ideas are sound, but the experimentalism of the production makes it difficult for staging.

NEVER NO MORE

One evening, James Knox Millen, an ex-cotton planter, leaving behind his unremunerative four thousand acres, stumbled across an orgy of the South— a Negro was being burned at the stake. The ghastly spectacle inspired *Never No More* (1932). This frontal attack upon lynching was too stark to last long in New York, and few other places would dare show it; but it is a significant and well written play. The quiet contentment of a Negro family with the crops laid by is sharply broken into when the young scapegrace son rushes in, having killed a white girl in unreasoning terror. A scene of almost intolerable tension follows as the family, barricaded in the cabin, have to hear the cries of the mob and the crackling and roar of the fire burning the boy. Threats to burn down the cabin and all the family cornered there meet with resistance; the mammy of the family rises to heights of strategy and bravery to save her flock. The characterization is admirably done. Fatalistically submissive, and grasping at the slightest aids to happiness when the play opens, these people become heroic at the play's end. "Can't God see out there?" asks one of the besieged. "God's gone somewhere else tonight," answers the elder son, easy-going once, but now made of sterner stuff.

BLOODSTREAM: THEY SHALL NOT DIE

Another play, groundbreaking in its significance, was *Bloodstream,* by Frederick Schlick (1932). Dealing with the tragic brutality of Negro and white convict labor in the mines, the play was a powerful social statement. Like *Never No More* in its failure to last on Broadway as long as its value warranted, *Bloodstream* has been recently revived by the Federal Theatre Project.

They Shall Not Die by John Wexley (1934) is a powerful dramatization of the earlier years of the Scottsboro case. The frame-up of the boys, the juggling of justice, the lynch spirit of the courtroom are graphically conveyed. The Negro boys are not so individualized as other characters, but full light is thrown upon what the Negro masses of the South have lined up against them. Langston Hughes' *Scottsboro Limited,* on the same subject, is a poetic mass chant done with bitter satire and prophecy. His *Troubled Island* (1936) dealing with revolutionary Haiti carries implications for modern American Negro life.

STEVEDORE

Even more successful as a social protest play was *Stevedore* (1934) by Paul Peters and George Sklar. Showing intimate acquaintance with Negro life—the scenes in Binnie's lunch room and on the wharves being rich in folk-humor and satire—the play's main theme is the necessity for the unity of black and white workers. The framing of a militant Negro by the

132

usual broadcast of the cry rape, the rampaging of southern hoodlums, and the concerted action of white and black dockhands in turning back the mob are conveyed with power. There is a gallery of memorable figures: Binnie, sharp of tongue and unsubmissive; Blacksnake, a man in full; Jim Veal, the hat-in-hand strawboss. The central figure is Lonnie Thompson who is slowly waking to class rather than race consciousness, and who, when the white boss calls him "a bad nigger", replies, "You mean I'm a nigger you can't cheat." Such a speech as the following shows a southern Negro hounded to the last ditch and turning on his pursuers:

> Every time de white boss crack de whip you turn and run. You let him beat you, you let him hound you, you let him work you to death. When you gwine to put a stop to it, black man? When you gwine turn on 'em? When you gwine say: You can't do dat. I'm a man. I got de rights of a man. I'm gwine fight like a man. . . . Ain't no peace fo' de black man, preacher—ain't never gwine be, till he fight to get it.

RADICAL PROTEST

They Shall Not Die and *Stevedore* were potent forces in dramatic history. They concentrated upon deeper problems than those of the "talented tenth", or of near-white persons whose lives have been made too woeful in drama. They show the oppression and exploitation of Negroes where these are most heavy, and they insist that as starvation, penury and shame are common to both white and black masses so their interests are identical. Alice Holdship Ware's *A Mighty Wind A-Blowin'* (1936) is a powerful one-act play of the plight of sharecroppers, both white and black, and the late-coming realization on the part of both that in union only is there strength. Ben Nelson, who believes in trusting in the Lord and the landlord, is challenged by his wife Hattie, who is slowly awaking to rebellion, and their son Sam, who cries out "Oh yes, Lawd! We're down here dependin' on you! Oh, yes, Lawd! We're down here bein' shot at, dependin' on you!" Many plays of Negro life are published by The New Theatre League, which seeks to stimulate drama reflecting contemporary life and struggle and to "participate in the gigantic social changes of our time." *Angelo Herndon Jones* by Langston Hughes, *Angelo Herndon Back In Atlanta* by Elizabeth England, and *A Million Black and White* by Irene Paul deal with the famous young Negro who was sentenced to the chaingang for twenty years because he led a protest march of the unemployed. *Bivouac* by Paul Peters attacks lynching. Langston Hughes' *Trouble With The Angels* shows up segregation and Negro submissiveness. *His Jewels* by Bernice Harris is another play of an evicted sharecropper, who has taken refuge in a church he helped to build. *Mess of Pottage* by John Rimassa and Richard Oliver, and *Smell The Sweet Savor* by Harold Anderson are other plays of Negro life sponsored by the League. Thomas Richardson has written an experimental mass-chant, *Protest,* which makes effective use of Gellert's *Negro Songs of Protest. John Henry,* by Herbert Kline, once editor of *New Theatre,* shows the epical triumph of the hero, and urges Negro and white workers to join their forces. It is written with grim power.

THE FEDERAL THEATRE PROJECT

Another *John Henry,* by Frank Wells (1936) covers the life of the hero from slavery days to his famous achievement. The incidents show a fine inventiveness and truth. John Henry embodies unsubmissiveness; the idea, eloquently developed, is that such

134

is, as it has been, the great need for Negroes. This play was produced by the Federal Theatre Project, which has been of inestimable value in developing Negro audiences, playwrights, technicians, and actors, and in presenting more completely the story of the Negro. Most famous, probably, of the Federal Theatre's plays was the Haitian *Macbeth* (less Shakespearean than gorgeous spectacle, but an experimental success). Similarly fine spectacles were *Black Empire* by Christine Amos Clarke and Obey's *Noah*. Besides productions of *Stevedore, The Emperor Jones* and *Roll, Sweet Chariot,* the Federal Theatre has produced plays of social content such as Frank Wilson's *Walk Together, Children* and Augustus Smith's and Peter Morrell's *Turpentine* which brought upon the stage the newer realism. *Battle Hymn* by Michael Gold and Michael Blankfort, deals with John Brown, showing the parallels between the abolitionist struggle and the present one against slavery. Negroes willing to fight for freedom are sympathetically treated. Conrad Seiler's *Sweet Land* is another play about southern sharecroppers, showing the natural hostility of some Negro workers to the ideas of black and white unity. *Natural Man,* of which the script was by Ted Brown and the entire production developed by project workers, is a folk opera version of the John Henry legend. The entire list of plays produced or planned is too long for inclusion here; a fact that is all to the good since it bears witness to a living theatre.

CONTEMPORARY MINOR ROLES

Although the Negro servant appears in comic relief in modern plays, notably those about Dixie like *Solid South,* his characterization though minor and conventional has gained because of realism in such works as

135

the opera *Deep River,* by Stalling and Harling, and in *Show Boat, The Front Page, Once In A Lifetime,* and *Three Men On A Horse.* In *The Last Mile* by John Wexley a Negro convict is portrayed with as much honesty and sympathy as any of his mates in Death Row, and the Negro gangster in *Petrified Forest* is recognizably realistic.

THE LIVELY ART

Most of the serious plays of Negro life have been the work of liberal and radical white authors; the Negro's own contribution has been largely to the livelier side of the theatre. In unbroken line from the Negro musical shows and the minstrel shows, the twentieth century Negro musical comedies have put a definite stamp upon American entertainment. *Shuffle Along* (1921) the work of Miller and Lyles, Sissle and Blake was the first and one of the best of a long line with such names as *Liza, Runnin' Wild, Chocolate Dandies, From Dixie to Broadway, Plantation Revue, Blackbirds, Hot Chocolates* and *Brown Buddies.* Of differing degrees of excellence, all of these shows were marked by wild infectious gayety in dancing and melody. The comedy scenes, in spite of traces of the minstrel, often came close to reality. Comediennes such as Florence Mills and Ethel Waters made reputations. The heyday of these shows seems to have passed; less lavish and more conventional musical shows, however, still go the rounds. Some of the musical shows feel duty bound to carry messages in defense of their race, at times an incongruous addition to their glorification of the Negro girl. *Brown Buddies,* for instance, was organized around the theme of the Negro's service in the World War. Negro vaudeville comedians and white blackface teams seldom

136

escape the trite situations and humor. Occasionally an artist of satiric genius like Ethel Waters breaks the pattern. Her monologue over the washtub of the ways of white folks has a bite to it, and her singing in *As Thousands Cheer* of "Supper Time", a protest at lynching, was a startling and effective innovation.

THE NEGRO IN MOVIES

The story of the Negro in movies deserves a brief, though admittedly inadequate word. It repeats the story we have traced in drama, with a lag natural to the more popular medium. The first appearances of the Negro in movies were minstrel caricatures, servants hysterically frightened at ghosts, or rapturously enchanted by their white masters and mistresses. *So Red The Rose* and *The Little Colonel* are the newest variations of such ancient themes. *Hearts of Dixie* and *Hallelujah,* performed by all Negro casts, combined good local color with conventional characterization and situations. *The Green Pastures* was, like the play, a charmingly naïve fantasy. *The Emperor Jones* was made more spectacular on the screen, and thereby suffered. An approach to a problem in Fannie Hurst's *Imitation of Life* was soon abandoned: the two central Negro figures were merely the old stereotypes of the contented slave and the tragic mulatto brought up to date. It would be too much to expect the movies to handle plays of social protest such as *Never No More* and *Stevedore,* for the box-office returns generally follow the glorifying of popular creeds, but the treatment of the Negro character with honest realism certainly does not seem too much to ask.

SUMMARY: PROSPECTS

A decade ago, Alain Locke prophesied a flowering of the drama of Negro life, basing his hopes upon the

137

successful plays of Ridgely Torrence, Paul Green and Eugene O'Neill. "The dramatic intensities of Negro experience" held forth promise for a needy American theatre. Part of the promise has undoubtedly been realized. Such plays as *Porgy, The Green Pastures, Run, Little Children* and *Stevedore* have brought color and vitality to the theatre, together with a deeper understanding of the Negro. The emergence of actors and actresses such as Paul Robeson, Jules Bledsoe, Rex Ingram, Leigh Whipper, Jack Carter, Todd Duncan, Rose McClendon, Abbie Mitchell, Georgette Harvey, Flo Mills, Ethel Waters, Fredi Washington, Edna Thomas and Anne Wiggins Brown have been all to the good. Veterans like Charles Gilpin, Richard Harrison, S. Tutt Whitney and Wesley Hill found opportunities long denied for roles that could bring out their finest abilities.

Of great service have been the advances in stage technique made use of in *The Green Pastures, Stevedore, Roll, Sweet Chariot* and the Federal Theatre *Macbeth*. More important has been the change in the conception of the Negro. From a shuffling clown or knee-bending servant, the development has been sure, although long-drawn out. Now a harassed Abraham McCranie can reveal his tragic perplexities; Porgy and Bess in a warmly, colorfully depicted Cat Fish Row can be shown as human—all too human, rather than as buffoons; Lonnie Thompson can stand up for his rights like a man; and group experience, as in *The Green Pastures,* can be perfectly rendered. A great deal has been done.

But the note of encouragement is not the only one. These plays, for all of their understanding and beauty, are beginnings, not ends. Vast areas of Negro experience and character remain unexplored. Although too many Negro critics believe that "well educated,

138

cultured Negroes" are all that is necessary for great drama, and that any play not dealing with this minority of the race is therefore trash, it is still regrettable that the life of middle class Negroes, with its comedy and tragedy, its quieter heroism as well as its frantic striving, remains scarcely touched. Drama has room for such representation, if done honestly and thoughtfully, without the usual middle-class self-advertisment. High lights of Southern life have been seen, but one could hardly say that the dramatic possibilities of the South have been fully realized. A deeper revelation of the folk, with the "folksiness" less stressed, is likewise waiting. Drama of the struggles of the working class are just starting to be written. The exploits of Negro history furnish a mine for the dramatist. There remains a great deal to be done.

Certain factors militate against any prophecy that this great deal will soon be achieved. Broadway, for all of its growing liberal attitude, is still entranced with the stereotypes of the exotic primitive, the comic stooge and the tragic mulatto. The anecdote of the manager who having read a serious social drama about Negro life, insisted upon the insertion of "hot spots," of a song and dance, is still too pertinent.

Furthermore, the intimacy with Negro life requisite for the types of drama still necessary is in the main to be expected from Negro playwrights. And, without a theatre for apprenticeship in their craft, Negro playwrights are sorely handicapped. Without their own audience, they are doubly handicapped. The tyranny exerted by the Broadway audience, however enlightened it is becoming, is hard enough for a playwright whose material is less controversial. The development of a Negro audience does not seem immediately forthcoming. There is a Negro theatrical tradition, that of the song and dance show, with blackface skits interspersed. Certain critics, among them Max Reinhardt, see great possibilities in combining the swiftness and vitality of these shows with something worth saying dramatically, and they prophesy a new dramatic form. So far this hope is unrealized; these shows remain farce and cabaret, and the audience is too well summed up by a Negro critic who says: "As soon as a Negro puts his money down for a ticket he starts laughing." Escape from drudgery and insult by laughter is what the Negro theatre means to too many Negroes. Serious drama of their lives is neither wanted, nor understood. And the movies and radio further these attitudes. Upper class Negroes frequently resent any picturing of Negro life, proudly and pathetically insisting that with the "folks down home" or with the workers they have nothing to do.

The story would not be complete, however, without mentioning certain counteracting forces. One of the most powerful of these is the "tributary theatre" which has done so much for American drama. Jasper Deeter's Hedgerow Theatre and Cleveland's Gilpin Players, directed by the Jelliffes, have been of great service. Frederick Koch of the Universities of North Dakota and North Carolina must be mentioned, not only indirectly because he did so much to make colleges drama-conscious, but also directly, since he was Paul Green's instructor and guide. His calling the attention of the student "to the dramatic happenings in the life with which he is most familiar" has borne fine harvest. With so many others of the tributary theatre he has had much to do with extending "footlights across America." As Lennox Robinson, of the influential Abbey Theatre, says: "Young American dramatists learned not to be afraid of accent and dialect; learned that the materials of the American play were the sticks and stones lying outside the American door."

In 1921 Alain Locke and Montgomery Gregory started the Howard Players at Howard University, hoping to lay the basis of a little threatre movement among Negroes. After a slow start, colleges throughout the country enthusiastically sponsored the movement. Dramatic associations, prominent among them the Negro Intercollegiate Dramatic Association and the Southern Dramatic Association (in the founding of both of which Randolph Edmonds was prominent) and the work at Atlanta University, the first to establish a summer theatre, are good signs of a dramatic awakening. The colleges have, of course, the necessity of acquainting the young actors with world drama as well as with drama of Negro life, but it must be stated that Negro plays and playwrights are hardly important in their repertories as yet. Little Theatre Groups such as The Krigwa Players in Washington and New York and on the coast have flourished and drooped; the more robust of these have been the Harlem Experimental Theatre, The Boston Players and especially the already mentioned Gilpin Players. In many cities talented groups have come together for one or two years, for study and production, but the productions are usually repeats of Broadway hits. Some of these groups would disdain the presentation of any play dealing with Negro material. Much more promising are the workers' theatres springing up throughout the country, with their unfettered programs and their encouraging of unknown playwrights to go down unbeaten paths. The Federal Theatre has been of great benefit, not only to the unemployed actors and technicians, but for the help extended to Negro playwrights to write unhackneyed social drama, and to

141

get the most valuable experience beyond the footlights. And it has brought Negro audiences into the theatre. These are portents of a better future for the drama of Negro life.

DISCUSSION QUESTIONS

What is the contribution of Eugene O'Neill?

Compare his purposes with those of Green, Heyward, and Marc Connelly.

How are the naturalistic plays unrealistic?

How do the first problem plays differ from *Never No More, Stevedore* and the radical plays?

Who are favorite heroes in recent drama? Account for this.

What are the achievements of *The Federal Theatre Project?*

Account for the fact that few Negro playwrights write drama of social protest.

What accounts for the popularity of the Negro show?

What have been the chief roles for Negroes in the movies you have seen?

What are the forces opposed to the development of Negro playwrights?

What are the forces of benefit to the development of Negro playwrights?

READING REFERENCES

Blake, Ben: *Awakening of the American Theatre*—New Theatre—1935.

Deutsch, Helen and Hanau, Stella: *The Provincetown: A Story of The Theatre*—Farrar and Rinehart, New York—1931.

"Negro Stars" essays by several writers in *Negro, An Anthology*—edited by Nancy Cunard.

Seldes, Gilbert: *The Seven Lively Arts*—Harper & Brothers—1925.

The Crisis, Opportunity, Stage, Theatre Arts, The New Theatre (especially for July 1935)

Also works, already cited, in Chapter VIII by Brawley, Gregory and Locke, James Weldon Johnson and Quinn.

142

The Negro in
American Fiction

EDITORIAL FOREWORD

This Bronze Booklet aims at a survey of the Negro in American fiction, both as character and author. It is the first full-length presentation of this subject, but differs from the usual academic survey by giving a penetrating analysis of the social factors and attitudes behind the various schools and periods considered. Sterling A. Brown, now associate professor of English at Howard University, born and educated in Washington, D. C., was graduated from Williams College in 1922 with Phi Beta Kappa honors and the Clark Fellowship to Harvard, received his master's degree at Harvard in 1923, and has since pursued graduate work in English literature at Harvard University. He has had wide experience teaching at Virginia Seminary and College, Lynchburg, Va., 1923–26, at Lincoln University, Mo., 1926–28, Fisk University, 1928–29, and at Howard University from 1929 to date. His volume of verse, *Southern Road,* published in 1932, put him in the advance-guard of younger Negro poets, and, as well, the then new school of American regionalist literature. In 1937, Professor Brown was awarded a Guggenheim Fellowship for creative writing and among other things, will complete for publication his second volume of verse, *"No Hiding Place."* Since 1936, he has been directing editor on Negro materials of the *Federal Writers' Project* at Washington headquarters. For the last five years, his literary book review comments in *Opportunity* under the caption: *"The Literary Scene,"* have revealed a critical talent of sane but progressive and unacademic tendencies,—a point of view that the reader will find characteristically carried through in this provocative and masterly study.

ALAIN LOCKE

TABLE OF CONTENTS

INTRODUCTION

The treatment of the Negro in American fiction, since it parallels his treatment in American life, has naturally been noted for injustice. Like other oppressed and exploited minorities, the Negro has been interpreted in a way to justify his exploiters.

> I swear their nature is beyond my comprehension. A strange people!—merry 'mid their misery—laughing through their tears, like the sun shining through the rain. Yet what simple philosophers they! They tread life's path as if 'twere strewn with roses devoid of thorns, and make the most of life with natures of sunshine and song.

Most American readers would take this to refer to the Negro, but it was spoken of the Irish, in a play dealing with one of the most desperate periods of Ireland's tragic history. The Jew has been treated similarly by his persecutors. The African, and especially the South African native, is now receiving substantially the same treatment as the American Negro. Literature dealing with the peasant and the working-class has, until recently, conformed to a similar pattern.

The blind men gathered about the elephant. Each one felt the part of the elephant's anatomy closest to him, the trunk, tusk, eyes, ear, hoof, hide and tail. Then each became an authority on the elephant. The elephant was all trunk, or all hoof or all hide, or all tail. So ran their separate truths. The single truth was that all were blind. This fable, pertinent to our study, might be continued to tell how some of the blind men returned to their kingdoms of the blind where it was advantageous to believe that the elephant was all trunk or tusk.

We shall see in this study how stereotypes—that the Negro is *all* this, that, or the other—have evolved at

1

the dictates of social policy. When slavery was being attacked, for instance, southern authors countered with the contented slave; when cruelties were mentioned, they dragged forward the comical and happy-hearted Negro. Admittedly wrong for white people, slavery was represented as a boon for Negroes, on theological, biological, psychological warrant. Since Negroes were of "peculiar endowment," slavery could not hurt them, although, inconsistently, it was their punishment, since they were cursed of God. A corollary was the wretched freedman, a fish out of water. In Reconstruction, when threatened with such dire fate as Negroes' voting, going to school, and working for themselves (i.e., Negro domination), southern authors added the stereotype of the brute Negro. Even today much social policy demands that slavery be shown as blessed and fitting, and the Negro as ludicrously ignorant of his own best good.

Many authors who are not hostile to the Negro and some who profess friendship still stress a "peculiar endowment" at the expense of the Negro's basic humanity. Some antislavery authors seemed to believe that submissiveness was a mystical African quality, and chose mulattoes for their rebellious heroes, attributing militancy and intelligence to a white heritage. Many contemporary authors exploit the Negro's quaintness, his "racial qualities." Whether they do this for an escape from drab, standardized life or out of genuine artistic interest or, in the case of Negro authors, out of race pride, their work suffers from the narrowness of allegory. It must be added that these authors play into the hands of reactionaries, who, once a difference is established, use it to justify peculiar position and peculiar treatment.

Whether the Negro was human was one of the problems that racked the brains of the cultured Old South.

2

The finally begrudged admission that perhaps he was, has remained largely nominal in letters as in life. Complete, complex humanity has been denied to him. He is too often like characters in the medieval allegories: now Loyalty, or Mirth, or Servility, or Quaintness, or Exuberance, or Brutishness, or Lust. Only seldom is he shown as Labor or Persecution, although he was brought here to supply the first, and as payment received the second.

Since there is no stereotype without some basis in actuality, it goes without saying that individuals could be found resembling Page's loyal Uncle Billy or Stark Young's William Veal, or Dixon's brutal Gus, or Scarlet Sister Mary or Van Vechten's Lasca, or even Uncle Tom and Florian Slappey. But when, as is frequent, generalizations are drawn from these about a race or a section, the author oversteps his bounds as novelist, and becomes an amateur social scientist whose guesses are valueless, and even dangerous. Fiction, especially on so controversial a subject as the American Negro, is still subjective, and novelists would do well to recognize that they are recording a few characters in a confined social segment, often from a prejudiced point of view. They cannot, like Bacon, take all for their province.

Fortunately for American fiction, however, there have been authors, even from the outset, who heard the Negro speak as Shakespeare heard Shylock:

> He hath disgraced me . . . laughed at my losses, mocked at my gains, scorned my nation . . . cooled my friends, heated mine enemies; and what's his reason? I am a Jew. . . . If you prick us, do we not bleed? If you tickle us, do we not laugh? If you poison us, do we not die? and if you wrong us, shall we not revenge? If we are like you in the rest, we will resemble you in that.

We shall see in the nineteenth century many writers, from Melville to Cable, who have shown sympathy and comprehension. Nevertheless it is to present-day realists, a large number of them southerners, that one must look for the greatest justice to Negro life and character. They have been less concerned with race than with environment; they have sought to get at social causes rather than to prop a social order.

In spite of the publishers' dicta that certain authors know *the* Negro better than Negroes themselves; in spite of certain authors who believe that slave-holding ancestry is necessary in order truly to know Negroes (on the theory that only the owner, or his descendants, can know the owned); in spite of the science of Negro mind-reading, flourishing below the Mason-Dixon line, it is likely that Negro authors will, after the apprentice years, write most fully and most deeply about their own people. As we go to the Russians, the Scandinavians, and the French for the truth about their people; as we go to the workers and not to the stockholders, to the tenants and croppers and not to the landlords, for the truth about the lives of tenants and croppers, so it seems that we should expect the truth of Negro life from Negroes. The Negro artist has a fine task ahead of him to render this truth in enduring fiction. So far, much of what seems truthful has been the work of sympathetic white authors. In all probability white authors will continue to write about the Negro. Sometimes similarly conditioned in America's class structure, sometimes extremely sensitive and understanding, they will get at valuable truth. But Negro novelists must accept the responsibility of being the ultimate portrayers of their own.

CHAPTER I

Early Fiction. When Americans started to write novels, at the end of the eighteenth century, the Negro was definitely part and parcel of American life. Colonial authors from Cotton Mather and Samuel Sewall to Benjamin Franklin, Crèvecour and John Woolman had protested his enslavement. He was the rock upon which the constitution nearly split. In the North, there were still a few slaves and a growing body of freedmen, some of whom, like Phillis Wheatley, Benjamin Banneker, Richard Allen, and Crispus Attucks, were more than locally known. The vast hordes of slaves, together with a good number of free Negroes, were a more integral part of southern society. They had cleared the forests and laid the roads, had built the fine houses and wrought the beautiful ironwork; had labored on the tobacco, rice, indigo and cotton plantations so that their masters could buy more slaves. Cotton was not yet king, the cotton-gin was not invented; but the broad backs of the slaves were still supporting a heavy load. Whether as house-servant grateful for easy favors, and contributing to the master's feeling of safety, or field-hand, or fugitive stealing away to the North, or intractable revolter, throwing both northern and southern communities into consternation, the Negro was recognizably part of the American scene.

But the first groping American novels were still tied to Mother England's leading strings. For all of their patriotism, the novelists were little concerned with American actualities. When the Negro character was

5

included, he was a shadowy figure in the background, an element of romantic side interest, closer to Aphra Behn's *Oroonoko* and Defoe's fiction than to what the novelists could have seen about them.

The earliest novels, William Hill Brown's *The Power of Sympathy* (1789) and Mrs. Susannah Rowson's *The Inquisitor* (1794), true to their sentimental models, have antislavery feeling. Hugh Brackenridge's *Modern Chivalry* (1792 to 1815) contains a good ironic attack upon the slave-trade, and a less successful character Cuff, whose jargon seems plucked out of Defoe:

> Now, shentiman, I say, dat de first man was da black a-man, an' de first woman was de black a-woman: get two-tree children; de rain vasha dese, an' de snow pleach, an' de coula came brown, yella, coppa coula, and at de last quite fite. . . .

Royal Tyler's *The Algerine Captive* (1797) deplores the "middle passage" horrors of the slave-trade in the sentimental mode: "I thought of my native land and blushed." Charles Brockden Brown's novels contain Negro characters only incidentally. There were no English models to make these early novelists aware that servitude and struggle could be subjects for fiction.

Irving. In the nineteenth century, interest in the Negro increased. In *Salmagundi* (1807) Washington Irving, a brisk young man-about-town, records the Negro curiosities he finds, such as the "Negro wench, principal musician at a ball." He describes a dance in Haiti with unctuous ridicule:

> In the middle of the rout, when all was buzz, slip-slop, clack and perfume, who should enter but Tucky Squash! The yellow beauties blushed blue and the black ones blushed as red as they could . . . for he was the pride of the court, the pick of all the sable fair ones of Hayti. Such breadth of nose, such exuberance of lip! his shins had the true cucumber curve; his face in dancing shone like a kettle. . . . When he laughed, there appeared from ear to ear a *chevaux de-frize* of teeth that rivaled the shark's in whiteness. . . . No Long Island Negro could shuffle you "double-trouble" or "hoe corn and dig potatoes" more scientifically.

6

Here we have the first comic Negro in American fiction, assured of long employment from Irving to Octavus Roy Cohen. *Salmagundi* likewise includes Caesar, a "weatherbeaten wiseacre of a Negro," who henpecks his masters, tell stories of ghosts, goblins and witches, and, like a good man Friday, accompanies his master to his sparking and dancing. Caesar is repeated in *The Knickerbocker History of New York* (1809) as an old crone who would croak:

> a string of incredible stories about New England witches—grisly ghost horses without heads,—and hairbreadth escapes, and bloody encounters among the Indians.

"Adventures of the Black Fisherman" in *Tales of A Traveler* (1824) tells us only that Black Sam or Mud Sam was "supposed to know all the fish in the river by their christian names," and that he had a "great relish for the horrible," such as executions, and that all of the urchins felt free to play tricks upon him. Irving does not attempt to give his speech, much less his character.

Cooper. The first American novelist to aim at fullness in his presentation of American life, James Fenimore Cooper naturally included the Negro. Although limited in information and skill, he expanded and improved upon the slight sketches of his forerunners. He presents Negroes of many types. First of all, there is Caesar Thompson, the loyal retainer in *The Spy* (1821). True to the prevailing literary attitude of the gentry towards underlings, Cooper burlesques his appearance with what passed for humor in those days:

> But it was in his legs that nature had indulged her most capricious humor. There was an abundance of material injudiciously used. The calves were neither before nor behind, but rather on the outer side of the limb, inclining forward. . . . The leg was placed so near the center as to make it sometimes a matter of dispute whether he was not walking backward.

7

Nevertheless Caesar is shown as crafty, and courageous in the service of his family. Cooper's interest in Negroes is continued in *The Pioneers* (1823) in Agamemnon, not a slave but a legal ward, a man-of-all work whose deference does not keep him from mirth at his master's expense, and Abraham, a free black who shares in the rough frontier life.

A different type is the free Sailor, Scipio Africa, one of the heroes of *The Red Rover* (1827). In physique, seamanship, self-control, and intelligence he is superior to his sailing mates, but this does not shield him from their petty insults. There is pathos in the scene of his death:

> If he is not (a Christian) I don't know who the devil is. A man who serves his country, is true to his messmate, and has no sulk about him, I call a saint, so far as mere religion goes. I say, Guinea, my hearty, give the chaplain a grip of the fist. . . . A Spanish windlass would not give a stronger screw than the knuckle of that nigger an hour ago; and now, you see to what a giant may be brought!

In *The Last of The Mohicans* (1826), Cora Munro, the offspring of a mixed marriage, is shown to be resourceful and strong, above the usual run of Cooper's "females." It is worthy of note, since she is the first of a long line of "octoroons," that her end is tragic.

Cooper thus anticipates later creators of Negro characters, presenting the faithful house servant, the courageous man of action, and the octoroon doomed to tragedy. Though crudely recorded, his dialect rises above the usually impossible Negro speech in early novels. No abolitionist, Cooper still did not favor slavery, and honest observer that he was, he refuses to see the Negro, even when grotesquely described, as subhuman.

Simms. William Gilmore Simms, of South Carolina, differed from Cooper, his northern model, in that he defended slavery ardently. In his fiction, however,

Negroes are presented without excessive argument. They range from the obsequious house-servant to the brave freeman. Hector, in *The Yemassee* (1832) is a heroic slave, participating gallantly in the Indian warfare, volunteering for perilous service, warning blockhouses, and rescuing his master. He is extremely loyal and refuses to be freed.

> I d—n to h—, maussa, if I gwine to be free. . . . 'Tis onpossible, maussa. . . .   Enty I know wha' kind of ting freedom is wid black man? Ha! you make Hector free, he turn wuss more nor poor buckrah—he tief out of de shop—he git drunk and lie in de ditch. . . .

This passage is the first and most influential example of a scene soon to be hackneyed. Caesar in *Guy Rivers* (1834) is subservient, but cunning and philosophical. *The Partisan* (1835) gains in interest because of the presence of Tom, who is such a good cook that Porgy, his gourmet master, will not brook his being abused. Tom repays by keeping his master fat and happy "so long as dere's coon and possum, squirrel, patridges and dub, duck in de ribber, and fish in de pond."

Simms' *Richard Hurdis* (1838) shows slaves accompanying their masters on the move to the Alabama frontier, dancing, singing, sometimes listening to a fellow slave's impromptu verses:

> In them he satirized his companions without mercy . . . and did not spare his own master, whom he compared to a squirrel that had lived upon good corn so long that he now hungered for bad in his desire for change.

In *The Forayers* (1855) Cato is a slave-driver, courageous and devoted to his family, and Benny Bowlegs, another driver, is

> a moral steam engine. He pushed his master as well as his brother slaves. . . . Push at the beginning, push in the middle, push at the end, and Ben's pushing made crops.

The Wigwam and The Cabin (1845) a collection of stories, is unusual in showing Negroes at the center of the picture. "The Loves of The Driver" casts sidelights upon plantation customs, and the "Lazy Crow" is the first to portray Negro superstition and folkways.

In numbers, and a certain rudimentary realism, the Negro characters in Simms' many novels go beyond those of any other early nineteenth century novelist. Simms bungles when he tries to record the Gullah dialect, but the effort is worthy of comment. Striving to be accepted as a southern gentleman, Simms shows his slaves, generally, to be well cared for and contented. Nevertheless, his urge to realism kept him from showing slavery to be an endless picnic. Masters held forth freedom as a reward for service; they knew, if the contented slaves did not. All in all, however, Simms is noteworthy more for the extensiveness of his gallery of Negroes than for any depth of characterization.

As Simms showed Negroes participating in the backwoods life and warfare of the South, so earlier writers of the westward movement included sketches of Negroes. Paulding's *Westward Ho* (1832) deals with southerners leaving what romancers were to consider Arcadia for a better land. In this novel, Pompey, like Simms' Hector, refuses freedom. *Nick of The Woods* (1837) a melodrama of bloody Kentucky by Robert Bird, includes several Negroes. Emperor is most fully characterized: like Cooper's Caesar he is loyal, worshipful of quality, and, grotesque. Although his "natural" cowardice is insisted upon, his actions belie this, as he fights for his "little missie" and dies the death of a hero, "gored by numberless wounds, and trampled by the feet of his slayers."

The Virginians. Virginia is the setting for such novelists as W. A. Carruthers, Beverley and George Tucker, and John Esten Cooke. Their novels describe

10

the gentry and their complaisant slaves who enter the books as unobtrusively as they entered the grand dining rooms to bring in sweet missives or decanters of old port. These mammies and butlers and coachmen are interchangeable, appearing in different books under different classical names, but always the same.

Toby in Poe's "The Journal of Julius Rodman" (1840) is "as ugly an old gentleman as ever spoke, having . . . swollen lips, large white protruding eyes, flat nose, long ears, double head, pot-belly, and bow-legs." He is another of Poe's sad attempts at humor. Jupiter, in "The Gold-Bug" (1843), traditionally refuses to leave his master, but threatens in all serious-ness to beat him, a hot-blooded cavalier, with a big stick. His dialect, an attempt at Gullah, is language belonging with Poe's masterpieces, "out of space and out of time." Poe revealed that his southern upbring-ing had borne fruit, however, when, defending slavery from "the fanaticism of the Northern Abolitionists" he writes that it is the will of God that the Negro should have a "peculiar nature," of which one charac-teristic is his tremendous loyalty to his master, "to which the white man's heart is a stranger." The master has a "reciprocal feeling of parental attach-ment to his humble dependent":

he who is taught to call the little negro his in this sense and *because he loves him,* shall love him *because he is his.*

Melville. A greater writer than Poe in his grasp of character, Herman Melville was above this sophistry in dealing with human beings. A northerner, Melville did not know slavery at first hand; but a mariner, he did know Negro seamen. *Moby Dick* (1851) reveals this knowledge.

[Daggoo] a gigantic coal-black negro . . . retained all his barbaric virtues and erect as a giraffe, moved about the decks in all the pomp of six feet five in his socks. There was a corporeal humility in looking up at him; and a white man standing before him seemed a white flag come to beg truce from a fortress.

11

If Daggoo is the "noble savage," Pip, as sympathetically created, is of another breed. Pip's cowardice is not considered racial but is naturally human.

> Poor Alabama boy! On the grim Pequod's forecastle ye shall see him, beating his tambourine, prelusive of the eternal time, when sent for to the great quarter-deck on high, he was bid strike in with angels and beat his tambourine in glory: called a coward here, hailed a hero there!

Negro sailors, generally courageous and praiseworthy, occur in Melville's other romances of the sea.

Benito Cereno (1855) is a masterpiece of mystery, suspense and terror. Captain Delano of the *Bachelor's Delight,* discovering a vessel in distress along the uninhabited coast of Chile, boards her to render aid. He is interested in the many Negroes he finds on the decks: "like most men of a good blithe heart he took to Negroes not philanthropically, but genially, just as other men to Newfoundland dogs." He is mystified, however, when the gamesome Negroes flare up in momentary rage, and especially by their continual clashing their hatchets together. Only when Don Benito, in desperation, escapes to Delano's ship, does the real truth dawn.

There had been a revolt on board the *San Dominick;* the Negro sailors and the slaves had killed many of the whites, and had kept the others alive only for their skill as navigators in order to reach a Negro country. The mutineers and revolters are overcome in a bloody battle, carried to Lima, and executed. The contrast between the reputed gentleness of Negroes "that makes them the best body-servants in the world," and the fierceness with which they fight for freedom is forcibly driven home. Certain Negroes stand out: Babo who, resembling a "begging friar," engineered the revolt with great skill and is almost fiendish in his manner of breaking down Cereno's morale; Francesco, the mulatto barber; Don José, personal servant

12

of a Spanish Don; and Atulfa, an untamed African chieftain, all filled with hatred for whites. Melville graphically pictures the slave mothers, "equally ready to die for their infants or fight for them"; the four old men monotonously polishing their hatchets; and the murderous Ashantees. All bear witness to what Melville recognized as a spirit that it would take years of slavery to break.

Although opposed to slavery, Melville does not make *Benito Cereno* into an abolitionist tract; he is more concerned with a thrilling narrative and character portrayal. But although the mutineers are bloodthirsty and cruel, Melville does not make them into villains; they revolt as mankind has always revolted. Because Melville was unwilling to look upon men as "Isolatoes," wishing instead of discover the "common continent of man," he comes nearer the truth in his scattered pictures of a few unusual Negroes than do the other authors of this period.

Frontier Humor. The southern humorists, thriving from the thirties to the sixties, introduce the Negro only incidentally in their picture of horse-swapping, gander-pulling, camp meetings, fights, and political brawls. Because they were realistic, the "plantations" they show are most often backwood farms. The hard-fisted frontier squires, with a love of horse-play, and a callousness necessary for survival, treat their slaves as one would expect: they are neither Legrees nor American versions of Sir Roger de Coverly. In *Georgia Scenes* (1835), Longstreet non-comittally shows a Southern backwoods "lady" knocking her servant around from mere habit. In *Adventures of Simon Suggs* (1846) Johnson Hooper gives good pictures of southern camp-meetings, at which Negroes and whites vie in religious hysteria, mingling indiscriminately in the hollow square, plunging and pitching about in the

13

"jerks" and screaming "glory" in unsegregated chorus.

George Harris in *Sut Lovingood Yarns* (1867) tells of a rowdy whose antics include poking a hornet's nest into a Negro camp meeting. At another time, Sut removes a corpse and lays a snoring, drunken Negro in the coffin. When the slave preacher Simon comes to the coffin he yells:

> "Oh Goramighty massy on dis soul; de debil hesef on top of brudder Seize! . . ." Jis then I moaned out in a orful doleful vise, "Hiperkrit, cum tu hell, I has a claim ontu you fu holdin the bag while Seize stole co'n." He jes rar'd backwards, an' fell outen the door wif his hans locked, an' sed he in a weak . . . sort of vise, "Please marster" an' jis fainted, he soon cum to a-runnin', fer I hearn the co'n crashin thru the big field like a in-gine were runnin' express thru hit. I hain't seen Simon ter this day.

Other humorists tell of frontier surgery upon slaves; if they were not ill before, they were near death's door after the barbarous operations.

The tone of the humorists is burlesque, which often sinks to the level of present-day "darky" jokes. Nevertheless, southern humor is significant. The assumption that Negroes are especially designed as butts for rough practical jokes is probably closer to the reality of the antebellum South than the sentimentality of more ambitious works.

True to the manner of cracker-box philosophers, Artemus Ward attacks the sentimentalized and the unconventional, and delivers many of the "common-man's" jibes at abolitionists and Negroes. "The Octoroon" is, at least, a refreshing departure from the shopworn tragic mode.

> "Hush—shese a Octoroon!"
> "No! sez I . . . yu don't say so! How long she bin that way?"
> "From her arliest infuncy," sed he.
> "Wall, what upon arth duz she do it fur?" I inquired.
> "She kan't help it. . . . It's the brand of Kane."

Oberlin College is lampooned for being rather "too strong on Ethiopians." Though a good Unionist in

14

the war, Artemus Ward, unlike his successor Nasby, does not reveal any sympathy for the Negro.

Summary. Irving's tellers of mysterious legends, Cooper's house-servants, Melville's mates in the foc'sle, and the obsequious servants of the Virginia cavaliers reflect their authors' interests and experience more than they interpret Negro life. Simms' blood and thunder melodramas and the farces of the frontier humorists give more varied types and experiences, with some crude realism. Melville's *Benito Cereno* goes more deeply into character. In the main, however, these subsidiary characters are not very convincing. They speak a pidgin English, closer to the speech of Robinson Crusoe's Friday than to that of nineteenth century Negroes. Cooper and Simms tried to record dialects; Simms is probably better since Gullah is nearer to pidgin English, but he is still inaccurate. Some authors presented the Negro with dignity and sympathy, but serious realism was still far off. It is worthy of note, however, that such favorite Negro characters as the fabler, the loyal servant, the buffoon, the tragic octoroon, the noble savage, and the revolter, appear in these early books.

Although in a few cases propaganda for or against slavery raises its head, these subsidiary characters are not made into walking arguments. Toward the end of this period, however, the slavery debate broke out, and, in the words of one critic, "the world of nature was lost in the world of controversy."

DISCUSSION QUESTIONS

1. Why were early American novels "tied to Mother England's leading strings?"

2. What tradition of English literature might account for Irving's and Cooper's humorous treatment of the Negro?

15

3. Since Simms was proslavery, what is inconsistent about his showing Negroes being set free as reward for heroic services?

4. What historical incidents could have suggested Melville's *Benito Cereno?*

5. What in Poe's life might have occasioned his attitude toward the Negro?

6. In which of the works mentioned is the Negro character a foreground character?

CHAPTER II

The Plantation Tradition. The growth and accuracy of the plantation tradition have been excellently studied in *The Southern Plantation* (1925) by Francis Pendleton Gaines. Gaines attributes the tradition's hold on America to a love of feudalism (in spite of our profession of democracy), the charm of the Negro characters as "native" literary material, and a romantic wish for an Arcadian past. He proves that "the tradition omits much plantation truth and exaggerates freely certain attractive features of the old life." But the tradition goes on unabashed; over a century old, it still guarantees best selling fame.

The setting is familiar:

> The old plantation; a great mansion; exquisitely gowned ladies and courtly gentlemen moving with easy grace upon the broad veranda behind stalwart columns; surrounding the yard an almost illimitable stretch of white cotton; darkies singingly at work in the fields, Negro quarters, off on one side, around which little pickaninnies tumbled in gay frolic.

It is used in advertisements for coffee, pancake flour, phonograph records, and whiskey. It is a favorite American dream. The characters are as constant as the cotton bolls: the courtly planter, the one hundred per-cent southern belle, the duelling cavalier, the mammy or cook, "broadbosomed . . . with vari-colored turban, spotless apron, and beaming face," the plantation uncle, black counterpart "of the master so loyally served and imitated," and the banjo-plunking minstrel of the quarters.

Since the plantation tradition tells of a glory that must have no blemish, slavery is explained away as a

17

benevolent guardianship, necessary for a childish people's transition from heathendom to Christianity. By stressing festivities such as harvesting, corn-shucking, hunting, fishing, balls, weddings and holiday seasons, slavery was presented as "an unbroken Mardi Gras." Since southerners, merely because they are born in the South, are a kindlier, gentler breed than other mortals, the possible abuses of slavery existed only in the minds of fanatical Yankees.

Plantation tradition fiction, reenforcing proslavery thought, was in turn reenforced by it. Occasionally southern economists admitted that slavery was the basis of southern commerce and civilization. But these dismal scientists were too outspoken for the sentimental romancers. Southern physiologists who proved that "by an unknown law of nature none but the black race can bear exposure to the tropical sun," justified the sippers of juleps on shaded verandahs. Theologians defended slavery as having Biblical support since Ham was cursed by God. In the main, however, the plantation tradition advanced less unfeeling arguments: the grown-up slaves were contented, the pickaninnies were frolicking, the steamboat was hooting around the bend, God was in his heaven, and all was right with the world.

The Tradition Begins. Swallow Barn, the first example of the plantation tradition, appeared in 1832. J. P. Kennedy, the author, was skillful, but his picture relies upon Addison, Goldsmith, Walter Scott, and proslavery thought more than upon observation and understanding. His mouthpiece in these sketches is Littleton, a northerner (Kennedy himself was a Marylander, southern in upbringing), who comes South with an "inky intent" to see the worst of slavery, but remains to worship it. The southern aristocrats

18

are not in love with the institution of slavery, but realize that it is necessary for the Negro who is

> essentially parasitical, dependent upon guidance for his most indispensable necessaries, without foresight or thrift of any kind. . . . I am quite sure they never could become a happier people than I find them here. . . . No tribe of people have ever passed from barbarism to civilization whose progress has been more secure from harm, more genial to their character, or better supplied with mild and beneficent guardianship adapted to the actual state of their intellectual feebleness, than the negroes of Swallow Barn.

In accordance with this ideal coloring, Negro children are shown "basking on the sunny sides of cabins [like] terrapins luxuriating on the logs of a mill-pond." Slaves seem to be kept busiest tending their own garden patches, of which they sell the produce. "I never meet a Negro man—unless he is quite old—that he is not whistling; and the women sing from morning to night." Negroes are shown as ludicrous:

> And when to these are added a few, reverend, wrinkled decrepit old men, with faces shortened as if with drawing strings, noses that seemed to have run all to nostril, and with feet of the configuration of a mattock, my readers will have a tolerably correct idea of the negro-quarter.

Hardships come chiefly from meddling abolitionists: "We alone are able to deal properly with the subject." Kennedy shows how he can add sweetening to the bitter by explaining the breaking up of families (Tidewater fortunes were frequently based upon domestic slave-trading) as follows:

> All before Abe had been successively *dismissed* from Lucy's cabin, as they reached the age fit to render them serviceable, with that satisfied concern that belongs to a negro mother who trusts to the kindness of her master. [Italics mine.]

Kennedy admits that the recording of dialect was beyond him. A great deal more was beyond him, but that does not keep *Swallow Barn* from being influential upon literature about Negro life and character.

In his plays, especially *The Gladiator* (1831), Robert Montgomery Bird took an antislavery stand,

19

but his satirical novel *Sheppard Lee* (1836) was pro-slavery. Part of the book deals with a Quaker philanthropist, confused and futile, who goes to the South to work for abolition. The slaves on the plantation are shown living happily under an indulgent master until an antislavery tract changes them into burners, ravagers and murderers.

Proslavery Humorists. Although, for the sake of the record, Sam Slick, the comic character of T. H. Haliburton's *Yankee Stories* (1836) announces that he dislikes slavery, most of his comments justify it. He objects to enslaving white men for debt, but "those thick-skulled, crooked-shanked, flat-footed, long heeled, woolly headed gentlemen don't seem fit for much else but slavery . . . they ain't fit to contrive for themselves." He ridicules the talk of

> broken hearted slaves killin' themselves in despair—task-master's whip acuttin' into their flesh—burnin' suns,—day o' toil—nights o' grief—pestilential rice grounds—chains—starvation—misery and death,—grand figurs them for oratory.

He is unwilling that abolitionists should be lynched, but they should learn how the cowskin feels. To prove slavery no hardship, he reasons that a married woman is a slave, and if she happens to get the upper hand, the husband is a slave, and leads a worse life than any Negro. Sam's brother, a lawyer in Charleston, S. C., forces an old white swindler to buy a Negro back into slavery, for the good of the Negro. These stories do not belong to the plantation tradition, for some mention "nigger-jockies," i.e., "gentlemen who trade in nigger flesh," and a planter who has "one white wife and fourteen black concubines." But they are proslavery in sympathy. Sam Slick is significant in that he represents a large number of northerners who were never too fond of Negroes and strongly opposed abolition. Some of these became catchers of runaway slaves.

and many expressed their hatred of the Civil War in the Draft Riots.

When William H. Thompson, Georgia humorist, sent Major Jones on his travels in the forties, he was able to get in many proslavery thrusts. Mary Jones wants to take along her slave Prissy, since she is unwilling to have white servants:

> I could never bear to see a white gall toatin' my child about, waiting on me like a nigger. It would hurt my conscience to keep anybody 'bout me in that condition, who was as white and as good as me. . . . A servant, to be any account as a servant, is got to have a different kind of spirit from other people; and anybody that would make a nigger of a white child, because it was pore, hain't got no Christian principle in 'em.

Uncle Ned believes that abolitionists have horns like billy-goats, eyes like balls of fire, and great forked tails like sea serpents. "Ugh, chile, dey wusser'n collery-morbus." When these fierce creatures get hold of Negroes, ruin is come; here is Major Jones describing the free Negroes of the North:

> Pore, miserable, sickly-lookin' creaters! it was enuff to make a abolitionist's hart ake to see 'em crawlin' out of the damp straw of the cellars, to sun themselves on the cellar-dores till they got able to start out to by or to steal sumthing to eat . . . many of 'em was diseased and bloated up like frogs, and lay sprawlin' about like so many cooters in a mud-hole . . . like lizards in a pile of rotten logs. . . This, thinks I, is nigger freedom: this is the condition to which the philanthropists of the North wants to bring the happy black people of the South!

First Answers to Mrs. Stowe. In the three years following the appearance of *Uncle Tom's Cabin* (1852), there were at least fourteen proslavery novels published, besides numerous pamphlets, articles, and a long poem. W. L. G. Smith's *Life At The South,* or *Uncle Tom's Cabin As It Is* (1852) was struck off while the iron was hot, borrowing illustrations from *Swallow Barn* and passages from *The Yemassee.* Uncle Tom, irked at being outdone in the fields by the younger, stronger Hector, and jealous of his master's favoritism, moodily listens to an abolitionist, and runs

21

away. In Canada he finds real slavery; in Buffalo he sees the freedmen in wretchedness, discovering one frozen to death in a snow storm. Finally he begs his master to return him to the South, which that gentleman does out of Christian consideration and forgivingness. The following passage shows Dinah refusing to join Tom in seeking freedom:

> Dinah: ". . . An' den wha' would be de feelin's of your own Dinah. She would curse de hour when she was born. No, no! I cannot consent to be a party to sich an arrangement."
> Tom : "How silly you talk. You will do noffin yourself, an' you will let no one help. I begin to think, you hab revoked your decision. . . . Dere you hab it; you now know'd my feelin's."
> Dinah did not know what to say in reply . . . "there is something in this idea of being free that I cannot comprehend," she thought to herself.

This passed for Negro speech and psychology in proslavery novels. Hector likewise refuses to be free in a speech stolen from the Hector of Simms' *Yemassee*. Allgood, a hypocritical philanthropist, and Bates, an abolitionist busybody, are types that later novels were to repeat.

In the same year, Caroline E. Rush sent forth her little book, *North and South,* or *Slavery and Its Contrasts,* to teach the Northern reader "boundless, illimitable love," that would make him "regret the necessary evils of the Slavery of the South, without bitter feelings towards those who are born amid the peculiar rights and duties of the slaveholders." The thousands of free Negroes in Philadelphia pain Mrs. Rush because of their lack of an "elegant degree of refinement and cultivation"; their poverty is racial debauchery, while the poverty of the whites is victimization. What are the abuses suffered by slaves

> to the real, bitter, oppression that in our own midst sweeps its thousands out of a life of penury into premature graves?

Tears should not be shed for Uncle Tom—"a hardy, strong and powerful Negro"—but should be reserved for helpless, defenseless, children—"of the same color as yourself." Writing of plantation Negroes she wishes that she too had "taken lessons of a colored professor, and was conversant enough with Negro dialect, to launch out boldly into their sea of beauties," but she is forced to leave the speech to her readers' imagination. Little is left to their imagination, however, when she describes the cabins of the field-hands, embowered in Cherokee roses. At this point, the book's illustration resembles a suburban paradise adjoining the White House. When the slave-mistress gently patted a quadroon's head, she "intimated a freedom which is not often shown to the servants in the North." Mrs. Rush is correct here; there was a great deal of such freedom.

Mrs. Eastman's *Aunt Phyllis' Cabin* likewise appeared in 1852. This popular novel glorified slavery and denounced abolitionists, particularly Mrs. Stowe, but it did attempt to describe slave life. Bacchus prays hard and drinks harder; many of his antics—his love for cast-off finery, the banjo, and big words—could grace a minstrel show. Aunt Phyllis is one of the first to appear of the mighty race of "mammies." The title character of John W. Page's *Uncle Robin in His Cabin* (1853) puts the author's beliefs into dialect: he does not want freedom for himself, and the Negro who is dissatisfied should go back where he came from:

"Dis, sir, is no country for free black men: Africa de only place [for] he, sir. . . ."

Sentimentality of The Old South. Mrs. Caroline Lee Hentz, a northerner married to a southern gentleman, turned out a number of blood-and-tears romances. In *Marcus Warland* (1852) and in *Linda* (1857) she celebrates the mammy:

Aunt Judy's African blood had not been corrupted by the base mingling of a paler strain. Black as ebony was her smooth and

23

shining skin, on which the dazzling ivory of her teeth threw gleams bright as the moon at midnight. Judy had loved—adored, reverenced her, as being of a superior, holier race than her own.

The Planter's Northern Bride (1854) by Mrs. Hentz shows the typically converted northern girl. After her appearance on the plantation has elicited rapturous cries of adoration from the slaves, she is won over to the peculiar institution. "Oh! my husband! I never dreamed that slavery could present an aspect so tender and affectionate!" The husband, though a perfect master, modestly says that he is "not as good as the majority of masters." His slaves are fat, sleek and good natured; on Sunday, at church, they are "fashionably attired" and there is "the rustle of tissues, the fluttering of muslin and laces, the waving of feathery fans, the glitter of jewelry." The planter proves that the Negro was divinely ordained for slavery since

> his skull has a hardness and thickness greater than our own, which defy the arrowy sunbeams . . . and his skin secretes a far greater quantity of moisture and throws back the heat absorbed by us.

Crissy, misled by an abolitionist, crosses the Ohio and finds freedom too much for her—"the only slavery she had ever known." An incipient revolt is nipped by Moreland, who, appalled by "the intolerable burden of the slaves' treachery and ingratitude" says:

> I would rather, ten thousand times, cultivate these broad fields myself, than be served by faithless hand and false, hollow hearts. I have hands that can work. I would do it cheerfully; if labor was the portion God had assigned to me in the world. Better, far better, the toiling limbs than the aching heart! He paused a moment in indescribable emotion.

The slaves, naturally, break down and weep. All are forgiven, except Vulcan, who had lifted his "rebel arm" against Moreland: "You must never more wield the hammer or strike the anvil for me. . . . Go— you are free!" Poor Vulcan. . . .

24

Mrs. M. J. McIntosh in *The Lofty and The Lowly, or Good in All and None All-good* (1854), hopes for the solution of the most difficult problem: "how the slave may be elevated to the condition of an intelligent, accountable being, without detriment to the master's interest." Mrs. McIntosh is sure that the solution cannot come from the fanatical North; she hopes that the South "with its greater sympathy, love and understanding will awaken to its responsibilities." Daddy Cato, who has grown gray in faithful service at Montrose Hall, Savannah, is set free and given a little homeplace. He is not proud of his freedom; he will be proud only when he can read the Bible and is free of sin. Following his beloved family to the North, he is highly insulted when he is approached by Boston abolitionists.

> Make me free! how can I free any more? Dem da nonsense people, and what dem want take me from Miss Alice for? . . . I wonder if I been sick and couldn't do any ting, ef dem would nuss me and take care o' me liken Miss Alice. . . . I tink dem crazy 'bout free. Free bery good ting, but free ent all; when you sick, free won't make you well, free won't gib you clo's, no hom'ny, let 'lone meat.

Needless to say, the other slaves at Montrose, away from these crazy people talking about "free," live their childish lives in happiness. *The Lofty and The Lowly* is full of piety toward southern divinity.

The Defense Sums Up Its Case. Mrs. Henry R. Schoolcraft's *The Black Gauntlet* (1860) is likewise a compendium of proslavery arguments. The comfortable, well-ventilated slave homes "with sitting and sleeping room" and a loft for storing provisions are compared with the dens, holes, cellars and tenements of poor whites in northern cities. Food is good and abundant, with game and fish caught in the slave's plentiful off time. Slaves were given an acre of ground for their own use and allowed to raise hogs

25

and poultry, of which the produce was sold at full market price. That slaves were ever knocked senseless is "purest fiction," since "their skulls are so thick that it is doubtful whether any white man's strength could consummate such a feat."

> I am so satisfied that slavery is the school God has established for the conversion of barbarous nations, that were I an absolute Queen of these United States, my first missionary enterprise would be to send to Africa, to bring the heathen as slaves to this Christian land, and keep them in bondage until compulsory labor had tamed their beastliness. . . .

Mrs. Schoolcraft was a bit late, however; for over two centuries countless ships had been sent, and millions of Africans had been brought "to school" in Christian lands.

Since "not a living man can swear that he has ever heard antislavery sentiment from a slave in the South," the suffering of the Negro, to Mrs. Schoolcraft, is a lie whipped up by northern politicans. Runaway slaves are always the good-for-nothing rowdies, who flee to escape work and discipline. The separation of slave husbands and wives is no tragedy, since all are polygamists as in Africa.

> It is not believed by the author that such a monstrosity (babies sold from mothers) has ever occurred in South Carolina, as a mistress *there* usually takes more care of her little Negro property than a black mother ever does of her children.

Poetic justice is in the book: the poor dupe of abolitionists is betrayed into crimes that "destroyed and grieved her conscience," but the faithful mammy is well rewarded. *The Black Gauntlet* is an extreme case of special pleading, where vilification of the accursed Negro alternates with praise of his blessedness in slavery. It is noteworthy, however, that Mrs. Schoolcraft's use of Negro dialect, in this case the Gullah of the low country, is as good as that of any preceding writer.

26

Suggested by "a popular work of fiction, abusive of southern slavery," *The Yankee Slave Dealer* by a Texan (1860) has for its subtitle *An Abolitionist Down South*. The theme is hackneyed: a northerner attempts in vain to aid slaves to freedom, is won over to the proslavery cause, and winds up by becoming a confirmed slave dealer, inhumane because he was born on the wrong side of the Ohio River. Justus, the Yankee, tries to lure three Negroes to freedom. Moses, the first, is a walking edition of *The Bible Defense of Slavery:*

> Well, heah's sump'n else, mastuh: we read in the book of Leviticus dat de childin of Isr'l was told dey should buy slaves. I marked de place, and I'll jes read it to you; doe I s'pose you's seed it many a time. It's in de twenty-fif' chapter, de forty-fif' and sixt' verse.

Truly religious, Moses says that he submits because the Bible tells him that such is his duty. Justus approaches the second Negro with ludicrous pomp: "Let an ardent desire to alleviate the woes of the suffering plead my excuse for the breach of decorum." To this the Negro responds: "What for massah make fun of puoh nigger dis way!" The third specimen, farthest down in the physical and mental scale, runs away with Justus, only to steal his horse and saddlebags and return to his master. Justus soon learns the proslavery creed that freeing the Negro will merely "people the penitentiary or feed the gibbet."

> Nature, by their inferior capacity and cheerful submission to their lot, has so well fitted them for this position. . . . The lot of the serving classes in all countries imposes a burden.

Grief is expressed for the white working class of the North; the female slave finds no parallel to the degradation of northern prostitutes. Abounding in such arguments, *The Yankee Slave Dealer,* though poor in characterization and plot, was the type of novel that the South wanted.

27

Summary. Less novels than fictional arguments, the first books of the plantation tradition are strikingly similar. Frightened by the success of *Uncle Tom's Cabin,* southern authors rushed counter-propaganda to the presses. To testify to their culture, they produced crude, ungainly works. They called Mrs. Stowe "a moral scavenger" and worse names; since she was a Yankee woman, the rules of chivalry could be suspended. The pattern seldom varied: scenes of bliss on the plantation alternated with scenes of squalor in the free North. The contented slave, the clown and the wretched freedman are the Negro stereotypes, who put into dialect the creeds of Chancellor Harper and Professor Dew in the *Pro-Slavery Argument,* and of the Reverend Priest in *The Bible Defense of Slavery.* A plantation with a kindly master was basis for generalizing about all plantations, of whatever type, in whatever sections. A pampered house-servant, who refuses uncertain freedom for a comparatively easy place, becomes *the* Negro slave; a poor unemployed wretch becomes *the* freedman.

The intractable, the ironic, the abused Negro is nowhere on these plantations. Congressmen might deplore in legislative halls the injuries done the South by the Underground Railroad, and southern newspapers might be filled with descriptions of runaways, some second offenders with branded scars on their faces. But runaways in these books are generally flighty creatures and half-wits, and even they finally steal back to the South. Judicial records might be full of instances of brutality, but the occasional whippings are shown to be for due cause such as stealing a ham from a poor woman who could not spare it. Miscegenation is missing in spite of the proofs walking about in the great houses or in the fields or the slave-pens. Slavery is shown as a beneficent guardianship,

28

never as a system of cheap and abundant labor that furnished the basis of a few large fortunes (and assured an impoverished, disfranchised class of poor whites).

In spite of the exaggerations and omissions, however, certain damning evidence creeps in. Though too kind to maltreat Negroes, the cavaliers are adept at tarring-and-feathering, riding on rails, and lynching abolitionist villains, probably out of consideration for the Negro's welfare. Slavery is sometimes considered as not the Negro's final state; at some indefinite time (probably after the planters had all become wealthy) he would be returned to Africa to bear witness to the civilization and Christianity he had seen in America. And lastly, the arguers are betrayed by their argumentative tactics: It isn't true; but since it is, you are worse. Thus: it isn't true that slavery is a bad system, it is really a fine thing—no worse than the northern and English system of wage-slavery, which is terrible. Proslavery authors were justified in protesting the exploitation of northern factory workers, but to argue that therefore slavery was blessed, is to prove that a man's broken leg is not painful since another man has a broken arm.

DISCUSSION QUESTIONS

1. Describe examples of the plantation tradition found in modern advertising.

2. List examples of the plantation tradition in popular songs.

3. Granting that *Swallow Barn* was the truthful picture of a Virginia plantation, why is its influence on literature dangerous?

4. What is damaging in Kennedy's admission that he could not record Negro speech?

29

5. List examples of what you consider the greatest exaggerations in the pictures of slavery given by these books, and state your reasons for so considering them.

6. List the similar situations and arguments of these books.

7. Which novelists defend slavery because of the physical traits of Negroes?

CHAPTER III

ANTISLAVERY FICTION

Growth of the Attitude. The opposition to slavery, which began almost as soon as the first slaves were brought here, found literary expression in colonial times and especially in the eighteenth century, when honorable voices denounced slavery as "the most unremitting despotism on the one hand, and degrading submissiveness on the other." It was not until the eighteen thirties, however, that the antislavery crusade took on full force, moving "from resistance to the slave power . . . to death to slavery." In 1831, the year of Nat Turner's famous revolt, the Antislavery Society was established, and William Lloyd Garrison published the first number of his *Liberator.*

In addition to the pamphlets strewn on "the wayside, the parlor, the stage coach, the rail car and the boat deck," slave narratives became a literary weapon. The experiences of fugitive slaves intrigued abolitionists who took down their stories, sometimes for newspaper sketches such as Isaac Hopper's *Tales of Oppression,* and sometimes for fictionalized biographies such as *A Narrative of the Life and Adventures of Charles Ball, A Black Man* (1838), *Recollections of Slavery* (attributed to a runaway slave, 1838) and *The Narrative of James Williams* (1838). In 1839 Theodore Weld, as important in the antislavery crusade as Garrison, produced *Slavery As It Is,* a book of facts "authenticated by the slave-holders themselves [yet containing] but a tiny fraction of the nameless atrocities gathered from the papers examined." Written to combat "the old falsehood that the slave is

31

kindly treated that has lullabied to sleep four-fifths of the free North and West," this was the most popular antislavery publication before *Uncle Tom's Cabin*.

When antislavery fiction appeared, therefore, it found an audience prepared, and the arguments, the characters and a literary form set up.

Before Uncle Tom's Cabin. The first antislavery novel was published anonymously in 1836 as *The Slave, or Memoirs of Archy Moore.* Enlarged in 1852, it was renamed *The White Slave,* and claimed by Richard Hildreth, the historian. Archy Moore, son of his master, Colonel Moore, marries an octoroon, Cassy. Forced to run away, since the colonel desires Cassy for himself, they are captured and sold to different masters. Archy is sold and resold, until in South Carolina he and Tom, an embittered rebel, take to the swamps, finding a colony of outlawed slaves. Ferreted out of there, Archy, because of his light color, manages to escape to the North; Tom becomes the wild scourge of the region. Archy goes to Europe, attains some education and wealth, and redeems his wife from slavery. Though written in highflown language, and not so dramatic as *Uncle Tom's Cabin, The White Slave* is still vigorous. Certain characters—the white slave, the octoroon girl, the insurrectionist, the unfeeling Yankee overseer, and the lustful planter—are to reappear in later novels. The arguments, though slowing up the action, are cogent and informed. Hildreth obviously studied the slaves in his sojourn: his delineation includes hypocritical humility, sullenness, vindictiveness, intractability, cunning, courage, the contempt of house-servants for field hands, and of mulattoes for darker Negroes. The loyalty of some slaves to their masters, and their treachery to their fellows, are explained largely as policy for gain. Although occasionally heightened and unfair, *The White Slave* is one

32

of the most important novels of this controversial period.

Herman Melville's allegory *Mardi* (1849) has bitter antislavery protest and wise prophecy in the sections that describe Vivenza (the United States). A slave with red marks of stripes upon his back is observed hoisting a standard, correspondingly striped, over the Capitol, the temple dedicated to Liberty. Hieroglyphics read "All men are born free and equal;" minute hieroglyphics add "Except the tribe of Hamo." In the south of Vivenza, the strangers see

> Under a burning sun, hundreds of collared men . . . toiling in trenches. . . . Standing grimly over these, were men unlike them; armed with long thongs, which descended upon the toilers.

After close scrutiny the strangers, in amazement, swear that the slaves are men. For this they are branded as "firebrands, come to light the flame of revolt." The southern spokesman exclaims: "The first blow struck for them dissolves the Union of Vivenza's vales. The northern tribes well know it." Melville warns northerners not to feel self-righteous, and does not malign southerners, since "the soil decides the man," and they have grown up with slavery. Some slaves even seem happy, but Melville adds significantly "not as men." Melville is perplexed about the solution, and fatalistically concludes that "Time must befriend these thralls," but he is certain that slavery is "a blot, foul as the crater-pool of hell."

The first woman to turn the novel to antislavery uses was Emily Catherine Pierson, who felt that too few readers knew of the thousands of runaways who had gained freedom. *Jamie, The Fugitive* (1851) introduces the hero in a newspaper advertisement of a runaway, and takes leave of him in an invoice as one of "Ten Bales of Humanity, in a thriving condition, late from three plantations in Virginia." In between we get descriptions of life in the cabins and fields, of "nigger-buyers," slave sales, slave-pens and caravans, and of the hazards of the fugitive stealthily pursuing his way under the "eaves of the Alleghanies," befriended only by the North Star. Mrs. Pierson's book is pious and sentimental, but her characters, though slightly sketched, are believable human beings.

The same author writes in *Cousin Franck's Household* (1852):

> Were we content to be an humble imitator, we know of no one whom we should be prouder to follow than the noble author of that wonderful work "Uncle Tom's Cabin." But we owe it to ourselves to say that our little book was projected before the publication of the latter; and our Jamie Parker, we think, had only one predecessor—and that we had not seen—in this species of literature.

Written as the letters of a northern woman visiting Virginia, *Cousin Franck's Household*, or *Scenes In The Old Dominion* is *Swallow Barn* in reverse. Slave-traders and fugitives are again described. In addition we have close observations of domestic life. Some of the slaves, with good right, resemble the master too much for his wife's comfort and she begs him to sell them or send them off to his Alabama plantation. A slave drover remarks:

> Fact is, I've got a specimen lot . . . of Anglo-Saxon blood, I reckon they calls it; at any rate, I'm takin' ter market some of the best blood in the "Old Dominion'". . . . Ingenus, ain't it now, for a body to tarn a body's own blood to sich account.

A Yankee overseer, who "calculates what a nigger is wuth, and how long he'll last on the hard drive plan;" a beautiful octoroon and her mother, crazy Millie, deranged by the tragedy of slavery, are types that will frequently be met with in later fiction. Although apologetic to "fastidious readers" who might object to her recording "dialectal peculiarities," Mrs. Pierson kept voluminous notebooks "to secure accuracy in the nondescript vernacular of the cabin and the hut." She sees the social setting, likewise, with accuracy; she records what southern novelists preferred not to show: the poor whites, not an accident but a logical result of slavery; and the worn-out, profitless land, with brought it about that Virginia's best crop was the crop of slave children in the quarters.

Harriet Beecher Stowe. In 1851, a little woman in Cincinnati sent the first chapter of *Uncle Tom's Cabin or The Man that Was a Thing* to the *National Era.* The daughter of a famed preacher, and the sister of another more famous for his antislavery sermons, Harriet Beecher Stowe had grown up in religious, humanitarian surroundings. Cincinnati, a border city, was a battleground for antislavery and proslavery forces; Dr. Bailey, abolitionist editor of the *National Era* was mobbed there, and Quakers spread the anti-slavery gospel in "sewing societies." Mrs. Stowe, whose home was at times a shelter for fugitives, had listened to pathetic or hair-raising stories of the South, and had written two antislavery sketches, "Immediate Emancipator" (1848) and "The Freeman's Dream" (1850). Her anger at the passage of the Fugitive Slave Law made her dissatisfied with such weak parables, and she set out to write a passionate protest. In preparation she read books like Weld's *Slavery As It Is,* and the autobiographies of Frederick Douglass, of Lewis Clark, who suggested George Harris, and of Josiah Henson, who suggested Uncle Tom.

In 1852 when the completed serial was published in book form as *Uncle Tom's Cabin, or Life Among The Lowly,* its success was instantaneous. Over three hundred thousand copies were sold in America in the first year; in a very short time there were forty editions in England, and over a million and a half copies sold in the Empire. It was translated in many foreign languages, including Bohemian, Welsh and Siamese. It

35

was acclaimed by George Sand, Dickens and Kingsley, who naturally were not annoyed by the sentimentality and melodrama; it set Heinrich Heine to reading the Bible; to Macaulay it was the greatest American literary achievement. Whittier rejoiced in the Fugitive Slave Law, since it gave occasion for the book. Lincoln later said to Mrs. Stowe, "So you are the little woman who brought on the great war." If this is overstatement, it is true that many of the voters who elected Lincoln in 1860 were greatly influenced by the household favorite. Tolstoy grouped it with the few masterpieces of the world, and Howells considered it the only great American novel produced before the Civil War. Detractors have for a long time been undermining its prestige, but it has probably been more widely read than any other novel in the world, and it is still popular.

In characterizing the Negroes in *Uncle Tom's Cabin,* Mrs. Stowe faced the dilemma of the propagandist. If she showed them as brutalized by slavery, she would have alienated her readers, whose preferences were for idealized heroes. If on the other hand, she made her characters too noble, her case against slavery would be weakened. She did this with Uncle Tom, and critics have stated: If slavery produced a Christian hero so far superior to free whites, then slavery is excellent. This dilemma was hardly recognized by Mrs. Stowe, however, as all of her training and inclinations were toward sentimental idealism. Eliza and George, if not models of Christian forgivingness, are still virtue in distress, to be saved by poetic justice. Eva's ethereal goodness, and Legree's cruelty are examples among the white characters of the same idealization. But Topsy must not be overlooked; although minstrel shows have made her into a Puck in blackface, Mrs. Stowe intended to show her as a pathetic victim of

36

slave-trading as well. Sambo and Quimbo, the slave-drivers, had been dehumanized by the system; Cassy is the octoroon whose beauty has crushed her; and Chloe, while traditional, is made realistic by the little touches of a woman well acquainted with kitchen-lore. Mrs. Stowe has a wide range of Negro characters, and one southern critic finds in *Uncle Tom's Cabin* just about all of the traits he is willing to grant the Negro. High spirits are shown on Shelby's Kentucky plantation, but tragedy lurks in the background. Mrs. Stowe handles the tragedy with the bold melodramatic strokes of Dickens; but she artfully blends the shocking with humor and pathos, with mystery and suspense; familiar domestic scenes with cotton-planting, steamboating on the river and gambling in New Orleans; pious moralizing with fascinating wickedness—all in all a successful recipe.

When Mrs. Stowe rattled the bones of the skeletons in southern closets, howls arose from the manors. A South Carolinian recorded the rumor:

> That the whole "nigger kingdom" of the South had been killed, smothered, torn to pieces by bloodhounds, ground up for bone manure; children dragged from mothers' breasts, and the whole plantations turned into slaughter-houses, we fully expected; and yet nobody had read it.

It is needless to say that no such pictures occurred in *Uncle Tom's Cabin,* yet Mrs. Stowe was called a defamer, a hypocrite, "snuffling for pollution with a pious air," a plain liar.

A moralist and debater, Mrs. Stowe returned the lie. She published *A Key to Uncle Tom's Cabin,* a book as long as the novel, giving sources for all of her charges. The *Key,* largely unread by the critics, remains unanswerable. Granting that such feats as Eliza's crossing the ice are sensational, although vouched for, in what did the lying in *Uncle Tom's Cabin* consist? Joel Chandler Harris goes too far in calling it a defense of American slavery as Mrs. Stowe found it in Kentucky, but his comment has point. Shelby and St. Clair are kindly owners, in the plantation tradition, whose humanity was overpowered by the system. The two Yankees,—the vicious Legree and the priggish, unsympathetic Miss Ophelia are certainly in line with southern gospel. It is no lie that there were slave auctions, slave cellars such as the ones where the flies "got to old Prue," public whipping posts, mothers separated from their children, and slaves like Cassy whose beauty was their doom. With allowances for sentimentality and melodrama, essential truth is in *Uncle Tom's Cabin.* To argue against its artistic faults and to consider it incomplete representation are possible. The charge of lying, however, is confusing. Mrs. Stowe showed that slavery was a great wrong, and that Negroes are human. Is it here that critics believe that she lies?

Mrs. Stowe's second antislavery novel, *Dred, A Tale of the Dismal Swamp* (1856) later published as *Nina Gordon,* was obscured by the lasting fame of *Uncle Tom's Cabin,* although many critics have preferred it. It lacks the pathos and sweep of the earlier work, but it adds pictures of the "poor whites" and of Negro outlaws in the Dismal Swamp. Harry Gordon is a fuller portrait of George Harris; another "white slave," he is the successful manager of a plantation while his white half-brother is a wastrel and carouser. His character is analyzed in conventional terms: "the rules about Ham do not pertain" to him, and at times he plaintively wishes to be "a good, honest, black nigger, like Uncle Pomp." Lizette, his quadroon wife, is similar to Eliza. Traditional Negroes are Old Hundred, the coachman, and Tiff, who in his love for his little white charges is like Uncle Tom. Dred, a fanatical fugitive, the son of Denmark Vesey, is created somewhat after the model of Nat Turner. A new figure for Mrs. Stowe, she does not portray him very successfully. Devoted to the creed of "turning the other cheek," she shows Dred doing little other than rescuing the virtuous, or urging slaves to escape. He is less an insurrectionist than a Negro Robin Hood. His supernatural appearances recall Scott's novels, and his longwinded chants are more those of a Hebrew prophet. Other fugitives are more real: Hark, sullen and inflexible, and Jim, the clownish house-servant, pampered but wanting to be free, especially so that he can have a wife all his own. There is local color in scenes like the camp-meeting, but the book is written with a reformer's zeal, more concerned with urging emancipation and denouncing "the great Christianizing institution" than with re-creating social reality. Antislavery feeling is likewise in *The Minister's Wooing* (1859), a tale of New England. Candace, "a powerfully built, majestic black woman, corpulent, heavy," is traditional in her loyalty to her family, but she is proudly and volubly free: "I ain't a critter. I's neider huff nor horns. I's a reasonable being . . . ."

Negro Novelists. Very shortly after *Uncle Tom's Cabin* the first novel by an American Negro appeared. This was *Clotel, or The President's Daughter* (1853) by William Wells Brown, an antislavery agent. The book was popular enough for three editions; in the second and third, the heroine is changed to the daughter of "a great statesman." *Clotel* is not well written or well constructed, but these failings are common to its type. Scattered throughout the book are intimate glimpses that only one who had been a slave could get: a few dialect rhymes, certainly among the first in American literature, a few comic interludes, and some Negro jokes on the master. But such things are all too scarce. The story is melodrama, and the chief characters, though vouched for by the author, are hardly distinguishable in gentility from the heroines of "blood and tears" romances. Clotel's mother jumps into the Potomac, committing suicide to elude the slave hunters. Her aunt, after marriage with a white Vermont doctor, who neglects to file papers of manumission, is sold with her beautiful daughters on the block, and dies of the shame. The surpassingly beautiful Clotel is luckier. Sold from one place to another, she finally becomes maidservant for an angelic girl, and falls in love with a handsome black slave. Helping him to escape execution for resisting a white man, she disguises him in her clothes, and remains undetected in the cell. (She is nearly white, and he is black.) She is flogged for this and sold to New Orleans, where an enraptured Frenchman steals her away. After his death, providential for the plot, she meets her former lover in Europe. Back in America, he dies leading a charge in the Civil War, and she becomes an Angel of Mercy to the Federal troops. The novel wanders far afield, and incidents that might have been impelling arguments are told too casually.

Two other Negro novelists took up the novel as their weapon. Frank J. Webb's *The Garies and Their Friends* (1857) takes place chiefly in Philadelphia. It has a new setting and problem, but is badly overwritten. Mr. Garie, a white man, has married a wife only partly white, and race prejudice makes the whole family suffer for it. In contrast, a Negro family lives a happier life in spite of hardships. Martin Delany, a versatile free Negro, began in 1859 a novel *Blake, or the Huts of America* in the *Anglo-African,* but the work was not completed. With a hero and heroine modelled upon George Harris and Eliza, and a number of horrors, *Blake* is an imitation of *Uncle Tom's*

40

Cabin, best in the pictures of the Southwest which Delany had visited. In 1859 Frances Harper's "The Two Offers" appeared, telling of a white heroine who devotes her life to the antislavery cause. This is the first short story by a Negro author, but otherwise unimportant.

Other Successors. *The Planter's Victim* (1855) by W. W. Smith, republished five years later as the *Yankee Slave Driver,* is the most gruesome antislavery novel. Richard Dudley, wishing his octoroon half sister for mistress, is infuriated when she marries a nearly white slave, George. He has Caroline flogged with one hundred and fifty lashes and George with four hundred. On such a scale are all the barbarities inflicted. Dudley smashes the skull of Caroline's baby and, when Caroline dies heartbroken, he insults her corpse. For many years he torments George, and finally after starving him in a New Orleans dungeon, stabs him. The slaves are extreme specimens, George being a "youthful and majestic Apollo in the full glow of masculine beauty and splendor," and Caroline being magnificently beautiful. Both speak highflown drivel. With all of his supposed manliness, George equals Uncle Tom in saintliness. The book hardly serves its purpose: the villains are too monstrous for belief, the hero too submissive for respect, and the incidents too uniformly gruesome for anything except a collection of horrors.

Among the antislavery authors who, like Mrs. Stowe, advocated colonization is H. L. Hosmer, author of *Adela, The Octoroon* (1860). Adela, a slave-mistress, though disliking abolitionist books which "merely ransack lawsbooks and newspapers for narratives of torture," condemns slavery as a fraud and curse. The misery of slaves on Mississippi plantations is pictured only a shade darker than the squalor of fugitives in the North. The happy opportunities of life in Liberia are set in contrast, but without conviction. One of the full length characters is Tidbald, distinguished champion of southern rights, but seducer of his own slave daughter. A mysterious worker of the underground, "broadbrim" Quakers, and an octoroon who preferred to be a kept woman in New Orleans instead of a plantation drudge, could well have been further developed at the expense of the argumentation. Mention is made of the melodies of the slaves and the rhythm of their dancing, but other local color is missing and the dialect is false. Many of the Negroes are true steel, game to the core. At the end Adela is proved to be herself an octoroon. To save her, a loyal body-servant, Captain Jack, heads an insurrection and kills her would-be ravisher. Although disgruntled at slavery, courageous, and intelligent, Jack rebels only when his mistress is in danger. *Adela, The Octoroon* is confused, incredible, and tedious, with only occasional originality.

More popular among the Union soldiers, according to report, than even *Uncle Tom's Cabin,* was a novel published in the Beadle Dime Novel Series, *Maum Guineas' Children,* by Mrs. M. V. Victor (1861). The author disclaims any political purpose, but her stress is antislavery. While planters and their families are shown in a sympathetic light, the abuses of slavery are told of in fuller measure. Maum Guinea, mysterious and embittered, has been deprived of her children and husband. She contrives the escape of Hyperion and Rose, a beautiful slave who has been sold by the "kindly" master to a libertine. The novel deals with the Christmas week in the lives of the slaves. Barbecuing, dancing, singing, and hunting are described to show the brighter side, but the stories told around the fire are grim and rebellious. One slave's husband had been in the Nat Turner uprising; another had attempted to kill his mistress, because she had jealously hounded his mother to death. The novel is simply written and evidently based upon intimate knowledge. Mrs. Victor seems to look upon the pure African type as happy-go-lucky, and finds rebels only among the mixed bloods, and the happy ending is forced. Even with these failings, however, the novel belongs with the most readable and convincing of antislavery novels.

Written to enforce the antagonism of many northerners to the Fugitive Slave Law, since "a human critter's of more account than all the laws in Christendom," J. T. Trowbridge's *Neighbor Jackwood* (1856) is far more convincing in its pictures of Vermont than of the deep South. Camille, the daughter of a Frenchman and an octoroon *placée,* is "jest dark enough to be ra'al purty." Enslaved after her father's death, untimely as in so many abolitionist novels, she is sold and is subjected to her master's advances. Robert Greenwood, a northerner, enamored of her, helps her escape to the North; but unwilling to become his mistress, she runs away from him. In Vermont she finds honest love in Hector, who marries her, and goes South to buy her freedom. Left in Vermont, she is hidden away by Neighbor Jackwood, until Robert, now a fullfledged scoundrel, tells the kidnappers where she is. She is rescued in the nick of time by Hector, who brings her papers of freedom. There is a great deal of mystery and suspense, Camille's hiding away in a haystack on a stormy night being vividly described. But the book is more sensational than revelatory of Negro life; and the southern scenes are hastily passed over and conventional.

The same author's *Cudjo's Cave* (1863), a stirring boys' book, tells of the conflicts between Unionists and

Confederates in Eastern Tennessee in the first year of the war. Three Negro characters are prominent: Toby, the faithful servant; Cudjo, ape-like in appearance, but cunning, powerful, and vindictive, the unbroken African; and Pomp, "magnificently proportioned, straight as a pillar, and black as ebony, of noble features." Pomp has been educated abroad by an indulgent master. As usual in these novels, the benefactor dies, and the new master is tyrannical. Pomp escapes to the ravines of the Cumberland Mountains, and there meets Cudjo, whose scarred back was "the most powerful of antislavery documents." They eke out an existence in the cave, with the connivance of slaves who keep them posted; in their turn they help runaways, succor abolitionists is distress, and finally aid in overthowing the Confederate guerrillas. The Negroes and the Unionists are too good, and the Rebels too villainous, but the novel has the suspense of escape and capture, and throws light upon an interesting chapter of history.

In spite of its unwieldy plot, Epes Sargent's *Peculiar* (1863) is one of the most rewarding of antislavery novels. It is not a mere recounting of horrors. "It ain't de whippins . . . dat make de wrong of slavery. De mos' kindest thing dey could do de slave would be ter treat him so he wouldn't stay a slave nohow," says one character. Another insists that if slaves were so brutalized as to be contented, slavery would be doubly cursed, and rejoices that "there is manhood in them to make them at least unhappy." The slave Peek, named for the "Peculiar Institution," has full share of this manhood, and is defiant, provident, intelligent, and, strangely for the antislavery gallery, skeptical of religion. Vance, the white hero, disguises himself as Gashface, a mulatto underground agent, out of hatred for the system that had killed his octoroon wife. He and Peek, as climax to their safeguarding the virtuous, and confounding wrong-doers, discover a beautiful white girl who had been sold into slavery, and rescue her from the lust of her master. The story is sensational, but Sargent shows an understanding of such historic matters as the kidnapping from northern States, the workings of the underground, and the easy acceptance of concubinage by southern society. He shows the slaves to be secretive, relying on their "grapevine telegraph" for mutual protection; slyly humorous, waging their own guerrilla warfare against a stronger enemy. Sargent goes below the surface and gets at social causes, and because of this his book is frequently persuasive.

Summary. Antislavery fiction naturally concentrated upon the abuses that proslavery fiction left unmentioned: slave-sales, the breaking up of families, shameful practises at the slave-mart, slave jails and coffles, whippings, overwork and concubinage. Slave discontent was stressed. Negro insurrectionists, outlaws, fugitives and underground agents are favorite characters, and since they existed in large numbers, antislavery fiction makes a contribution here to realism. Unfortunately the rebellious and militant are generally shown to be of mixed blood, like George Harris, whereas the more African type is shown as docile, like Uncle Tom. Some novelists depart from this pattern, but the pattern persists and has remained wrongly influential. Moreover, the heroine is frequently a quadroon or octoroon, a concession, unconscious perhaps, to race snobbishness even among abolitionists. As one critic says:

This was an indirect admission that a white man in chains was more pitiful to behold than the African similarly placed. Their most impassioned plea was in behalf of a person little resembling their swarthy protégés. . . .

The plots are strained and melodramatic. Too often the kindly disposed master dies suddenly, without having chance to fulfill his promises of freedom. Too often, on the other hand, the slave's problems are solved by breaks of good luck at the book's end.

Antislavery fiction set up the stereotypes of "the victim", "the noble savage" sometimes "the perfect Christian," and the "tragic octoroon." The items of its denunciation are true enough to history, but they do not represent the real gamut of Negro life and character. The large plantation, where the abuses incidental to absentee ownership throve, is still the chief setting, and the smaller, more typical farm is neglected. The workaday life of the average slave, who, through fear, ignorance, loyalty or habit did not revolt or run away, and who learned to accommodate himself so that the whippings and penalties would be less, is missing. Often, too, antislavery fiction, by stressing physical punishments, underemphasizes the greater wrongs, the destruction of manhood, and the ugly code of morality that slavery fostered. Certain articles of the southern creed were accepted too easily, such as the belief that the slave-trader was a low boor, unaccepted socially by the aristocrats. Modern scholars, such as Frederic Bancroft in *Slave Trading in the Old South,* have shown how some of the "finest" southern families built up their wealth from slave dealing.

It might be expected in the "battle of the books" that proslavery authors would have an advantage in being on the scene. But full or even partial use was not made of this advantage, the dialect and local color of the proslavery authors being very little better than and frequently not so good as those of the abolitionists. Except for Mrs. Schoolcraft, Harriet Beecher Stowe writes better dialect than proslavery authors.

Hildreth and Mrs. Victor obviously knew southern life. In their total presentation of social setting, the abolitionists have not been so one-sided as their detractors have made out. Many show good masters as well as bad, attacking a system rather than the people. For comic relief, or for honest realism, many present happier scenes, but wisely present these as holidays, not as the reality of slavery. Most important, however, is the difference in characterization. Lowell said that Mrs. Stowe's genius "instinctively goes right to the organic elements of human nature, whether under a white skin or black;" and at their best the other antislavery authors do like wise. When a mother is separated from her child, they show the grief of a bereft mother, not a mother of peculiar racial endowments who cannot love her children because she and they happen to be black. If she is not grief-stricken, they lay the blame upon the brutalizing of slavery, not on a racial characteristic that it soothed slave-holders to believe in. The antislavery authors may not ever have owned Negroes, but they started from the premise that Negroes were human. Finally, it must be said that although both sides went in for melodrama and idealizing, the antislavery case was much more credible. Facts, even in spite of *Gone With the Wind,* are abolitionist.

DISCUSSION QUESTIONS

1. What noted Americans outside of the novelists, were antislavery in sympathy?

2. What are probable reasons for the private first printing of *Memoirs of Archy Moore* and its later reissue and enlargement?

3. What might explain the fact that the first publisher approached turned town *Uncle Tom's Cabin?*

4. List the books that make use of the hero and heroine of mixed blood.

5. How did the use of these characters strengthen the antislavery argument? How did it weaken?

6. List the books making use of the pure African type as hero.

7. What, according to Melville, would cause Civil War in Vivenza?

CHAPTER IV

RECONSTRUCTION: THE GLORIOUS SOUTH

The Triumph of The Tradition. If *Uncle Tom's Cabin* triumphed in the antebellum "battle of the books," being widely remembered while its opponents are forgotten, the plantation tradition was to score a signal victory in the Reconstruction. Although no longer needed to defend a tottering institution, it was now needed to prove that Negroes were happy as slaves and hopelessly unequipped for freedom, so that slavery could be resurrected in practise thought not in name. Ancestor worshippers, the sons of a fighting generation, remembering bitterly the deaths of their fathers, uncles, or brothers, the sufferings of their families and themselves, brought the passion of the defeated to their descriptions. Many, politically astute, used the plantation tradition to further their ambitions.

The authors of the reconstruction were better writers than their antebellum predecessors. Moreover, they were farther from slavery, and since their memories were often those of childhood, they idealized to a much greater degree. Some proslavery authors, like William Thompson, had admitted, for instance, that many slaves had the harshest kind of masters; others unconsciously allowed facts to enter that their descendants considered too uncouth for mention. Nostalgic yearning brought it about that, according to Gaines:

> Slavery was softened until whatever may have been evil was regarded as accidental. . . . The scale of life was steadily enlarged, the colors were made increasingly vivid. Estates swelled in size and mansions grew proportionately great. Gentlemen were perfected in courtly grace, gay girls in loveliness, slaves in immeasurable devotion.

49

With the seductiveness of any past seen through "the golden haze of retrospect," with realism to the surface of Negro life, disarmingly affectionate references to Negroes of the old school, and a mastery of the tricks of fiction, the plantation tradition came into its own. The Negro was established as contented slave, entertaining child and docile ward, until misled by "radical" agitators, when he became a dangerous beast.

Local Color. Following Bret Harte's discovery of the picturesque and quaint in California's past, local colorists sprang up all over the nation. Many southern regions were staked out as claims worth mining. Charles Egbert Craddock in the Tennessee mountains, Mark Twain in the Mississippi valley, George Washington Cable in fabulous New Orleans brought the wealth of their discoveries to a literature that had fallen on lean years. Coincidentally with the rise of the local colorists, a new interest in the South, the scene of America's greatest war, was awakening. Magazines, especially *Scribner's,* attempted to slake this curiosity. A great outburst of dialect stories resulted. Among the first of the writers to realize the picturesque interest of the southern Negro was Sherwood Bonner (Mrs. Katherine McDowell), a pioneer in local color fiction as Russell was in poetry (she had even written dialect poetry of the Negro before Russell's book appeared). Many of her *Dialect Tales* (1878) and *Suwanee River Tales* (1884) are about Negroes. They are interesting as first attempts, but they illustrate the chief weaknesses of local color: they reveal odd turns of speech and customs but the characterization is superficial and condescending. Southern local colorists were soon to sweep the North with a different formula; fidelity to speech and manners was to be combined with regret "for the dear dead days beyond recall."

50

Thomas Nelson Page. Most elegiac of these authors, and probably most persuasive in casting a golden glow over the antebellum South is Thomas Nelson Page. With a mastery of pathos and stirring melodrama, his *In Ole Virginia* (1887) sets a pattern that time has not been able to wear out. The three best known stories of this volume are "Marse Chan," "Meh Lady," and "Unc' Edinburg's Drownin'." They are told in the dialect of eastern Virginia, accurately recorded. The literary device used in all three stories is quite simple: an old Negro, garrulous in praise of the old days, tells a tale of handsome cavaliers and lovely ladies, with stress upon the love between master and slave. Marse Chan saves a slave's life at the cost of his own sight; Uncle Edinburg is saved by his young master from a raging torrent; Uncle Billy defends his charges from marauding Yankee soldiers, and supports them after the war. The stories end in lovers' meetings; as in Shakespeare, the courtship of lord and lady is balanced by the comical courtship of the servants. Page has his three ventriloquist's dummies agreeing upon the blessedness of slavery. Sam says:

> Dem wuz good ole times, marster—de bes' Sam ever see! Dey wuz, in fac'! Niggers didn't hed nothing' 'tall to do. . . . Dyar warn' no trouble nor nothin'.

Uncle Edinburg seconds the emotion:

> Oh! nuttin' warn' too good for niggers dem times; an' de little niggers wuz runnin' roun' right 'stracted. . . . Dis nigger ain' nuver gwine forgit it."

And Uncle Billy:

> I wuz settin' in de do' wid meh pipe, an heah 'em settin' dyah on de front steps, dee voices soun'in low like bees, an' de moon sort o' mellow over de yard, an' I sort o' got to studyin' an' hit pear like de plantation live once mo', an' de ain' no mo' scufflin', an de ol times done come back agin. . . .

"No Haid Pawn," a ghost story in the same volume, has a Negro character who differed from other slaves in that he was without amiability or docility, superstition or reverence. Page adds significantly, "He was the most brutal negro I ever knew." *The Negro: The Southerner's Problem* states Page's lavish praise for the "old time darky" and his virulent disgust at the "new issue," ruined by emancipation; *Red Rock* (1898) embodies this hatred in fiction. The docile mastiffs have become mad dogs; the carriers of the rabies are Yankee soldiers and schoolmarms, carpet-baggers, and scalawags. Mammy Krenda, Waverly, Tarquin, and Jerry are sympathetically treated because they despise the northern interlopers, and stand hand-in-hand before quality. Less servile Negroes are called insolent swaggerers. Moses, a mulatto trick doctor, is the worst of these. He orates: "I'm just as good as any white man. . . . I'm goin' to marry a white 'ooman and meck white folks wait on me." Within a few pages he is likened to "a hyena in a cage," "a reptile," "a species of worm," "a wild beast." He attempts to assault one of the heroines, the daughter of an abolitionist mother; this Page considers a fit harvest for interference with the most chivalrous of civilizations. Page thus anticipates such authors as Thomas Dixon whose stock in trade is the brute Negro, and whose pat response to any assertion of Negro rights is the cry of intermarriage or rape.

Such a volume as *Pastime Stories* (1894) deals less with the good times than with Page's own days. The Negro characters are petty thieves and drunkards, but are dealt with jocularly. There is ridicule in Uncle Jack's "Views on Geography":

> You knows de way to de spring and de wood-pile, an' de mill, an' when you gits a little bigger I's gwine to show you de way to de hoe-handle, an' de cawn-furrer, an' dat's all de geog-aphy a nigger's got to know.

One story shows approvingly how a mulatto office-seeker is thwarted by a faithful Negro for the sake

52

of his master's political advantage. *Bred in the Bone* (1904) adds nothing to Page's usual characterizations, dealing largely with the antics of comic menials.

Harris. It was from the slave quarters that Joel Chandler Harris started his trip to literary immortality. As a lonely boy, shy with people of his own race, he turned for companionship to the cabins on a Georgia plantation. There he met Uncle George Terrell, the original of Uncle Remus; there he started his long study of Negro lore, and there he learned something of the story-telling art and something of his wisdom. For years the slaves had been telling fables of Brer Rabbit, Brer Fox and Brer Terrapin, some of the stories having come from Africa. But no one had dug in this mine before Harris. A true artist, he recognized the value of what he found. He is more than a reteller, however; he altered, adapted, polished and sharpened until the products differ from folk tales. For all of the fascination of Brer Rabbit and company, the fabler is stressed more than the characters. Instead of being by the folk for the folk, Uncle Remus tells the stories to entertain a white child. Harris lost something authentic when he adopted this framework, but he gained Uncle Remus. And Uncle Remus is worth gaining. By no means the typical product of slavery, as Harris implies, he is still finely conceived: a venerable, pampered Negro with a gift for quaint philosophizing and for poetic speech, having (or allowed to have) only pleasant memories, fortunate above his brothers—one of the best characters in American literature.

In folk-idiom, the tales are kept close to the people. No author before Harris had recorded Negro speech with anything like his skill. Walter Hines Page stated: "I have Mr. Harris' word for it that he can *think* in the Negro dialect. He could translate even Emerson, perhaps Bronson Alcott in it. . . ." Any random excerpt will reveal this ability:

> Bimeby, one day, after Brer Fox bin doin' all dat he could fer ter ketch Brer Rabbit, en Brer Rabbit bin doin' all he could fer to keep 'im fum it, Brer Fox say to hisse'f dat he'd put up a game on Brer Rabbit, en he ain't mo'n got de wuds out'n his mouf twel Brer Rabbit come a lopin up de big road, lookin' des ez plump en ez fat, en ez sassy ez a Moggin hoss in a barley patch. . . .
> "All right, Brer Fox, but you better holler fum whar you stan'. I'm monstus full er fleas dis mawnin'," sez Brer Rabbit, sezee.

Strewn through the stories is much local color, well-observed and true. Fine turns of speech reveal the slave's mind. The use of Brer Rabbit as the hero is noteworthy. Forced to pit his cunning against enemies of greater physical strength, he was perhaps a symbol for people who needed craft in order to survive. But whether victor over Brer Wolf, or victim to the Tar-baby, he is a likeable scamp, who has come loping lickety-split down the years.

Before finishing his long cycle of tales, Uncle Remus revealed himself more thoroughly than any preceding Negro character. But Harris was a journalist, as well as a writer of fiction, and he was called upon to give his version of the critical times. It was here that his ability to translate anything into Negro dialect was misused. He made Uncle Remus the mouthpiece for defending orthodox southern attitudes. Needless to say, Uncle Remus diminishes in stature; he becomes less a man, more a walking delegate. The old man keeps his hat in his hand too much. He defends the glory of the Old South, he admires his white folks, he satirizes education for Negroes:

> Hit's de ruinashun er dis country. . . . Put a spellin'-book in a nigger's han's, en right den en dar' you loozes a plow-hand. . . . What's a nigger gwineter 'larn outen books? I kin take a bar'l stave an' fling mo' sense inter a nigger in one minnit dan all de schoolhouses betwixt dis en de State er Midgigin. . . . Wid one bar'l stave I kin fa'rly lif' de vail er ignunce.

54

When Negroes migrated for better working conditions, or out of fear, Uncle Remus almost frantically begs them to "stay off them kyars." That an old Negro, spoiled by his white-folks, and patronized by southern journalists, might say what his hearers want to hear, and even believe it, is quite probable. But as racial adviser, Uncle Remus forfeits our trust in him; he is too fluently the mouthpiece of southern policy. He did better telling how Brer Rabbit fooled Brer Fox by slick talk, or when he said: "Watch out we'en you'er gittin' all you want. Fattenin' hogs ain't in luck."

Many of Harris's other stories repeat usual characters in usual situations. In "Aunt Fountain's Prisoner" the old auntie saves a Yankee's life and presides over his successful courtship of a southern girl. "Mingo" tells of a slave of "meritorious humility," "a cut above" the Negroes who accepted freedom. In "Balaam and His Master," Baalam, of a "fearlessness rare among slaves" fights alongside his roistering master in tavern brawls and digs a hole in the wall of a jail to be near him. Although Ananias is mean-looking, his sacrifice for his master, ruined by the war, proves him to be an old familiar, merely with a new face. Like the typical southern authors of his time, Harris does not show the Negro who would fight or work or exercise his wits in his own cause.

A few runaways and freed Negroes attracted his attention. Free Betsey in *Sister Jane* and Mink in *On the Plantation* are as devoted to their little missy and massa, however, as Uncle Remus. "Free Joe" is the pathetic story of a freed Negro, feared by the whites and avoided, but hardly envied, by the slaves. After his wife was sold by a master well nicknamed Old Spite, and his faithful little dog was killed by Old Spite's hounds, he dies, heartbroken. Humane and intelligent, Harris uses "Free Joe" to attack the popular notion that Negroes always "grin at trouble." The forces making a free Negro an outcast are clearly indicated. But dyed-in-the-wool southerners could use Joe's shiftlessness to prove that a freed Negro could not stand alone, and Harris's picture of the laughing, singing slaves who despised Free Joe might bear them out. Joe is certainly not a typical free Negro, but the sympathy in his portrait is deeper than any of Harris's contemporaries dared show.

"Mom Bi" tells of an unusual mammy. In spite of her withered arm, Mom Bi is a black Amazon, with eyes that "shone like those of a wild animal not afraid of the hunter." She was not religious:

> Ef de Lawd call me in de chu'ch I gwine, ef he no call I no gwine, enty? I no yerry him call dis long time. . . .

Whoever crossed her—white or black, old or young —got a piece of her mind. She outspokenly scorns the South Carolina "sandhillers" or "tackies," and laughs at them for going to war to "fight for rich folks' niggers." In the Civil War she is a grim prophet of Yankee victory, and therefore is considered a lunatic. Again, however, Harris cannot shake off the heavy hand of tradition. Mom Bi forgives the sale of her daughter Maria, but is grieved that her young master Gabriel was killed in battle, fighting alongside of poor white folks. Emancipated, she goes down to live with Maria, her daughter; when smallpox kills off Maria and her children, she returns (as do most of the Negroes whom Harris likes) to the old homeplace. "I done bin come back," says she. "I bin come back fer stay, but I free, dough!"

Like "Mom Bi," "Blue Dave" promises much more than it gives. Dave, an inky black powerfully built runaway, has become a legend before the story opens

56

for fearlessness and terrorism. In the story proper, however, we merely get a Hercules devoted to a family because the young master resembles a former Virginian owner. Dave has said over and over again that slavery "ain't no home for me," but he is bought by the family he has served, and lives happily ever after as a model slave. "Where's Duncan," more than any other of Harris's stories, touches upon the sinister and repellent. A swarthy dark-bearded vagabond fiddler tells mysteriously of a planter who sold his son to a trader. The last scene, recalling Poe's effects, shows an old mansion afire; in the light of the flames, a mulatto woman cries out "Where's Duncan?" and stabs the white father of her son with a carving knife. Crooked-leg Jake saw Duncan, the fiddler, sitting in a corner, seemingly enjoying the spectacle.

The last story shows that Harris saw in slavery something more than a perpetual Mardi Gras; he knew that there was hatred as well as mutual affection, the ugly as well as the pleasant. Harris promised "scenes such as have never been described in any of the books that profess to tell about life in the South before the war." But with all of his value as a realist, Harris never came fully to grips with the reality of the South or of Negro experience. He was a kindly man, and wished the wounds of war bound up. He could give some praise to Negroes struggling to achieve property and education. But he was a southerner, living in vexatious times, and therefore his fiction almost always glorified the faithful self-denying slave of the old South, for whom the old ways of slavery were the best. He achieved a fine portrait in Uncle Remus, but Uncle Remus had brothers and children of a different stamp, whom Harris touched gingerly, if at all. Harris came a good distance down the road toward fairness if compared with Thomas Nelson Page. But compared with

George Washington Cable and Mark Twain, he still lagged behind.

Harris recorded some of the folk-lore of the "salt-water" Negroes with success, but it remained for Charles C. Jones to do the fuller job in *Negro Myths from the Georgia Coast* (1888). These tales are worthy to stand by those of Uncle Remus and, lacking the editorializing, are closer to the originals. They are told in the unique lingo of the rice-field and sea-island Negroes. The first in the "untrodden field of the swamp region of Georgia and the Carolinas," Jones discovered what later folk-lorists like Samuel Stoney, Gertrude Shelby and Ambrose Gonzales have found attractive.

Edwards. Harry Stillwell Edwards belongs to the long line of Georgians from Longstreet down to Erskine Caldwell who write of the Old South with more realism and less worship. His Major Crawford Worthington, for instance, is a portly, profane, self-willed sportsman who considers the Negro an unfailing source of amusement. Worthington's slave Isam is an annual runaway, not because slavery is harsh, but because he likes vacations. "The Two Runaways" tells of a vacation on which master and slave, boon companions, live high on stolen corn and melons. They enjoy seeing each other in difficulties. When a buck deer and the fat major are wrestling, Isam, a safe, happy ringsider, cries out:

> Stick ter 'im Mass Craffud, stick ter 'im! Hit's better fer one ter die den bofe! Hole 'im Mass Craffud. . . . Wo' deer! Stick ter 'im, Mass Craffud, steddy!

Tables are turned in "The Woodhaven Goat" when a goat, maddened by bees, butts and drags Isam all over the yard. From beneath the house, the Major

> looked out through tears with a sudden delight at the negro's predicament, sobbing and choking with emotion . . . he frantically

58

beat the dry soil about him with his fist for some moments. "Better for one to die than two. . . . Stick to him, Isam. . . . Whoa, goat!"

"Aeneas Africanus" (1920) humorously tells of a black Eneas, who confused by the duplication of town-names, covered 3350 miles through seven states, over a period of eight years, trying to get back to his quality whitefolks. Like his Major, Edwards seemed to have studied the Negro only on his amusing side. But he was willing to poke fun at some of the absurdities of the Old South, and his robust horseplay is a relief from sentimentality.

F. Hopkinson Smith. Few authors dealt with a rough-and-ready friendship between a swearing master and a none-too-obsequious slave in the manner of Edwards. More typical is the sentimental, genteel treatment of mutual affection as in *Colonel Carter of Cartersville* by F. Hopkinson Smith (1891), a portrait of a quixotic Virginia gentleman and his devoted servant, Chad. Chad exists only to prepare choice dishes of canvas-back duck and terrapin for his money-less but epicurean master, to support the colonel's hospitality with his pitiful stored earnings, to be a bulwark against the harsh Yankee world, and to express his disdain for people who are "not quality." With his wife Henny, a similar model of loyalty, he furnishes comic relief and glorifies the "good old days." *Colonel Carter's Christmas* (1903) adds little to the characterization of the sentimental pair.

James Lane Allen. Sentimentalist and idealist, James Lane Allen could find little blemish in the ante-bellum South according to "Uncle Tom At Home in Kentucky", his refutation of Mrs. Stowe. "Two Gentlemen of Kentucky" (1888) tells of the great affection between a sweet Kentucky Colonel—so unworldly that when he runs a store he chivalrously gives away the wares—and his faithful servant, Peter Cotton. Peter is completely self-forgetful, but must be made ludicrous as well. His blue-jeans coat, with very long and spacious tails, is embroidered with scriptural texts, the word "Amen" being located just "over the end of Peter's spine." The master's death is followed in a year by Peter's. The world after the Civil War was no fit place for these two, which is no great reflection, since too often they act like halfwits. In "King Solomon of Kentucky" (1891) a free Negro woman, who has made some money selling cakes and pies, buys a white vagabond on the block, because he was a friend of her dead Virginia master. The vagabond is regenerated and becomes the town hero in a cholera epidemic. The introduction of the auction block is almost unmatched in plantation tradition literature, but it is significant that a white man is the one sold from it.

Grace King and Kate Chopin. In resentment at Cable's attacks upon the plantation tradition, discussed in the next chapter, many southerners set up Grace King and Kate Chopin as more truthful observers of Louisiana. Undoubtedly both are more traditional. Few troubles fret the slaves in Grace King's stories, except in the case of octoroons who grieve that they are not white. "Monsieur Motte" tells of a Negro woman, Marcelite, who supports in a fashionable school the daughter of her dead mistress, pretending that money comes from a non-existent uncle, Monsieur Motte. In *Balcony Stories* (1893), Joe is likewise the devoted servant, begging to be sold because his master's widow is in need of money. "A Crippled Hope" tells of a Negro girl, whose value as a nurse for sick slaves in the auction mart keeps her from being sold to "delicate ladies," whom she would have loved to serve. When freedom comes she does not want it; she only wants to succor the ailing. "The Little Convent Girl" is about a sad-faced girl, who is suddenly discovered to have a negro mother. The girl drowns, escaping her fate. Even at the age of twelve, a tragic octoroon! Negroes not octoroons have a merry time:

> And then what a rolling of barrels, and shouldering of sacks, and singing of Jim Crow Songs, and pacing of Jim Crow steps; and black skins glistening through torn shirts, and white teeth gleaming through red lips, and laughing, and talking . . . bewildering, entrancing!

Kate Chopin was a sensitive, skillful teller of tales. Her *Bayou Folk* (1894) is a collection laid in and around Natchitoches Parish near Red River, of which she presents the local customs and patois admirably. But the Negroes she portrays are still models of loyalty and self-denial. In "A No Account Creole," La Chatte, a broad black mammy, is guardian over the love affairs of the white creoles. "In and Out of Old Natchitoches" shows a fiery plantation owner who for a time flouts the community taboo of consorting with mulattoes. "In Sabine" depicts Uncle Mortimer protecting a white woman who is abused by her hard drinking husband. "Beyond the Bayou" shows a gaunt, black woman overcoming her extreme fear of the bayou to carry home a little white child whom she loves. "The Benitou's Slave" pictures extreme devotion. "Desirée's Baby", probably Mrs. Chopin's best known work, deals with a young creole husband and wife to whom is born a child who gives evidence of Negro blood. The outraged husband sends his wife away in disgrace. He then, discovers, through an old letter, that the Negro blood came from his own mother; she was thankful, she said, that her son would never know.

Of the numerous short stories defending the Old South space forbids more than mention of a selected few. Maurice Thompson in "Ben and Judas" (1889) wrote a good story of a mutual affection between owner and owned. In "The Balance of Power," Thompson has a crafty Negro, who walks on "bofe sides of de fence," managing it so that the young man wins the beautiful girl while her father is conceded the election. The story is inconsequential, but it does show the colonel winning political support by stating that his rival is supported by Negroes. Of a different type is "An Incident" by Sarah Barnwell Elliott, which dramatizes the terror at the "brute" Negro, and is concerned with "what answer the future would have for this awful problem."

Summary. Plantation tradition fiction of the Reconstruction added realism of speech and custom, but with few exceptions, this realism was subordinated to the purpose of showing the mutual affection between the races which the North had partly destroyed in a foolish war. Negro characters, at their best, are shown only in relationship with kindly southern whites; at their worst, in relationship with predatory Yankees. They are never shown in relationship to themselves. They are confined to the two opposite grooves of loyalty or ingratitude. The authors, remembering their childhood when it is likely that they had Negro playmates as boon companions, made slavery a boyish romp. It was flattering to believe that their fathers and mothers were objects of universal love and worship. It was charming for a man accustomed to deference and submission to believe these to be ordained in heaven. It was uncomfortable to believe that irony, or shrewd appraisal could lurk behind the bland smile, the pull on the forelock, the low curtsey. Perish the thought! A kindly critic of the South paraphrases the legend:

> Way down upon the Suwanee River the sun shines bright on my old Kentucky home, where, bound for Louisiana, Little Eva

has a banjo on her knee, and Old Black Joe, Uncle Remus and Miss Sally's little boy listen to the mocking-bird and watch a sweet chariot swing low one frosty mornin'. The gallant Pelham and his comrades bend forever over the hands of adorable girls in crinoline; under the duelling oaks Colonel Carter of Cartersville and Marse Chan blaze away at each other with pistols by the light of the silvery moon on Mobile Bay . . .

And we might add: the happy slaves are forever singing in the beautiful fields of white cotton, and forever black mammies fondle their little marses and missies and exude love for all the rich folks in Dixie, and body servants rescue the perishing, care for the dying, serve their beloved masters until death let them depart in peace, to serve in heaven, forever and ever.

DISCUSSSION QUESTIONS

1. Why was the earlier plantation tradition fiction less persuasive than that written in Reconstruction?

2. What were reasons why the "brute" Negro was seldom mentioned in antebellum fiction, and so frequently mentioned in Reconstruction?

3. What in the testimony of Page's three Uncles supports the fact that Virginia was a slave-breeding state?

4. Compare Harris and Page.

5. Why is Edwards closer to the "frontier humorists" than to Allen?

6. Since instances of mutual affection in slavery could undoubtedly be found, why should not literature celebrating it be considered a trustworthy guide to the Old South?

7. List the runaways and "bad Negroes" mentioned in this chapter, with the authors' characterizations of them.

8. Account for the absence of characters of mixed blood.

CHAPTER V

Cable. Although he had served as an officer in the Confederate Cavalry, George Washington Cable was aware of much that was wrong in the old South and the new. His *The Silent South* and *The Negro Question* are antidotes to Page's dangerous drugs; against the convict lease system, for instance, Cable wrote with startling pertinence even for our own day. Cordially hated in the South, he took up residence in Massachusetts, but though in "exile" he kept close to his heart the best interests of his section.

Praised as the first southerner to include just and sympathetic recognition of the Negro, Cable portrays Negroes or the background of slavery in most of his novels. For our purposes *Old Creole Days* (1879) and *The Grandissimes* (1880) are most important. *Old Creole Days* re-creates, with vivid local color, early nineteenth century Louisiana. In "Posson Jone", a faithful servant outwits the sharpers who were preying upon his master; if the situation is old, the details are sharply observed. Less kindly pictures of slavery appear in " 'Tite Poulette" and "Madame Delphine", stories of octoroons of a warm seductive beauty, cultivated with care so that they may be "protected" by some Louisiana grandee. This "protection" does not keep tragedy from their lives, however. To these women, says Cable, "every white man in this country is a pirate." Therefore, both mothers in these stories pretend that their daughters are not really theirs, in order that the girls may get around the law that rigorously forbade marriage of

64

octoroons to "pure whites." Bitterly acquainted with what faces her lovely daughter, Delphine cries out against the law "to keep the two races separate": "A lie, Pere Jerome! Separate! No-o-o! They do not want to keep us separated; no, no! But they *do* want to keep us despised!"

In *The Grandissimes*, a long novel of old Louisiana, we have the background of slavery well worked in, and in the foreground, individualized Negro characters, far more convincing than the abolitionist victims. Outstanding is Honoré Grandissime, "free man of color," educated, successful in business but an ineffectual victim of caste. Though true to New Orleans history, his type has been neglected in fiction for the more fascinating octoroon heroine. Palmyre is one of the best characterized octoroons in fiction.

> This woman had stood all her life with dagger drawn, on the defensive against what certainly was to her an unmerciful world . . . And yet by inexorable decree, she belonged to what we used to call "the happiest people under the sun." We ought to stop saying that.

Under domineering and insult, Palmyre is shown as silent; "and so," says Cable, "sometimes is fire in the wall." Clemence, illiterate and superstitious, has folk-shrewdness:

> You mus'n b'lieve all dis-yeh nonsense 'bout insurrectionin'; all fool-nigga talk. W'at we want to be insurrectionin' faw? We de happiest people in de God's worl'! Yes, we is; you jis oughteh gimme fawty an' lemme go! Please gen'lemen!

Her cunning does not help, however, in this drastic case; she is told to run, and is coolly shot, stone dead.

One of the most unusual figures is the gigantic Bras Coupé, captured king of the Jaloffs, a legendary figure with counterpart in Louisiana history. He is contemptuous of whites, and kills the Negro driver who first tells him to work. Driven to the swamps for striking down his master, he puts a curse on the plantation. When he is captured he is "hamstrung", in accordance with the *Code Noir*. When the name of his worst enemy falls upon his ears, even though dying, he spits upon the floor; when he is begged to forgive, he merely smiles. "God keep thy enemy from such a smile", says the author.

Cable's fiction shows full acquaintance with folksongs, speech, lore and superstition, but unlike his contemporaries, Page and Harris, he does not use the material to support old traditions. He makes clear-eyed, telling observations on the South. A blow, punishable in a white offender by a small fine or conviction, assured Bras Coupé the death of a felon, by the old Code Noir.

> (We have a Code Noir now, but the new one is a mental reservation, not an enactment). . . . The guests stood for an instant as if frozen, smitten stiff with the expectation of insurrection, conflagration and rapine (just as we do today whenever some poor swaggering Pompey rolls up his fist and gets a ball through his body). . . .

"It seems to be one of the self-punitive characteristics of tyranny, whether the tyrant be a man, a community, or a caste, to have a pusillanimous fear of its victims." But Cable does not over-idealize the Negro. He is sharp toward the mulatto caste—"the saddest slaves of all."

> Your men, for a little property, and your women, for a little amorous attention let themselves be shorn even of the virtue of discontent. . . . I would rather be a runaway in the swamp than content myself with such a freedom.

Although Cable helped to establish the tragic mulatto stereotypes, his portraits of this caste are drawn from a specific situation in the past, more pronounced in New Orleans though widespread in the South. The stereotype has fascinated later writers who have fallen under Cable's charm. But they are without his information and sympathy, and are therefore less truthful. All in all, Cable is one of the finest creators of Negro character in the nineteenth century.

Twain. Like Cable, Twain was of southern birth and upbringing, and fought in the Confederate army (but for a short time only, in a spirit of horseplay, learning only how to retreat). The two men lectured together. Both had sympathies for the underdog and both attacked the sham chivalry of the South. Mark Twain insisted that he was almost completely without race prejudice and that the color brown was "the most beautiful and satisfying of all the complexions vouchsafed to man." He loved the spirituals best among music. In his youth he grew up with slave boys as playmates; in his manhood he paid a Negro student's way through Yale, as "part of the reparation due from every white to every black man."

Twain's first treatment of Negroes in *The Gilded Age* (1873), however, is largely traditional, unlike "A True Story (Repeated Word For Word As I Heard It)" which is a bitter memory of cruelty and separation, contradicting Thomas Nelson Page's formula stories.

In *Huckleberry Finn* (1884) the callousness of the South to the Negro is indicated briefly, without preaching, but impellingly. Huck informs Aunt Sally that a steamboat blew out a cylinder head:

> "Good gracious! anybody hurt?"
> "No'm. Killed a nigger."
> "Well, it's lucky because sometimes people do get hurt . . ."

In this book Twain deepens the characterization of Jim, who, like Tom and Huck and the rest of that fine company, was drawn from life. He is no longer the simple-minded, mysterious guide in the ways of dead cats, doodle-bugs and signs of *The Adventures of Tom Sawyer*. Running away from old Miss Watson, who, though religious, "pecks on" him all the time, treats him "pooty rough" and wants a trader's eight hundred dollars for him, Jim joins Huck on the immortal journey down the Mississippi. His talks enlivens the voyage. He is at his comic best in detailing his experience with high finance—he once owned fourteen dollars. But the fun is brought up sharp by Jim's

> Yes, en I's rich now, come to look at it. I owns myself en I's wuth eight hund'd dollars. I wisht I had de money, I wouldn't want no mo'.

But he did want more. He wanted to get to a free state and work and save money so he could buy his wife, and then they would both work to buy their children, or get an abolitionist to go steal them. Huck is "frozen at such thoughts;" torn between what he had been taught was moral and his friendliness for an underdog. Jim is the best example in nineteenth century fiction of the average Negro slave (not the tragic mulatto or the noble savage), illiterate, superstitious, yet clinging to his hope for freedom, to his love for his own. And he is completely believable, whether arguing that Frenchman should talk like people, or doing most of the work on the raft, or forgiving Huck whose trick caused him to be bitten by a snake, or sympathizing with the poor little Dauphin, who, since America has no kings, "cain't git no situation." He tells of his little daughter, whom he had struck, not knowing she disobeyed because she had become deaf from scarlet fever:

> . . . En all uv a sudden I says pow! jis' as loud as I could yell. She never budge! Oh, Huck, I bust out a-cryin' en grab her up in my arms, en say, "Oh, de po' little thing! De Lord God Almighty forgive po' ole Jim, kaze he never gwyne to forgive hisself as long's he live!" Oh, she was plumb deef en dumb, Huck, plum deef en dumb—en I'd been a-treatin' her so!

From the great tenderness and truth of this portrait *Pudd'nhead Wilson* (1894), Twain's last novel concerning Negroes, falls a great way. In violent, ugly Dawson's Landing a fantastic tale is set. Roxana, only one-sixteenth Negro, a handsome earthy Amazon, is the mother of a son, Valet de Chambre, fathered by a gentleman of the F.F.V.'s. This baby was born on the same day as her master's son, Thomas à Becket Driscoll, and looks exactly like him. In order to save the baby from slavery, Roxy exchanges the two. The boys grow up with their positions reversed; the false Valet is ruined by slavery, and Tom, ruined by pampering, becomes a liar, coward, gambler, thief and murderer. In desperate straits, he tricks his mother and sells her down the river. Although Tom's character could be attributed to a rigid caste system that granted excessive power to petty people, Twain leaves many readers believing that he agrees with Roxy who, astounded by her son's worthlessness, muttered: "Ain't nigger enough in him to show in his finger-nails, en dat takes mighty little, yit dey's enough to paint his soul." Twain has little good to say for slavery in this book. Roxy's terror of being sold "down the river," and her experiences there under a vicious Yankee overseer are grimly realistic. Roxy is a first-rate preliminary sketch. By no means faultless, a petty thief and a liar, she is capable of sacrifice, and has intelligence, pride, and courage. If Twain had spent more time in developing her portrait, *Pudd'nhead Wilson* would have been a better novel.

Humorists. One of those humorists whose misspellings and satiric temper pleased Abraham Lincoln, Petroleum V. Nasby (David Ross Locke), wrote *Nasby: Divers Views, Opinions and Prophecies* (1866) and *Ekkoes From Kentucky* (1868), both showing post-war attitudes to the Negro. Pretending to be a Copperhead postmaster, Nasby reveals himself as an ignorant, besotted politician, forever dragging in the race question for personal gain. Some of

69

Nasby's shafts could well be used at southern rabble-rousers today. Nasby shows how the cry of Negro domination and amalagmation rose whenever the slightest effort was made for justice to the freedmen. Severely satirical of southern chivalry, Nasby shows the white daughters of John Guttle, a gentleman of Mobile, fighting against their Negro half-sisters over their father's tomb, and concludes that "there wuz some disadvantages attending the patriarkle system." To those who saw the Negro as unfit for freedom he wrote:

> Three hundred niggers . . . wuz wrencht from paternal care to starve, which the most uv 'em are industriously doin' at about $3 per day.

He advises the legislatures to forbid Negroes to leave their country, and then to pass laws setting up a maximum wage for Negroes of five dollars a month. Thousands of Negroes will then die by midwinter and the rest will beg to be reenslaved.

> We kin . . . pint 2 their bodies and say in a sepulkered tone: 'Wen niggers wuz wuth $1500, they wuz not allowed to die thus —behold the froots uv Ablishun philanthropy.'

For all of his burlesque, Nasby saw clearly and prophesied sanely. A whole school of southern writers came along and did in dead earnest what he had counselled in bitter jest.

Samantha On The Race Problem by Marietta Holley counsels colonization even so late as 1892, recounts the tragedies of a few superior mulattoes, and most important, shows the Florida Ku Klux Klan at its work of burning schools and terrorizing Negroes who were forging ahead.

Northern Novelists. John William DeForest's realistic novels of the South immediately after the Civil War, *Miss Ravenal's Conversion From Secession*

70

to Loyalty (1867) and *Kate Beaumont* (1872), contain minor Negro characters, but these are generally typical. In 1867, Rebecca Harding Davis wrote the dramatic, sympathetic *Waiting For The Verdict*, the first novel to deal with the dilemma of the fair Negro who attains a superior position without being suspected of having Negro blood. Constance Fenimore Woolson's short stories of the South, written in the eighties, have been praised for their sane balance. In "Rodman The Keeper" she describes with sympathy the freedmen—bent, dull-eyed and ignorant, singing "Swing Low Sweet Chariot" on their way to the graves of Federal Soldiers "who had done something wonderful for them and their children." Generally, however, Miss Woolson is irritated by the freedmen, reserving her liking for those who are traditionally loyal to their white-folks, and seeing little in "the glories of freedom" except the "freedom to die." "King David" shows a Northern educator who gives up in the face of "universal, irresponsible ignorance." Miss Woolson recognizes the shiftlessness and chauvinism of the planter class, but keeps her sharpness for the "misguided and untimely idealism" of northerners. She tries so hard to be just to the fallen ex-planter that she is less than just to the rising ex-slaves. In these grievous times, the second stood in the greater need of justice.

Tourgée. Albion Tourgée differed from Miss Woolson sharply in his discoveries. He had a good chance for observation. He was an officer in the Union Army, and after the war remained in North Carolina as a judge. If he is a typical example of a carpetbagger, then his class has met with grave underestimation. He was thoughtful, considerate, courageous and honest. Like Miss Woolson, he recognized the gravity of the problem facing the South. Unlike her, however, he did not believe that the problem existed only because the freedmen were irresponsible, ignorant and unready for citizenship. He had seen too often what she omitted from her picture: the mob violence of the Regulators and the Ku Klux Klan, the determination to restore slavery, the ostracism of the "misguided" school teachers, the burning of the schools. He was a humane man, and he could not hold his peace. But he spoke on the unpopular side, and today he is barely mentioned in histories of American literature.

A Fool's Errand, by "One of the Fools" (1879), is largely autobiographical, and has been called "The Uncle Tom's Cabin of Reconstruction." Colonel Servosse, an officer of the Federal Army, took up residence in the South, foolishly believing that, with the end of the war, the North-South hostility would end. He soon learns better; for lending aid to Negroes in need he is called a "nigger lover," for making a speech urging justice to Negroes he barely escapes being horsewhipped. Yankee schoolmarms are insulted. When northern troops are withdrawn, terrorization of Negroes quickly follows. A Union League organizer is killed by the Klan, which is composed of prominent southerners. Negroes are shown hard at work, struggling to make their living, enthusiastically welcoming schools, lurking about the edges of crowds at political meetings, listening intently to the speeches, or organizing for protection. In a section hotly intent that there shall be no "nigger witnesses, no nigger juries, no nigger voters," all of this is insolence and insult.

Jerry is the type of uncle not before met with in American fiction. He is religious and devoted to Servosse, not out of loyalty of slave to master, but out of gratitude that Servosse was helping his people to true freedom. Jerry has his dignity; when whites ridicule his church services he says:

> An' when you all laughs at us, we can't help tinkin' dat we mout a done better ef we hadn't been kep' slaves all our lives by you uns.

But in one of his sermons, he tells too much about the Klan's most recent murder, and he is swung from a tree to prove that "It don't do fer niggers to know too much." Another different Negro is the blacksmith, Bob Martin, who makes such a good living that he becomes a marked man for the night riders. He scornfully ridicules the superstition that the Klan is ghostly, showing his scarred back as proof of the Klan's "humanity." He tells a shocking story of his own beating, the abuse of his wife and daughter, the death of his baby, and the destroying of his home, all supposed to teach him to be more respectful of white folks and less anxious to vote for radicals. Bob is of the stuff of heroes, however; he was in the Union Army at Fort Wagner, and he doggedly swears that "ef dere's any mo' Kluckers raidin' roun' Burke's Corner, dar'll be some funerals too." Later editions of *A Fool's Errand* included documentary evidence of the sinister workings of the Klan, a key to the truth something like the *Key to Uncle Tom's Cabin*.

The title *A Fool's Errand* lays blame only on the folly of rash hopes for improvement in the South, not on the effort to get justice. *Bricks Without Straw* (1880) is a more developed attempt to show the desperate problem, to prove that without support from the rest of the country, those few who were struggling were "making bricks without straw." Nimbus, the outstanding Negro character, is uneducated, but he fought in the Civil War, and is a man of courage and good, hard sense. Industrious and thrifty, he is disliked by the whites because he has a good house, a tobacco barn, a fine crop and valuable stock, and a church and schoolhouse on his place. He adds to these injuries the insult of wanting pay for his wife's services, and schools and the vote for all of his people. When the Klansmen, among whom are many aristocrats—"the freedmen's best friends"—come after him, Nimbus, aided by his wife Lugena, who fights with an axe, resists fiercely, and finally gets away. Returning years later, broken in health but not in spirit after experiencing riots, peonage and prison camps, Nimbus will not stay, but leads an exodus to Kansas. Elijah Hill, the schoolteacher, and Berry Lawson, good-natured avoider of trouble, but wily and loyal to Nimbus, are interesting minor figures.

Tourgée's other books on the Negro are not so valuable as these. *A Royal Gentleman* (1881), written earlier as *Toinette,* is pretentious, with a crowded plot. Mabel, mother of Toinette, is crazed by her unhappy life as the mistress of a white slave owner, and tries to murder those who would inflict upon her daughter the same fate. But Toinette, a refined olive-skinned beauty, is in love with, and beloved by her owner. Since he is a "royal gentleman," marriage cannot take place, and tragedy follows. The characters are idealized, and the incidents far-fetched. *Hot Plowshares* (1883) is a historical novel on the state of the nation preceding the Civil War. Great attention is paid to the rise of antislavery sentiment and the Underground Railroad. *Pactolus Prime* (1890) shows the economic hardships faced by Negroes in Washington, D. C. Pactolus is the father of a girl whom he disclaims in order that she may live as white, may be lifted "from shame to honor." Upon her discovery of the real truth, she takes the vows as Sister Pactola, and dedicates her life to her race. The story is not completely convincing, but Tourgée again reveals himself as well conversant with problems faced by Negroes. These novels have more argument than characters in action, but the argument is what has been too easily forgotten today.

Hearn. To Lafcadio Hearn the southern novel was "gushy-floriated English—written in bad taste, wishy-washy trash." With his sympathy for the underdog, strengthened by his connection with the quadroon Althea Foley, he admired Cable's defense of the Negro. Nevertheless, Hearn did not censure the South openly. He held stock beliefs such as that the Negro would disappear in freedom—"dependent like the ivy, he needs some strong oak-like friend to cling to"—and that it was only the mulatto influence that made slaves unmanageable. Always attracted by the unusual and picturesque, Hearn became an authority on Louisiana lore, making friends with the *bonnes vielles negresses,* who sold homemade sweetmeats in New Orleans, and the mysterious Voodoo Queen, Marie Laveau. But the teeming levees come to life only in sketches like "Dolly, an Idyl of the Levee" and "Banjo Jim's Story" (1876). In the West Indies Hearn was struck by the "appetizing golden bodies of the Martinique Quadroons, sensuous but childlike," gossiped with the washerwomen and treasured their soft slurring talk; and watched

> the *porteuses* on their way to market in the early morning, huge baskets of fruit and vegetables balanced on their heads, their skirts tucked into a belt in front, showing the shapely muscled bronze of their legs, as they walked with all the lithe feline grace of some wild animal.

Youma, "La Giablesse" and "Un Ravenant" are good fiction of the West Indies, but the wealth of Hearn's sensitive observation appears in his travel reporting. He was better in describing settings than in presenting character.

Howells.   The serious phase of Negro life that William Dean Howells thought worthy of inclusion in his canvas of the American scene was the age-worn tragedy of the octoroon.   In *An Imperative Duty* (1892), Rhoda, the beautiful daughter of a northern physician and an accomplished octoroon, bore no evidence of Negro blood. On the eve of her marriage, she is told her lineage by her duty-bound aunt.   Later, passing for an Italian and happily married to a man who is undisturbed by her lineage, she is still wretched at her "disgrace."   The novel is sympathetic, but there were graver, less romantic problems of Negro life that a novelist of Howells' scope and ability might have presented.

Negro Novelists.   Two Negro authors who had given their best energies to the antislavery struggle turned to fiction in the post-Civil War years. William Wells Brown's *My Southern Home* (1880) included sketches of southern Negro folklife, before the successes of Page and Harris.   Frances Harper, whose antislavery poetry was popular, now defended her race in *Iola Leroy* or *Shadows Uplifted* (1892). Iola, granddaughter of a Creole planter, has the experiences usual to fiction of the beautiful "white slave." She is kept ignorant of her race, and educated in the North.   When her white father's marriage to her quadroon mother is called illegal, she is sold as a slave.   After indignities in slavery, she is rescued, and serves as a nurse in a Civil War hospital. She rejects the love of a white New England physician, who, though knowing her race, wishes to marry her.   With her brothers and long-lost uncle, all of whom refuse to "pass for white," she dedicates herself to her people.   The book is "uplifting" but is far from convincing in incident, speech, and characterization. Iola is another of the octoroon heroines too angelic for acceptance. Some of the minor characters are better, but they cannot redeem the novel.

Dunbar. Dunbar has aptly described the typical setting for his fiction:

> Happy Hollow. . . . Wherever Negroes colonize in the cities or villages, North or South, wherever the hod-carrier, the porter, and the waiter are the society men of the town; wherever the picnic and the excursion are the chief summer diversion, and the revival the winter-time of repentance. . . . Wherever laughter and tears rub elbows by day, and the spirit of labour and laziness shake hands, there—there—is Happy Hollow.

In Old Plantation Days (1903) repeats the Thomas Nelson Page formula. Negro house servants comically ape the "quality," or intervene in lovers' quarrels, or in duels between cavaliers. One slave deceives his beloved master into believing that the good times of slavery still prevail. The planters, highbred and chivalrous, and the slaves, childish and devoted, rival each other in affection and sacrifice. These anecdotes of slavery, but a step above minstrel jokes, are all too happy for words, and too happy for truth.

The harshness of Reconstruction and of Dunbar's own time is likewise conventionally neglected in his other volumes of short stories: *Folks From Dixie* (1898), *The Strength of Gideon* (1900), and *The Heart of Happy Hollow* (1904). Freedmen discover that after all their best friends are their kindly ex-masters. In "Nels Hatton's Revenge," an upstanding Negro gives his hard-earned money and best clothes to his destitute master, who had abused him when a slave. The venality of Reconstruction politicians, which certainly existed, is satirized; but the gains of Reconstruction, which certainly exist, are understressed. Probably with due cause, Dunbar feared the rising poor-whites; therefore, like many Negro spokesmen of the period, he idealized the ex-planter class, the "aristocrats," *without* due cause.

Dunbar's fiction veers away from anything more serious than laughter or gentle tears. "At Shaft 11" shows the difficulties of Negro strikebreakers; but, afraid of organized labor, Dunbar idealized owners, operators, and staunchly loyal Negro workers who get to be foremen, thus carrying over the plantation tradition formula into the industrial scene. "The Ordeal at Mt. Hope" faces the loose-living of a "Happy Hollow," and then is lost in sentimental compromise. Dunbar wrote two stories of lynching, "The Lynching of Jule Benson" and the unusually ironic "The Tragedy at Three Corners." But Dunbar usually places the hardships of Negro life in the city, as in "Jimsella," with pastoral distrust of the city and faith in rural virtue. Fast livers, quacks, politicians and hypocritical race leaders are occasionally attacked.

The Sport of the Gods (1902), Dunbar's most ambitious novel, is the only one that is chiefly about Negroes. The first of the book is trite, but the latter section, though confused and melodramatic, has a grimness that Dunbar seldom showed. Berry, the innocent victim of a degenerate white man's crime in the South, and his family, the victim of hostile New York, are treated somewhat in the manner of Hardy's tragic laughing-stocks. The book has serious weaknesses, but it gives promise that Dunbar, but for his untimely death, might have become a prose writer of power. Judged by his accomplishment, however, Dunbar in fiction must be considered as one who followed the leader, not as a blazer of new trails.

Chesnutt. Charles Waddell Chesnutt, however, deserves to be called a pioneer. Writing to counter charges such as those made by Page in *Red Rock,* Chesnutt is the first to speak out uncompromisingly, but artistically, on the problems facing his people. One careful critic has stated that Chesnutt "was the first

Negro novelist, and he is still the best," and another has said that his books contain early drafts of about all of the recent Negro novels.

In Chesnutt's *The Conjure Woman*, seven tales based upon Negro superstitions, Uncle Julius recalls Uncle Remus and Page's Uncle Billy, but differs from them in his craftiness. He tells his stories not merely to entertain, or to bewail the beautiful past, toward which he is ironic, but to gain his point in the present. His dialect is worked out in great detail, but is not so readable as that of Uncle Remus. There is good local color throughout, and some interesting characters emerge.

The Wife of His Youth, and Other Stories of the Color Line (1899) deals mainly with problems of race. The title story tells of a successful Negro in Groveland (Cleveland), the "dean" of the "Blue-Veins," who, on the eve of his engagement to a beautiful widow, theatrically acknowledges a little old black woman who had been his wife in slavery days and had helped him to freedom. A Negro mother denies her octoroon daughter in order for her to marry a New Englander of Mayflower lineage in "Her Virginia Mammy," a story like Cable's "Madame Delphine" but less convincing and gripping. In "The Sheriff's Children" a mulatto prisoner, falsely accused of murder, is defended from a mob by a sheriff who turns out to be his father. Desperate and cynical, the son is about to kill his father to escape when he is shot by the sheriff's daughter. In "The Web of Circumstance" a Negro blacksmith, falsely accused of stealing a whip, is sentenced to five years in the penitentiary on the same day that a white murderer is sentenced to one year. "The Passing of Grandison" shows a cunning slave, pretending to despise the abolitionist North, returning to his "understanding" master.

79

He does so, however, only to manage the escape of all his kith and kin. "A Matter of Principle" satirizes the color line within the race: Clayton, an uppercrust near-white Negro, who "declined to associate with black people," pretends that his house is quarantined in order to keep a black Congressman from calling on his daughter. The Congressman turns out to be a mulatto, "well worthy" of Clayton's daughter.

The House Behind the Cedars (1900), Chesnutt's first novel, is concerned likewise with the color line. Rena, another octoroon heroine, is insulted by whites and oppressed by her mother and a mulatto suitor. Honorable devotion comes to her only through an upstanding black hero, but this cannot forestall her pathetic death. *The Marrow of Tradition* (1901), less conventional, is better. White characters range from the aristocratic General Delamere to his debauched grandson Tom; Major Carteret, demagogue for white supremacy; and McBane, ex-slave driver who knows one solution: "Burn the nigger." Negro characters range from Dr. Miller, a skillful physician, to the militant Josh Green; the loyal Sandy, and Jerry, a "white man's nigger." Sandy is framed for a murder in the first part of the book. A bloody riot, based on the one at Wilmington, N. C., is described in the second part. The white demagogues whip up the mob to fury, because a Negro newspaper has denounced lynching. Josh Green, who is willing to die rather than be shot down like a dog, who puts aside "fergetfulness and fergiveness," leads the aroused Negroes, when the upper-class Negroes believe that nothing can be done. The novel closes, however, on a note of forgetting and forgiving: Dr. Miller, whose own child was killed in the riot, goes to the home of his wife's white half-sister, to save her child with his very great medical skill. With all of its melodrama, the story has power; badly plotted, it still tells a great deal about social life in the South. Chesnutt idealizes some Negro characters, but candidly faces the weaknesses in others. Most important, however, is his going beneath the surface to social causes.

Chesnutt's last novel was *The Colonel's Dream.* Colonel French, an ex-Confederate officer of "family," dreams of resurrecting his native section and bringing it into the ways of prosperity and justice. As in so many novels of the time, his dream is not realized. He has opposed to him William Fetters, convict labor contractor, mortgage shark and political boss, together with the reactionary traditions and the inertia of the South. When the casket of his aged Negro slave, who had given his life for the Colonel's son, is dug up from the family burial plot and placed on his porch with a K.K.K. warning that the color line must continue even in death, he sees that his crusade is doomed. After this novel Chesnutt fell into an almost unbroken silence. Perhaps he felt the doom of his own crusade to bring about justice.

Whether he was pessimistic about his crusade or not, his achievements in fiction were worthy. Answering propaganda with propaganda, he might be expected to have certain faults. He was overinclined to the melodramatic, to mistaken identity, to the lost document turning up at the right or wrong moment, to the nick of time entrance. His characters are generally idealized or conventional. His "better class Negroes" speak too literary a language and are generally unbelievable models in behavior. Although attacking the color line within the race, he makes great use of the hero or heroine of mixed blood, and at times seems to accept the traditional concepts of Negro character. Even so, however, his characters stand

81

nearer to the truth than those of Thomas Page or Thomas Dixon; he does not force them into only two grooves. There is no gainsaying his knowledge of the southern scene, or of the Negro upper class in northern cities. Unlike Dunbar he is opposed to the plantation tradition, sharply critical of southern injustice, and aware of the sinister forces at work in Reconstruction. Deploring the abuses of that era, he still sees, like Tourgée, that the story of a South victimized by carpet-baggers and scalawags is only a convenient half-truth. He gives high praise to the Yankee schoolmasters and schoolmarms who swarmed over Dixie to lift a second bondage from the freedmen. He shows exploitation, riots and lynching mobs, as well as the more refined exercising of prejudice. Often pompous and roundabout, in the manner of his times, he nevertheless knew how to hold a reader's interest. We must concede that he was melodramatic in plotting, but evidences of a skillful master's hand can still be found. He knew a great deal, and all things considered, he told it well.

Summary. Deriving somewhat from the abolitionists, the best of the authors of this chapter attacked the plantation tradition, but with the sharper weapons of the growing realism. Twain's Jim and Roxana, Tourgée's Nimbus, Chesnutt's Josh Green, and even Cable's Bras Coupé and Madame Delphine (though they belong to a nearly legendary past) are far more convincing than Uncle Tom, Topsy and Hildreth's Archy Moore. Unlike their more popular contemporaries who defended the plantation tradition, these authors, at a risk, recorded the injustice that Negroes met with everywhere in "the tragic era." They knew that worshipful house-servants or depraved freedmen were not the sole actors in the story, and as lovers of truth and justice they wanted the full story told.

1. Why was Cable considered untrue to the Old South?

2. In what respects is Bras Coupé unusual in fiction about Negroes?

3. Compare the octoroons in antislavery novels with those in novels by Cable, Twain, and Tourgée.

4. Since Twain characterizes Jim as superstitious and illiterate, how can Twain be considered sympathetic?

5. Why are Hearn's beliefs about Negroes termed "stock"?

6. Compare William Wells Brown's *Clotel* with Frances Harper's *Iola Leroy*.

7. Compare Dunbar and Chesnutt.

8. What new characters appear in this chapter?

CHAPTER VI

OLD PATHS

Beautiful, Amusing Servitude. In the early twentieth century, under the influence of Thomas Nelson Page, a legion of writers wept over the vanished glory of the old plantation and presented Negroes of extreme devotedness to their masters. One writer in her book of sketches grieved:

> Aunt Phebe, Uncle Tom, Black Mammy, Uncle Gus, Aunt Jonas, Uncle Isom, and all the rest—who shall speak all your virtues or enshrine your simple faith and fidelity? It is as impossible as it is to describe the affection showered upon you by those whom you called 'Marster and Missis.'

Impossible though it may have been, countless authors attempted it, turning back time in its flight to sweetness and splendor that belong to another world than this.

Of the short stories in abundance that idealized the Negro, *in his place,* a few examples must serve. Betty Reynolds Cobb, in "The Coward" shows little Nemi conquering his great fears, and facing a raging torrent in order to get a doctor for "li'l Missy." (Cf. Kate Chopin's "Beyond The Bayou.") In Will Harben's "The Sale of Uncle Rastus", a nearly dead slave shams perfect health in order to fetch a better price for his bankrupt owner. His heroism reconciles his beloved master to an estranged brother, who bids two thousand dollars for him. "Dem boys done made up, en I fotch two thousand dollars! Whooee!" croaks Uncle Rastus at death's door. "Abram's Freedom," by Edna Turpin, shows Emmaline, who has struggled to buy her husband's freedom, saying: "Me an' Abram ain't got nothin' to do in dis worl' but to

84

wait on you an' master." These are merely duplicates of stories by more talented Reconstruction authors, with names and settings changed. Their authors have little to say, but say it over and over.

Ruth McEnery Stuart rises a notch above these. Although she glorified the past in *The River's Children* (1903) most of her work was local color of the deep South. In such works as *Napoleon Jackson* (1902), *George Washington Jones* (1903) and *The Second Wooing of Salina Sue* (1905), Negro life in the picturesquely shabby towns is quaint and droll, an unending source of mirth and satisfaction for the white-folks. Napoleon Jackson, the gentleman of the plush rocker, whose mother swore that he should never lay hand to a plow, worships old Marse and is therefore charming in Mrs. Stuart's sight. His wife Rose Ann, a visionary, is astonished that people pity Negroes since "we see mo'n white folks sees." Marital difficulties and burlesques of Negro church services furnish much of the drollery. Salina Sue, forced to marry her common-law husband, speaks of her fifteen-year old daughter: "Hit'll be a mighty good an' 'ligious thing for her to remember in after-years. Tain't every yo'ng gal dat kin ricollec' her pa an' ma gittin' married."

Better known writers preserving the tradition include the gifted Sarah Orne Jewett, whose *The Mistress of Sydenham Plantation* is like Constance Woolson's *East Angels* in showing a northern woman's respect for a servant's loyalty; Frank Stockton, who turned his facile invention to the Negro in *The Cloverfield's Carriage* and *The Late Mrs. Null;* and Booth Tarkington who invests the old picture with charm in *Penrod and Sam.* All of these are superior writers to such southern writers as Mrs. Burton Harrison, Opie Read and Marion Harland, but they give

85

no new interpretation. Some authors, like Virginia Frasel Boyle in *Devil Tales* (1900), followed Harris into the fertile field (and the wilderness) of folklore. Ed Mott's *The Black Homer of Jim Town* (1900) is a collection of folk tales from the Cape Fear country of North Carolina. Most of them are trite. Slavery is remembered as a good time, and in one of the tallest of the tales, a Negro in the Federal army arrives at the battle just in time to intercept a bullet intended for his Confederate master, in whose arms he dies.

Women writers of the South have been particularly attracted to literary exercises about the legendary chivalry, the perfect masters and slaves. In their prefaces, they seem to consider it their duty to "interpret the Negro race" and to lecture upon the modern Negro's deficiencies. Among these might be mentioned Emma Speed Sampson for *Mammy's White Folks* (1919) and *Miss Minerva On The Old Plantation* (1923); Jane Baldwin Cotton for *Wall-Eyed Caesar's Ghost* (1925) and Virginia McCormick for *Charcoal and Chalk* (1931). Pity for "the child who never had a fat, brown mammy with elastic lap and warm enfolding arms," alternates with beaming appreciation of happy-hearted pickaninnies living an endless picnic. "A real understanding of our colored people" generally amounts to having great fun out of them. The dialect is often carefully recorded, but the Negroes say about the same things that Page had them say long ago, to flatter their white-folks and to make them laugh.

Although willing to poke gentle fun at his native South, O. Henry kept to its old tradition about Negro character. Uncle Bushrod in "The Guardian of The Accolade", remembering Miss Lucy's words for Marse Robert: "a little child but my knight, pure and fearless and widout reproach," prevents Robert from absconding with what he thinks to be the cash of the bank, but what turns out to be two quarts of old silk velvet Bourbon. "The Fourth in Salvador" has a

buck coon from Georgia who had drifted down there from a busted-up colored colony that had been started on some possumless land in Mexico. As soon as he heard us say barbecue he wept for joy and groveled on the ground.

"The Emancipation of Billy" has an ancient body-servant, Old Jeff, a member of "de fambly," who despises "Yankee rascality enduring' the war," speaking "de fambly's" language *to a T*. "A Municipal Report" shows a faithful Negro coachman, Uncle Caesar, who supports his impoverished mistress, and kills her worthless husband (a professional southerner) for robbing her. A master of surprises, O. Henry has no surprises for us when he handles Negro characters. They belong to an endless line.

Irvin Cobb and The Professional Humorists. Irvin Cobb, whom some consider heir to the roving shoes of O. Henry, once had a favorite character declaim: "I ain't no problem, I'se a pusson. I craves to be so reguarded." But when Cobb regards Jeff Poindexter, he sees little more than a loyal and ridiculous servant, who says the right things. Jeff advises a white moving picture producer as follows:

Ef you kin git hold of a crowd of cullid actors w'ich is willin' to ack lak the sho'nuff ole time cullid an' not lak onbleached imitations of w'ite folks, it seems lak to me the rest of it oughter be plum easy. Mostly I'd mek the pitchers comical, ef I wuz you. You kin do 'at an' still not hurt nobody's feelin's, w'ite nur black. Ef you wants to perduse a piece showin' a lot of niggers gittin' skinned, let it be another nigger w'ich skins em. . . .
Then, w'en at the last, they gits even wid him it'll still be nigger ag'inst nigger. An' ef, oncet in awhile, you meks a kind of serious pitcher . . . 'at ought to fetch there yere new-issue cullid folks w'ich is seemingly become so plentiful up Nawth. But mainly I'd stick to the laffin' line ef I wuz you. An' whatever else you does, don't mess wid no race problem.

Irvin Cobb takes Jeff's advice, fondly affectionate toward the "old time cullid," derisive of the new-issue "onbleached imitations of w'ite folks," unwilling to hurt the feelings of any of his large white audience. As a result, his books such as *J. Poindexter, Colored* and those about Old Judge Priest rise little above the joke-book level when dealing with Negroes, in spite of Cobb's undoubted knowledge of his native Kentucky. McBlair's *Mister Fish Kelly* (1924) is similarly traditional, with some surface truth to comic elements in Negro life, but too set upon tickling America.

But that is a well paying business, as such writers as Hugh Wiley, Arthur Akers, Octavus Roy Cohen and E. K. Means have discovered. Belonging to light entertainment literature, their stories would hardly deserve serious attention, were it not for their undoubted social influence. With situations ranging from the improbable to the unreal, the comedy, the farce are not "pure," but are mixed all up with propaganda for Negro inferiority and subordination. These authors stem from Page and the Reconstruction: although they stress the comical, they likewise urge the mutual affection between funny Negroes and their fine white-folks, and bear witness to the sunny life of the South. Guy Johnson has written that there is a sort of

> folk attitude of the white man toward the Negro. . . . He must have his fun out of the Negro, even when writing serious novels about him.

How much more fun the professional marketmen of humor have out of the Negro is apparent when one reads the stories of Wiley, Akers, and Cohen, to name only three who write for wide circulation magazines such as *The Saturday Evening Post* and the *Red Book*. With the help of the radio, these family magazines see to it that there is a comic Negro in every middle class home.

Hugh Wiley in the twenties presented Wildcat, inseparable from Lady Luck, his unsavory goat. Like O. Henry, Wiley uses outrageous metaphors, but one does not have to believe the language to be Negro merely because it is amusing. Pet expressions are such as "crematized or secluded in de ground" for burial rites, "paraphernalia of chance" for dice, and other minstrel joke-book relics. The humor is broad, concerned with perspiring three-hundred pound black Amazons, "battling brunettes," a goat outsmelling creation, whose butting causes Wildcat to "skid over the curb in a pose which cost his army pants half of their seating capacity." Wildcat is a "champion ration battler," barely making it on four meals a day, lazy except at the irresistible crap game, where he wins fabulous sums with other-worldly luck. Characters are named Miss Cuspidora Lee, Vitus Marsden, Honey Tone, Dwindle Daniels, Punic Hunter, Presidump Ham Grasty, Festus Roach. There are many jobs (generally unwelcome) and a great deal of money and food in circulation; the law is loud-mouthed but gentle; things are "hotsy-totsy" down in Dixie, Lady Luck and the whitefolks will see to that. It all strives very hard, but it could be more amusing.

Of these professionally funny men, Octavus Roy Cohen is probably most widely known and industrious. Cohen and his large following are entranced by the comedy of what Cobb called "onbleached imitations of white folks." The idea of Negro doctors, lawyers, bankers, movie-magnates and society belles in Birmingham is too funny, but not too funny for words. Some of his annual books are *Assorted Chocolates* (1922) *Dark Days and Black Knights* (1923), *Bigger and Blacker* (1925), *Black and Blue* (1926) and *Highly Colored* (1921). All are highly colored: he names his characters Orifice Latimer, Callous Deech,

Magnolius Ricketts, Excelsior Nix, Forcep Swain, Exotic Hines, Unit Smith, Jasper De Vord, Chromo Bridal and Atlas Brack. His dialect is one unheard on land or sea: "Got to ain't has got;" "I ain't sawn her right recent;" "Does anybody discover that I ain't you, you is suddenly gwine to become ain't;" "salisfried, straduced, light bombastic, applicatin, foolisment; oh, whoa is me!" The plots and counterplots generally turn around the axis of money or love; the honest hero defeats the slickers, the boy gets the girl. Florian Slappey, in Harlem, is fleeced in the cold winter by two Harlem number men, but the happy ending is usual. The Sons and Daughters of I Will Arise, The Enter Paradise In Style Life and Death Sassiety, and The Over The River Buryin' Sassiety figure prominently. There seems to be a great deal of money in Negro Birmingham, but when Cohen speaks of a Negro star being paid one hundred dollars a week by a Negro movie company, he reveals his myth-making powers. One of Cohen's recent heroes, Epic Peters, is a pompously talking Pullman porter, proud of his service to "quality white folks" whom he can tell at a glance, happy, amusing, and about as real as his speech: "Goodness, goshness, Miss Agness, Mr. Foster—I suttinly thought I was gwine see you become ain't."

Arthur K. Akers' world is less unreal, but equally droll. Jeff thus explains his connubial woes:

> Hit's on account of me bein' weak in de'rithmetic. Dat's huccome I cain't ricollect is I got two weddin's and three d'voces, or three weddin's an' two d'voces. Emmline come in dar somewhar.

Akers has a fondness for names like Shakespeare Shackleford, Columbus Collins, Aspirin Edwards and Halfportion. His intricate plots invariably end happily for the dull-witted, inept heroes such as Gladstone Smith who is "numb from the neck up." Ipecac Ignalls, looking like "something dark that had been left under a tent—an orange-colored tent with LIFE GUARD lettered across it" does not know how to swim, but he saves the life of a belle by letting her stand on him while he is on the bottom of the pool drowning. Other comedy is furnished by lodge-life and financial high-jinks performed by the Worthymost Master Samson Bates and Horace Tombs, who are Get Rich Quick Wallingfords in blackface.

E. K. Means, whose stories were collected in volumes called *E. K. Means, More E. K. Means,* and *Further E. K. Means,* insists that he wrote out of a whimsical fondness for the Negro "to whom God has given two supreme gifts—Music and Laughter." He seems to agree with one of his white characters, how-ever, that the Negro "has a one-cylinder mind and a smoky spark-plug." Nigger-Heel Plantation, Hen Scratch Saloon, Shoofly Methodist Church, Tickfall and Dirty Six are treated with a mixture of true local color and far-fetched tom-foolery. The characters have ludicrous names like Whiffletree Bone, Limit Lark, Vakey Vopp, Dazzle Zenor, Coco Ferret, Ready Rocket, Vinegar Atts, Skeeter Butts. Means attacks conventional dialect, yet he makes use of invented phrases: "explavacatin'", "permittunce," "coming wid a looseness,' "de orgies" (for church services), "ax her inquirement," "ain't right in her intellectuals," "I warn't studyin' how to save by grace; I was pon-derin' how to save my grease." Means regrets that the good life lived by these naïve villagers is depart-ing; "Ethiopia is stretching out her hands after art, science, literature and wealth," Negroes are becoming "play-like white folks." He wishes to leave a record of the "sable sons of laughter and song, in Fiction's beautiful temple of dreams." The laughter, however, is chiefly the haw-hawing of the white folks; the dreams are practical jokes. Something of the sinister and ugly is recognized; Negroes at their Uplift League election wrench legs off of tables in a free-for-all, shot-guns and razors are frequently used, but the picture remains quaint and comical. In almost every story we have panic-stricken Negroes "skedaddling," their "ponderous feet beating a wild tattoo of panicky retreat upon the sodded turf;" oddly enough, one cause for fright never mentioned is a southern mob.

These authors contrive a rapid-fire dialogue, now near to life (as in Akers) and now to the minstrel show (as in Cohen). The white folks are tolerant, until tenants burn the porches off their homes, or servants mix up affairs too much, when they wax comically profane. The Negroes are superstitious, helpless, cowardly, utterly ridiculous children. Life is easy and indolent except for shrewish wives and scheming crooks; the razors do not cut, the scantlings used by white masters on their menials never hurt, since they strike the head, and tl "law" is only a mythical threat. What could be pathos and tragedy sets off laughter. The settings are supposed to be found in Demopolis or Birmingham or other southern cities, but they belong to a *never-never,* cloud-cuckoo land. All in all these stories reveal far less of Negro life and character than of middle class American taste.

The Rising Tide of Color. But there were others who took the Negro in dead earnest. Negroes were becoming educated, getting property, leaving the South, and asking for civil rights; they constituted, therefore, a menace. Southern civilization sought to preserve itself by peonage, disfranchisement, segregation, and lynching. The authors aided and paralleled the politicians, who confounded attempts at democracy by dragging the herring of intermarriage over

92

the countryside.   In proportion as Negroes showed themselves as seeking economic advancement and civil rights, authors portrayed them as insulting brutes and rapists.

This stereotype shot up to full growth in these first decades of the twentieth century.   But the seeds, as we have seen, had been sown long before.   Answering abolitionist onslaughts, the *Bible Defense of Slavery* had "proved" that Sodom and Gomorrah were strongholds of *Negro* vice, and that "the baleful fire of unchaste amour rages through the Negro's blood more fiercely. . . ."   Hinton Helper, in *Nojoque* (1867), had set up black and beastly as synonyms. *The Negro A Beast* (1900) by Charles Carroll which proves the Negro to be "a beast, created with articulate speech, that he may be of service to the White man," brought this type of book to a rabid climax.   As already pointed out, Page in *Red Rock* and *The Negro, The Southerner's Problem* had shown Reconstruction to be a holiday for Negro brutes.

Thomas Dixon.   After Page, the best known author of Ku Klux Klan fiction is the Reverend Thomas Dixon.   *The Clansman* and *The Leopard's Spots,* because of their sensationalism (cf. chapter titles "The Black Peril," "The Unspoken Terror," "A Thousand Legged Beast," "The Hunt For the Animal") seemed just made for the mentality of early Hollywood, where D. W. Griffith's *The Birth of a Nation* made for Dixon a dubious sort of immortality, and finally fixed the stereotype in the mass-mind.

The Leopard's Spots (1902) is Dixon's masterpiece of hatred.   This long novel has its share of sugary love affairs done in the best southern tradition, but is chiefly important for its political bearings. Characters are brought in from *Uncle Tom's Cabin;* Legree quits drink for the greater vice of becoming

93

a scalawag and a mill owner. Eliza's son, George Harris, is educated at Harvard, falls in love with Senator Lowell's daughter and is ordered from the abolitionist home. Tim Shelby, a silk-hatted Negro politician, boasts that he will one day marry a white woman and is lynched as "Answer of the Anglo-Saxon race to Negro lips that dare to pollute with words the fair womanhood of the South." Dick, an imbecile, crushes with a rock the head of a white child and then attacks her. The assaulted child and the burning of the Negro are described with gusto. Drunk Negro soldiers drag white brides from their homes; criminal Negroes rove the countryside, forcing whites to take to the cities. Included in the list of hateful outragers of the fair Southland are the Yankee schoolmarms, whom Dixon would like to see shipped back to Boston in glass cages like rattlesnakes. The Negro is not to be educated, not even industrially, for this drives him to crime or suicide. A few Negroes like old Nels obey their white-folks, but Dixon is surprised to find no Negroes in the mob that lynched Dick. Negro "dominion" and the threat that "the South will become mulatto instead of Anglo-Saxon" are overthrown when the Red-Shirts ride.

The Clansman (1905) is another hymn of hate. President Lincoln, considered pro-southern, is fearful lest "mulatto citizenship be too dear a price to pay even for emancipation." Stoneman, a libellous portrait of Thaddeus Stevens, is shown in the toils of Lydia Brown, a mulatto of extraordinary animal beauty. Other villains are Silas Lynch, a mulatto, "with the head of a Caesar and the eyes of the jungle," Augustus Caesar, "whose flat nose with enormous perpetually dilating nostrils, sinister head and enormous cheekbones and jaws reminded one of the lower order of animal," and Yankee soldiers whom faithful

94

ex-slaves obligingly knock down. "A new mob of onion-laden breath, mixed with perspiring African odour, became the symbol of American democracy." Against this reign of terror, culminating in a rape, painstakingly described, the knights of the Ku Klux Klan rise in righteous wrath. Gus, whose image was discovered upon the retina of the dead mother's eye by strange southern science, is not lynched, but "executed by the Grand Turk who flung his body on the lawn of the black Lieutenant-Governor of the State." In this way civilization was restored. Reconciliation is exemplified in northern-southern love affairs, but only when the Negro is returned to serfdom can there be true reunion.

The School of Page and Dixon. Emory's *A Maryland Manor* (1901) is important only as a sign of the trend. The slaves are shown as lighthearted, needing compulsion to teach them good habits. Chloe, who runs away frequently, is obeying an inherited love for the woods: "It was often the case . . . fugitives fled from those they loved best." From emancipation "the negroes suffered most of all, sinking into a condition little short of their original barbarism." Caesar is too intelligent to accept freedom, "What you take me fur, anyhow?", etc. As a reward he is allowed burial in the family graveyard, at his master's blessed feet.

In *The Northerner* (1905) by Nora Davis, a reconciliation novel, Falls, a Yankee businessman, establishes the Tennessee Valley Improvement Company to develop electric power in the South, and wins the Alabama belle in the meanwhile. Falls and Watson, a southern aristocrat, battle a mob to save an innocent but craven Negro, who, given a pistol to defend his life, thinks only: "Lawdy, don't I wisht I had er piece er M'lindy's cawn bread." Miscegenation is a great concern of the author, who calls it the "Curse of Dixie," "The Nameless Shame," "The Hidden Pain." Watson, in his cavalier youth, had been seduced by the brown Lesby, "a snake in the grass." He loathes his beautiful quadroon daughter, Rosebud. Miss Davis has him say: "Every drop of blood in my body turns cold with disgust at the thought—the sight of her!" And to his daughter, before she is relegated to the future in store for one "cursed with the black drop," he declaims:

> You should be just, child, to this man—try to see how he is placed. He has done, and he will do, his duty by you as God gives it to him to see it. . . . That was a sin of the flesh, you know, and in the flesh will he repay. But in the spirit, in all those things which belong to his higher nature, you can have no part. . . . He could not love you, cherish you: his very nature would recoil. It is instinct, child, blood!"

Rose meekly concurs. Some comic use is made of Pete, a state Congressman in Reconstruction, now happier as a valet for his white-folks.

Robert Lee Durham is even more concerned over the "Hidden Shame" in *The Call of The South* (1908). John Hayward, the central figure, is of barely perceptible Negro blood. Of fine ancestry on the white side, he is a first-rate student and athlete at Harvard before he leaves for heroic service in the war in Cuba. Becoming footman for a president who champions liberal democracy, he is thrown in contact with the president's daughter. After rescuing her from a runaway horse, and revealing his heroic past at Harvard and in battle, he wins her, like a modern Othello, by tales of dangers overcome. They marry secretly, platonically. Up to this point the novelist has been sympathetic toward Hayward's undoubted abilities and undeserved rebuffs. But the platonic husband and wife, waylaid in a storm, are forced to seek refuge in a hut.

96

> In a flash of light she sees his face—distorted: with a shriek
> of terror she wildly tries to push him from her; but the demon
> of the blood of Guinea Gumbo is pitiless, and against the fury
> of it, as against the storm, she fights and cries in vain.

The tragedy rushes on: Helen is delivered of a very
dark child, explained as a "recession"; her father dies
of heart failure; she goes mad. A South Carolina
cavalier points the moral and adorns the tale:

> How shall sickly sentimentality solace your shame if in the
> blood of your mulatto grandchild the vigorous red corpuscles of
> some savage ancestor shall overmatch your gentle endowment?

For "however risen, redolent of newly applied polish,"
the leopard cannot change his spots, nor the Ethiopian
his skin. It seems that the skin must be changed for
him. Even so, the fundamental savagery is still there,
lurking. Social equality means the "mongrelization of
the superior breed," of which one "blood deep charac-
teristic is chivalrous respect for women." So rings
out the Call of the South.

Although a much later book, Jean Sutherland's
Challenge (1926) is equally fantastic and insidious.
The Polish-English Prince Kareninoff, who is famous
as an opponent of race-mixture, has had a son by a
woman who, unknown to him, was part Negro. The
son, however, does the proper thing; he shuts himself
in a monastery to save his aristocratic fiancée from
pollution, and then, like his octoroon sisters, goes to
Africa to help his people.

Negro characters in John Trotwood Moore's novels
such as *Ole Mistis* and *The Bishop of Cottontown* are
in the mildewed tradition. Mammy, in the second of
these, has a new mission: she keeps the children of her
impoverished master from the cotton mills.

> You're down heah preachin' one thing for niggahs and prac-
> tisin' another for yo' own race; yo' hair frizzles on yo' head at
> th'ort of niggah slavery, whilst all the time you're enslavin' the
> po' little whites that's got yo' own blood in their veins. . . . I
> come for my child!

97

Frenzied at the wrongs of the cotton factory, she sets fire to the "Sodom." For this she is nearly lynched, but is saved by the heroes of the novel. "Thirteen dead men lay, and the back-bone of lynching had been broken forever in Alabama." This was written in 1906. Moore condones lynching as

> the result of the sudden emancipation of ignorant slaves, who, backed by the bayonets of their liberators . . . perpetuated an unnameable crime as part of their system of revenge for years of slavery. . . . And is not the honor of a white woman more than the hide of a broncho?

Inconsistently, he goes on:

> And so these people flocked to the burning—the Negro haters, who had never owned a slave and had no sympathy—no sentiment for them.

In one scene a group of Negro night-riders, instigated by the villains of the Union League and a mulatto politician, terrorize the faithful Negroes. The latter, who had been overseers, had "absorbed many of the virtues of the best class of whites," while the Negroes who wished to vote were "but a few generations removed from the cowardice of darkest Africa." Lushly overflowing with love for the poor millhands, Moore has a kind word for the Negro only as serf.

Summary. These authors urged reconciliation of North and South, *but on southern terms.* They shuddered at the rising tide of bad Negroes, dreading amalgamation, but too often "bad Negroes" to them were the educated, or the propertied, or the militant. Their books seem to be conceived in fear and written with hate. They reflected the thought of the South of their day, from planter aristocrat and political boss down to the poor-white on the farm or in the mills. They wanted the South left alone to deal with the Negro in its own way, and this way, since the Negro was needed as ignorant laborer and scapegoat, was the way of exploitation and cruelty. These authors merely

98

transferred melodrama of action into written melodramas. They were sometimes vicious, sometimes
stupid, and as in the case of Dixon, sometimes mob
inciters rather than novelists. But still, be it recorded
to democracy's shame, they got what they wanted.

DISCUSSION QUESTIONS

1. Account for the vogue of Thomas Nelson Page
at the beginning of the century.

2. Why was Cobb anxious to show "Negroes
always skinned by Negroes"?

3. What is significant in the fact that after Jeff
Poindexter makes his greatest speech he is given ten
dollars?

4. In the recent filibuster on the Anti-Lynching Bill,
what arguments were advanced that are to be found
in this chapter?

5. What is the relationship of Page's *Red Rock* to
the problem fiction of this chapter?

6. What were the chief problems that concerned
southern authors in this chapter?

7. In what respects do the comic writers and the
melodramatists of this chapter agree?

CHAPTER VII

Negro Apologists.—Aroused by the libels of Thomas Nelson Page and his school, Negro novelists stepped forward with race defense and glorification. Explaining weaknesses as the heritage of slavery and oppression, they wished to hold up to the world "the millions of honest, God-fearing, industrious, frugal, respectable and self-respecting Negroes, who are toiling on for the salvation of their race." They urged what Kelly Miller wrote in "An Open Letter to Thomas Dixon, Jr." (1905):

> Within forty years of only partial opportunity . . . the American Negro has cut down his illiteracy by over fifty per cent; has produced a professional class, some fifty thousand strong . . . some three thousand Negroes have taken collegiate degrees, over three hundred being from the best institutions in the North and West. . . . Negro inventors have taken out four hundred patents . . . scores of Negroes . . . take respectable rank in the company of distinguished Americans.

And, as another put it,—"This farm land that they own and operate if put acre to acre would make a strip of land five miles wide . . . from New York to San Francisco." They believed that the Negro who had succeeded in the American way should have his day in court. Some agreed with Booker Washington, more with DuBois, but all stressed the Negro's persecution and his achievement. The times demanded propaganda of them, they felt; and propaganda they gave, in good measure. The race was their hero, and preaching a solution their business, upon which they were grimly intent.

Sutton Griggs, one of the earliest, assured the readers of *Unfettered* (1902) that neither angels nor demons, but mere human beings made up his cast of characters. But this is not so. Morlene is described:

> A wealth of lovely black hair crowning a head of perfect shape and queenly poise; a face, the subtle charm of which baffles description; two lustrous black eyes, wondrously expressive, presided over by eyebrows that were ideally beautiful; a neck which, with perfect art, descended and expanded so as to form a part of a faultless bust; as to form, magnificently well proportioned; when viewed as a whole, the very essence of loveliness . . .

It is no wonder then, that she speaks to one of the villains: "Sir, it takes no prophet to foretell that terrible sorrows await you." The hero, Dorlan Warthell, is likewise faultless: "As to color he was black, but even those prejudiced as to color forgot that prejudice when they gazed upon this ebony-like Apollo." Dorlan, a power in politics, deserts the Republican party for betraying his race, and incurs the hatred of the white Congressman Bloodworth. The ills heaped upon ills of the southern Negro, a very idealized love affair, long discussions of the race problem, and Dorlan's plan to solve it (partly worked out on a balloon ride) make the book a hodgepodge. The prose is trite and pompous.

Griggs' *The Hindered Hand* (1905) is also a bad novel. The characters are models of decorum. In a passionate love scene at the end, the hero Ensal takes one of Tiara's hands in his, and then overwhelmed, takes the other:

> We fain would draw the curtain just here. . . . They were married that night, and the next day set out for Africa, to provide a home for the American Negro.

All of the darker phases of the South appear in the book, but melodramatically, unrealistically. The action is slowed up by long dissertations on "the problem," including a review of Thomas Dixon's *Leopard's Spots*. Even the two heroines are race orators. George McClellan's *Old Greenbottom Inn* (1906) is subtler propaganda. Most of the stories tell of the pathetic love affairs of beautiful Negro girls, but there is some rewarding local color of the Tennessee Valley and of the earliest Negro schools.

An argument in the guise of fiction is J. W. Grant's *Out of the Darkness* or *Diabolism and Destiny* (1909). Answering Booker T. Washington's conciliatory school of thought, the author writes "What are houses, land and money to men who are women?" But the mettle of the author deserves a better novel. His chief characters—the orator, the salutatorian and the valedictorian of their college class—become noted as preacher, statesman, and physician respectively. The physician discovers a cure for yellow fever, saves a beautiful white girl's life, and is lynched before the love affair between them ripens. He is nearly white and bitter towards the white world; his two classmates are likewise militant. The author continually stresses the grace, refinement, wealth, palatial homes and property of upper class Negroes, decries the masses, and demands that the Negro be measured not by his worst but by his best. Needless to say the wrongs of the Negro are listed in full, but are seldom shown movingly. *As We See It* (1910) by Robert L. Waring deals with a young black hero, Abe, who leaves scholastic and athletic honors at Oberlin College to avenge the lynching of his mother and sister. There is a Damon-Pythias bond between Abe and a white boy, Malcolm, and between their two fathers, one an Alabama aristocrat and the other his body-servant. The aristocratic class of the South is praised highly, while the poor-whites are treated with contempt and hatred. Waring's generalizations about the "cracker" are very much like Dixon's about Negroes.

From Superman to Man (1917) by J. A. Rogers has only a thin thread of narrative running through long discussions of the race problem, in which a Pullman porter embarrasses and refutes white passengers with his anthropological and sociological information. Quips such as "The white man's burden is composed largely of plunder" and " 'To educate the Negro is only to make him unhappy' really means 'Do not educate the Negro and make the white man unhappier' " carry force, but the book is more pamphlet then novel.

The apologist whom these authors praised for his uncompromising attitude was W. E. B. DuBois. His fiction, superior to theirs in literary value, is similar in many respects. *The Quest of the Silver Fleece* (1911) is part fantasy, part propaganda. Zora, who sees visions of the "little people of the swamps," rises from a degraded environment to become a race leader, fit companion for Bles Alwyn, a noble black boy from Georgia who becomes a force in politics. The plot is unconvincing; the characters are stiff and talk stiltedly: "Bles, thou almost persuadest me to be a fool." But DuBois' social understanding gives the novel value. The New England schoolmarms, the southern attack upon the schools, the scheming to get control of Negro education to render it harmless, the tie-up of Northern capital with cotton barons, the shame of Negro treatment, the conniving of political Negroes,—all of these are revealed by a keen social analyst. DuBois sees how poor-whites are used "to keep niggers in their place, and the fear of niggers to keep the poorer whites in theirs." One white character says "Derned if I don't think white slaves and black slaves had ought ter git together." But this radical lead is not followed up; the novel is too taken up with a priggish hero and an unbelievable heroine, and social reality is subordinated to symbolism. It is a significant book, however, and if DuBois answered Dixon's melodrama in kind, it was at least melodrama pleading for humanity and blasting injustice.

103

DuBois' *Darkwater: The Twentieth Century Completion of "Uncle Tom's Cabin"* (1919) contains five tales in a prose that echoes the Bible and medieval romance. Two modern fairy-tales attack race-hatred and oppression. "The Second Coming" tells of the birth of a black child in a Georgia stable while three bishops—"the wise men"— look on. "Jesus Christ in Texas," like Upton Sinclair's "They Call Me Carpenter," deals with the return of Christ to a hate-ridden community, where he is unrecognized by the preacher, but is known to the despised and rejected. Like H. G. Wells, DuBois, in "The Comet," makes use of pseudo-science to drive home social ideas. When Manhattan is destroyed by the gases of a comet, only two people survive, one a Negro bank messenger, and the other a white girl, "rarely beautiful and richly gowned, with darkly-golden hair and jewels." Alone on earth, the "Bride of Life" and "great All-Father of the race to be" are broken in upon and returned to the world of prejudice by the crass "honk-honk" of rescuers from the world outside of New York City. These stories are without the usual drive of DuBois' work; even within the frame of allegory and fantasy, they lack conviction.

James Weldon Johnson's *The Autobiography of An Ex-Colored Man* (1912) (first published anonymously) urges that

> log-cabins and plantations and dialect speaking 'darkies' are perhaps better known in American literature than any other single picture . . . [Too little known] are coloured people who live in respectable homes and amidst a fair degree of culture.

The hero, a sensitive, light-skinned Negro, expresses an upper-class snobbishness toward the Negro masses:

> The unkempt appearance, the shambling, slouching gait and loud talk and laughter of these people aroused in me a feeling of almost repulsion.

Ashamed of "being identified with a people that could with impunity be treated worse than animals," he decides to "pass" for white. He travels widely through the South, to New York and to Europe, mingling generally with artistic people. Economic security and a happy marriage with a white woman do not quiet his regret, however, and he calls himself a "coward, a deserter . . . [with] a strange longing for my mother's people." Although the central figure is complex and interesting, the novel seems to exist primarily for the long discussions of race, and the showing of the Negro in different milieus. The descriptions of the "big meeting" and of Bohemian life in New York are valuable realism. *The Autobiography of An Ex-Colored Man* was a ground-breaking novel in its dealing with the "aristocratic" mulatto, the problem of "passing," the Negro artistic world, the urban and European scene, and its subtler assertion of points where Negroes "are *better* than anybody else."

Summary. After the long years of caricature and contempt, it was natural that Negro novelists of the first generation after slavery should write as apologists. Not literary men, with the exception of DuBois and Johnson, but most often preachers and teachers, they had a charge to keep instead of a story to be told. They resented the use of the "Jim-Crow Negro," seen in Harris and Page, Dunbar and Chesnutt. DuBois reveals a refreshing faith in the people at times, but they all preferred the "talented tenth," at its most genteel. The heroines are modest and beautiful, frequently octoroon; the heroes are handsome and priggish, frequently black. Their characters have high-flown names like Dorlan Warthell, Ensal Ellwood, Tiara and Bles Alwyn; between these and comic names like Shakespeare Shackleford, Vakey Vopp, and Epic Peters there is little to choose. The villains are

too often poor-whites.   The incidents are romantic
and often fantastic.   The injuries of the Negro are
seldom conveyed with full power; like the abolitionists,
these novelists felt that listing could make up for
rendering.   The race problem, at the core of their
work, turns their novels into tracts.   Acceptance of
certain traits as racial, such as optimism, loyalty and
faith, and underestimation of the Negro masses in-
validate much of their discussion.   All are concerned
with refutation of Thomas Dixon and his school.
They were fighting in a good cause, but the novel
was not their weapon.

The Tradition of The Abolitionists.   Negro apologists found allies among northern white liberals who
joined in the struggle for Negro rights.   Mary White
Ovington, one of the important figures in the National
Association For The Advancement of Colored People,
wrote persuasive propaganda fiction.   *The Shadow*
(1920) makes out a case for Negroes against the white
world.   A white girl, abandoned by her aristocratic
family, is brought up as colored, until a letter informs
her of her lineage.   Her experiences in the white
world, complicated by coincidental meetings with her
Negro "brother," disillusion her, and she says:

> White people are wicked. . . . They hate goodness. . . . And
> they say they're so good! . . . We black people, we are bad. . . .
> Well, I want to be with bad people. I've been with good people
> as long as I can bear. . . .

The novel is worked out romantically.   Its pattern
and many of its situations, however, have been taken
over by later novelists.   Miss Ovington is likewise
the author of *Hazel* (1913), a story of a little colored
heroine, and the much better *Zeke* (1931), which is an
informed and sympathetic novel of the life of Negro
boys in a southern school.   Her "The White Brute"
has been called one of the most memorable stories
against lynching.

106

Dorothy Canfield's *The Bent Twig* (1915) refers to race prejudice in a midwestern town. When two shy, well-bred girls are discovered to have Negro blood, their schoolmates taunt them gleefully. An intelligent liberal—grieved at the humiliation—feels like gathering up his family and going away from the intolerable question, to Europe, but his wife grimly remarks: "And what we shall do is, of course, nothing at all."

Typical of the many works urging the solution of the race problem by applied Christianity is *Of One Blood* (1916) by Charles Sheldon, the author of the religious best-seller *In His Steps*. Sheldon admits that he has pictured the "heroic, the beautiful and the great of each race," but insists that he has not done them justice. The Negro hero is shown as triumphant college orator, great athlete, and finally agricultural expert instructing his people. Although nearly lynched in the South, being rescued melodramatically by a southern member of the "World Brotherhood," he will not be "angry, sullen, bitter or revengeful." The author concludes that race hatred would be abolished if "all the white men in the United States were like Abraham Lincoln and all the black men like Booker Washington," a hope as extreme as his characterization and plot. Likewise full of praise for Booker Washington, *The Testing Fire* by Alexander Corkey (1911) optimistically prophesies a redeemed South.

Early Southern Liberalism.—Groping and hesitant liberalism found expression in the work of some of the southern novelists. Some were aware of the heavy hand of the dead past and wanted to shake it off, others wanted to set down honestly what they saw about them. *The Southerner* (1909) first appeared as a serial, *The Autobiography of a Southerner Since the Civil War,* by Nicholas Worth, whom readers soon identified as Walter Hines Page. The attack of this book upon the "mummified" South, its dedication to the laying of the three ghosts of "The Confederate Dead, of Religious Orthodoxy and of Negro Domination," shows how opposed Walter Hines Page of North Carolina was to the ghost-ridden Thomas Nelson Page of Virginia. The novel is long and tract-like. Negro characters play an important part. Uncle Ephraim and Aunt Maria, worshippers of their white family, remember slavery as a happy state. Balancing these are Sam Worth, the runaway slave who becomes head of an industrial school; Lissa, another tragic mulatto, who bears a child to the future governor of the state; the Rev. Doctor Snodder, meek hang-dog "teacher of the oppressed"; John Marshall, an intelligent Hampton graduate; gullible office seekers, and a murderer of a Confederate firebrand. The author of *The Southerner* had, for his time, advanced ideas regarding education, civil rights, and democracy, and these are reflected in his characterizations of Negroes, which, though not done at full-length, are suggestive departures from the old and outworn.

Ellen Glasgow, who "carried realism across the Potomac" to the interpretation of her beloved Virginia, naturally pays attention to the Negro. He appears, however, as part of the social background, not as central character. He is viewed with shrewd insight: in *The Miller of Old Church* (1911) a Negro farmer, told to be thankful for his crop instead of complaining, responds:

> Dar ain't nuttin' 'tall ter be thankful fur in dat, suh, case de Lawd He ain't had no mo ter do wid dat ar co'n den old Marse Hawtrey. I jes ris dat ar co'n wid my own han' right down de road at my front do', and po'd de water on hit outer de pump at my back un. I'se monstrous glad ter praise de Lawd for what he done done, but I ain't gwine to gin 'im credit fur de wuk er my own fis' en foot.

Barren Ground (1925) contains some honest pictures of Negroes, not greatly different from the impoverished whites of the broomsedge, except that they are better and thriftier farmers. With courage Miss Glasgow introduces the common-law wife of old man Graylock. Once a handsome Negro woman, she is now slatternly and smoulderingly resentful, especially when the old man in a drunken fit takes a horsewhip to his mulatto brood.

The Negro character as a very different sort of background appears in *Hagar's Hoard,* by George Kibbe Turner (1920). This gripping novel tells of the horror of yellow fever as it came to the close-shuttered houses of Memphis. Negroes serve as a mysterious, sinister chorus. Memphis is conjured vividly before the reader: "that long ragged line of old brick blocks—that rendezvous of niggers and thieves—the bad niggers, and the murderers and the nigger thieves." Then there are the sanctified Negroes, "The Hollering Saints," who are certain that the yellow fever is "the punishment of God acomin' down on Memphis." Individualized Negroes are Arabella, the faithful house servant, fanatically awaiting the coming of the Lamb; Make Haste Mose, the driver of the dead wagon, and a saddle-colored Negro with an immense scar, lying in wait to rob. All of these, according to the southern boy who tells the story, are unfathomable:

> All white folks knew was what they generally know about niggers—that bowing and scraping; those brown masks—those faces with all their muscles trained since the sin of Ham in the Bible; since they went out in slavery and subjection—to lie still and show nothing. And those old brown eyes, watching, watching.

Under the pen name of "George Madden Martin," Mrs. Atwood R. Martin wrote many stories of southern Negro life. "Her Husband" concerns a lynching. When Edith Thornberry, a white woman of gentle birth, discovers that her husband, a poor white, has reverted to type and led the lynchers, she is set against

109

him. She was "bracketed with those thousands of southern men and women who speak a universal language of decency," but her husband was bracketed with "a pusillanimous multitude, skulkers ever behind the decent South, lynchers, night-riders, white caps, Ku Klux." Unfortunate in its connection of heredity with decency, the story is still significant for the sharp protest of an intelligent southern woman against mob-violence. *Children of The Mist* (1920) decries the work of agitators upon Negroes, but is by no means merely Thomas Nelson Page brought up to date.

Stirrings of Realism.—When, at the turn of the century, authors showed a willingness to deal seriously with uneasy segments of American life, the Negro made his demand upon them. It is significant that most of the early figures prominent in the history of twentieth century realism dealt in some measure with the Negro. Among them are Stephen Crane, Upton Sinclair, Theodore Dreiser and Gertrude Stein.

Stephen Crane's work was generally too advanced for the sentimental readers of his age, and "The Monster" (1897) was particularly so. This story of horror lashes out at the stupidity and heartlessness of a small American town. Henry Johnson, a Negro hostler, rescues a small boy from a fire. Falling, overcome by the fumes in the burning laboratory, he has his face eaten away by acid. The boy's father, Dr. Trescott, exercises his best skill and keeps Henry alive. When Henry was thought to be dying, he was lauded as hero and martyr; but kept alive, a faceless imbecile, he meets with terror and hatred, among the better class as well as in Watermelon Alley. "The Monster" is more a sharp satire of a small town's intolerance than a study of Negroes, but it has secondary meanings that pertain to Negro life in what it tells of service, sacrifice, and false affection that goes

110

over into revulsion. The few pictures of Negro life here and in *Whilomville Stories* are done with the vividness to be expected from Stephen Crane.

Negro characters in Upton Sinclair's *The Jungle* (1905) are only incidental, but they are drawn in grim earnest. He shows Negroes as strikebreakers, brought into Packingtown from the levees or the country districts of the far South on promises of five dollars a day and board, with special rates from railroads. The harsh life of scabs makes them surly and dangerous; most of them have knives, ground to fine points, hidden in their boots. "Whiskey and women were brought in by the carload and sold to them, and hell was let loose in the yards." After the strike, these "green" Negroes, together with foreigners and criminals, are turned loose in thousands upon Chicago. This sketch of the Negro worker, denied admission to unions and thereby forced to the role of strikebreaker, anticipates much of present-day proletarian fiction.

Carl Van Vechten considers Gertrude Stein's "Melanctha" in *Three Lives* (1909) to be "perhaps the first American story in which the Negro is regarded . . . not as an object for condescending compassion or derision." "Melanctha" is a slowly unwound character study of a "subtle, intelligent, half-white girl, Melanctha Herbert," who "always wanted peace and quiet, and always she could only find new ways to get excited." Her chief love affairs are painstakingly set forth. The characters talk in a mannered dialogue; they all sound like each other, and like the white people in the other two stories. Gertrude Stein speaks of "the wide abandoned laughter that gives the broad glow to negro sunshine," but her major characters do not have it. The people she calls "decent," she likewise calls unmoral and promis-

111

cuous or shows them in razor brawls. White blood in one character "made her see clear," and gave "her grit and endurance and vital courage," but the power and breakneck courage in Melanctha came to her from her big black virile father. In spite of these dubious generalizings, "Melanctha" is important. Though not realistic in the usual sense, it gives a convincing portrait of a mysterious, uncertain girl, "wandering in her ways," doomed to tragedy, a Negro Madame Bovary or Esther Waters.

Setting out early to chart "tragic America," Theodore Dreiser wrote "Nigger Jeff" (1918) about a lynching. Dreiser does not make the Negro innocent, but he shows with somber power the mob hysteria in a town ironically called Pleasant Valley, the bravery of the sheriff, the horror of the captured Negro, and the final hanging to the bridge. And then he goes farther, to the mother and sister of the victim, and without sentimentality shows their grief. "I'll get it all in," exclaimed the young reporter who covered the case. And Dreiser got it all in, to make one of his best stories.

Again The Tragic Mulatto.—Two writers of some repute returned to the theme of the tragic mulatto. Less romantic than their predecessors, they still cling to old stereotypes. Margaret Deland's "A Black Drop" (1908) tells of Lily, who, although brought up in Nigger Hill, a section of a midwestern town, by Mammy, a fair Negro woman, "cushiony and weighing two hundred and fifty pounds," is considered white. Lily's love affair with Framely Stone, son of abolitionists, is broken up. Miss Wales, his New England Sunday School teacher, points out proof of the girl's Negro blood, clinching her case by mentioning her use of "heavy perfumery." Miss Deland believes that intermarriage is forbidden by disgust,

112

"a race protest, a race horror . . . organic, biological."
Instinct, it seems, revolts at intermarriage, but not at
liaisons. Confusing and unconvincing, "A Black Drop"
is still not entirely without sympathy and insight.

In the short story "Carter" (1921) Don Marquis
is likewise concerned with one of the many mulattoes
who in fiction tragically yearn "oh to be white, white,
white!" After "passing" for a short while in New
York, he returns to Atlanta, resolved to live and die
among Negroes. He arrives there at the time of a
riot, and witnesses "the conflict which was forever
active in his own nature." He is happy when he is
taken for a white man of the better class by his own
white half-brother, but is plunged into misery when,
dying, he is re-identified as "a yaller nigger." Carter's
abjectness, and the flattery of whites are laid on a bit
too heavily. Although the story abounds in clichés
about mulatto character, it does approach Negro life,
especially the Atlanta riot, with seriousness.

John Bennett's *Madame Margot* (1921) is the
legend of a golden Creole who, in order to keep her
ivory daughter from dishonor and betrayal, "to keep
her white to all eternity," sells herself to Satan.
Margot's sultry beauty turns to grotesqueness. As
old Mother Go-go, in the dirty Negro quarters, black
now instead of ruddy gold, she is claimed by the devil.
An other-worldly romance, *Madame Margot,* for all
of its imaginative remoteness, conveys something of
what women like Madame Margot knew in bitter
actuality.

Summary. The tendencies seen in this chapter are
diverse, ranging from the race-glorification of Negro
apologists to social realism by important American
novelists. At times, as in the case of the tragic
mulatto, the work seems conventional, but in the main
we notice that authors are beginning to take the Negro

113

seriously, revising earlier stereotypes, and breaking the ground for later realism. The work that they did is little known, but it is important in the evolution of the Negro character in American fiction.

DISCUSSION QUESTIONS

1. Why are the weaknesses of the Negro apologists to be expected?

2. Why do novels of the "talented tenth" fail to overthrow the plantation tradition?

3. Why are novels by southerners included in this chapter?

4. In what respects is Gertrude Stein's story traditional?

5. What similarities are in all of the stories of mulattoes written by white authors?

6. Compare DuBois, Chesnutt, and Johnson.

7. What is significant in the final quotation from *Hagar's Hoard?*

CHAPTER VIII

REALISM AND THE FOLK

Sociological Realism.—T. S. Stribling's *Birthright* (1922) brought something new in the treatment of Negro life. The novel looks back in its problem and its preaching, and has its share of superstitions about "race" such as that Negroes howl their agony aloud and white men bottle up their grief, and that "to a white man absolute idleness is impossible . . . he must . . . do something to burn up the accumulating sugar in his muscles." Peter Siner is not completely credible: a Harvard graduate, he comes back South talking like a dictionary, urging "autonomous development" of his people, and yet he is easily swindled by a white banker. His marriage to Cissie, light-fingered and ruined by a white lout, is strained, to say the least. His opposite, Tump Pack, is caricatured. But Stribling does protest against the southern belief that all Negroes are carefree and happy. His description of Negro lodges, funerals, and workaday life are authentic. Most important of all, *Birthright* places the Negro at the center of the picture, attempts to show the influence of environment upon character, is ironic at the vaunted southern understanding of Negroes, and attacks injustice. The following description is quite different from the pastoral shabbiness that delighted Ruth McEnery Stuart, E. K. Means, and Paul Laurence Dunbar:

> On the edge of Hooker's Bend, drawn in a rough semi-circle around the Big Hill, lies Niggertown. . . . The grimy cabins lean at crazy angles, some propped with poles. . . .

115

Up and down its streets flows the slow negro life of the village. . . . The public well itself lies at the southern end of this miserable street, just at the point where the drainage of the Big Hill collects. . . . [To this hole in soft clay, where occasionally pigs fall in and drown] come the unhurried colored women, who throw in their buckets, and with dexterity that comes with long practice draw them out full of water. . . . The inhabitants of Niggertown suffer from divers diseases; they develop strange ailments that no amount of physicking will overcome. . . . About once a year the state health officer visits Hooker's Bend and forces the white soda-water dispensers on the other side of the hill to sterilize their glasses in the name of the sovereign State of Tennessee.

Nigger by Clement Wood (1922) compresses a very great deal into its less than three hundred pages. This, too, is a sociological novel, picturing a Negro family from its origins in slavery to modern life in Birmingham. After freedom, Jake's burden of debt on his little place grows heavier each year. Forced to flee when white hoodlums run rampant on a periodic lynch-fest, Jake takes his seven grandchildren to Birmingham, to realize the "emancipation" he has heard of so often. But one son, Pink, dies in France, a hero; another, Louis, decorated in France for bravery is shot down by the law; Tom, embittered and violent, becomes a criminal, and Dave's love of learning is dulled by the steel mills. The daughters fare no better. The characters are completely convincing: the trustful Jake is balanced by Jim Gaines who kills a white man to defend his daughter. Reverend Elisha Kirkman—"who had seen slavery . . . was weazened and sharp-tongued and wise; black and white feared the sting that hung in his words"—is new in books about Negroes, but is not, because of that, unconvincing. Even the "bad Negroes" are not Dixon's brutes; having seen lynchings and the flagrant hypocrisy of the law, they are desperadoes through complete cynicism. Wood presents his characters with great knowledge and sympathy; the little family's anguished but doomed efforts to get along are tragically moving. There is

116

humor in the book, but it is mainly grim. Louis, called upon by white examiners to recite the Constitution before he can vote, orates Lincoln's Gettysburg Address. The examiner is amazed and half apologetic: "I'm damned. I didn' think you knew it . . . I didn' think any nigger knew it."

White and Black (1922) by H. A. Shands gives a realistic picture of Texas plantation life, where instead of kindly whites and affectionate uncles and mammies, there are landlords struggling to get money, and Negroes at work in the Johnson and Bermuda grass trying to get a bare living. Joe Williams, an aspiring Negro share-cropper tries to bring up his daughters decently and is almost frenzied when Ella is seduced by the planter's son. Ulysses Mulberry who "ain't done a thing except lay around ever since he's been back and has been runnin' me down to the niggers and stirrin' em up about the low wages paid on the farm, and jes' playin' the big Ike gen'r'lly," is lynched for outraging a poor-white girl, in a scene powerfully presented. Richard Sanders, the preacher, starts as a new character, forward-looking and thoughtful, if over-academic in his language, but ends up typically, finding his Bathsheba in a fast woman who affects penitence. The revived Ku Klux Klan is shown punishing Henry Thompson, a white man who openly acknowledges his Negro children, although its ranks are filled with men having clandestine affairs with Negro women. Shands has gleams of irony, but he does not let his sympathies develop to fullness, and his book therefore lacks drive. Dorothy Scarborough's *In The Land of Cotton* (1923) also deals with Texas, containing snapshots of Negro life and some fine folksongs, presented with the sympathetic approach of a folk-lorist. The picture is generally pastoral. Realistic pictures of Negroes in turpentine camps help to

117

redeem Vara Majette's *White Blood* (1924), but the melodrama of the swamp octoroon is still traditional and unconvincing.

South Carolina Folk. The work of Ambrose Gonzales, begun at the end of the last century but mainly accomplished in the nineteen-twenties, is an example of southern anecdotage. Gonzales writes as two people: one, intent upon pugnaciously defending the lost cause, and the other, keenly interested in the little dramas of the Gullah folk of South Carolina. *The Black Border* (1922) contains a passage on Thomas Nelson Page's failure to deal fully with Negro life, but this book and *The Captain* (1924) are merely extensions of works like Page's *Pastime Stories* and go in no new directions. The hunting and fishing, the marital irregularities, the hog and chicken stealing of the black-border Negroes are told with gusto, but hardships and tragedies are glossed over. Gonzales gets closest to realism in his care for the language. He has studied the Gullah dialect with so much zeal that the reader's task is uneasy. *With Aesop Along The Black Border* is a sly, witty rendition of the old fables into the odd speech; the following concludes "The Fox And The Grapes":

> Bumbye 'e git up en' 'e walk off, en' 'e walk berry sedate. Attuwhile 'e biggin fuh grin. 'E suck 'e teet, en' 'e say to 'eself, 'e say, "Me yent hab time fuh w'ary me bone en' t'ing fuh jump attuh no sour grape lukkuh dem. Soon es Uh smell' 'um Uh know dem *done* fuh sour! No, suh! Ef Uh haffuh chaw t'ing lukkuh dat, Uh gwine hunt green possimun. . . ." Buh Fox smaa't!

At the same time that Gonzales was publishing, DuBose Heyward, sensitive and sympathetic, was taking notes upon Negro life in Charleston to appear as *Porgy* (1925). This novel is rightly influential. In a poem at the outset Heyward pleads for "great hearts to understand." His characterization is admirable;

118

he knows a great deal, and he sees the pity as well as the laughter. His hero is Porgy, a crippled beggar, whose love for Crown's Bess regenerates her. The setting, Catfish Row, a squalid tenement; the saucer-burial scene, the spirituals and the folk-speech, the steamboat picnic, the furtive fear of the "white" law are conveyed with brilliant poetic realism. One of the best bits of writing is the description of the September storm when Catfish Row sends out its doomed riders to the sea. The finale of the novel, presenting a Negro as *tragic hero* is worth quoting:

> The keen autumn sun flooded boldly through the entrance and bathed the drooping form of the goat, the ridiculous wagon, and the bent form of the man in hard satirical radiance. In its revealing light, Maria saw that Porgy was an old man. The early tension that had characterized him, the mellow mood that he had known for one eventful summer, both had gone; and in their place she saw a face that sagged wearily. . . . She looked until she could bear the sight no longer; then she stumbled into her shop and closed the door, leaving Porgy and the goat alone in an irony of morning sunlight.

The same willingness to see Negroes as heroic is also in *Mamba's Daughters* (1925). "Libel on the South—nothing less than plain libel. . . . Who, in pity's name, from a section which is famous for its aristocracy, elected to go and hunt up Negroes to be sung about?" are the words of one of the novel's patrician ladies. Heyward so elects, giving us a heart-warming chronicle of two women, Mamba and Hagar, whose selfless devotion to Lissa transcends the usual characterization of Negroes. Mamba is the untraditional mammy: sly, ironic and ambitious for her own. Hagar, an illiterate and grotesque Amazon, attains nobility in her fierce laboring and fighting for her daughter. Lissa, who owes her career as a singer to Mamba's generalship and Hagar's sacrifices, does not reach the stature of these, but is nevertheless a new figure in the gallery of Negro characters. Heyward's setting—Catfish Row, the phosphate mines,

119

upper Negro circles striving for gentility, are conveyed with authenticity, if not finality. Despite a few incidents of exaggerated humor, such as Mamba's appropriating the Judge's false teeth, the tone is serious. The exploitation in the mines and the travesty of justice meted out to the Negro are dispassionately noted. Heyward's "The Half-Pint Flask" (1927), one of America's best stories of terror, is skillfully set against a background of Gullah superstitions, authentically handled.

Another South Carolinian, Julia Peterkin, is like DuBose Heyward in her intimacy with her material, and her dealing with Negroes as foreground *characters* and not as background *types*. Only occasionally do white people enter her narratives: here are Negroes seen in terms of their own quite important lives. Mrs. Peterkin, who is the mistress of a plantation like the "Blue Brook Plantation" of her fiction, insists about her Negro characters: "I like them. They are my friends, and I have learned so much from them." *Green Thursday* (1924) bore witness to the liking for these people. It is a simple and touching group of connected short stories. Kildee, the central figure, with his growing love for Missie; Rose, cross in her perplexity, but human; Maum Hannah who burned the new house of the "po' buckra" who was dispossessing her, all are pictured with tenderness and insight. Folk-beliefs and ways are set down without condescension; the speech is Gullah, but modified from Gonzales' phonetic transcriptions; and the description of natural scenery is done with beauty and originality. *Green Thursday* is, all in all, a minor classic.

Black April (1927) differs. Here the colors are stronger. Although the upbringing of the boy Breeze has the simplicity and poetry of *Green Thursday,* the other half of the novel is at times violently primitive.

In spite of the church, Blue Brook Plantation is amoral. The foreman, Black April, is a great man for working and fighting, and a greater for love affairs, his "outside" children far outnumbering what he calls his "yard children." The book furnishes a storehouse of folk-lore; long catalogues of signs and folk-cures alternating with scenes of hunting, fishing, fighting, conversion, and love-making. For all of its horror Black April's death scene approaches the heroic. Dying after his feet have rotted off from gangrene, he forces out these words:

> "Bury me in a man-size box—You un'erstan?. . . . I—been—six feet—fo'—Uncle—six feet—fo'!" The blaze in his eyes fell back, cold, dim. A long shudder swept over him. The tide had turned.

Scarlet Sister Mary (1928) won for Mrs. Peterkin the Pulitzer Prize. There is no denying the grasp of her material nor the power of certain scenes in this work and the succeeding *Bright Skin* (1932), but something just as noticeable is the increasing accent upon exotic primitivity. Sister Mary, abandoned by July, who is wild and footloose, becomes the scarlet woman of the quarters, having love-affairs and love-children with startling regularity. Mary's pagan freedom endears her to Mrs. Peterkin, who deplores Puritan hypocrisy. Nevertheless the book has lapses into condescension; "Unex" for "unexpected" is one of the children's names, and Mary has twins the same night that her unmarried daughter bears her child in a woodshed. This is belaboring with a vengeance. *Bright Skin* is not so concerned with the plantation birth-rate as with the death-rate, which is very high from violent causes. A quiet death in bed seems as unusual for these folk as for the ancient Anglo-Saxons. Mrs. Peterkin is much less sympathetic to Cricket, "the bright-skin," and to bizarre Harlem, than to Blue, the pure type Negro, and primitive Blue Brook.

What these two books leave suspect *Roll Jordan, Roll* (1933) brings out into the open. Acclaimed by her publishers as the "outstanding chronicler of the American black man's life," Mrs. Peterkin in this book advances trite generalizations that go back to *Swallow Barn,* contradicts her own evidence, and is more concerned with apologetics for white southerners than with revelations of Negro character. The picture she gives is one of Arcadian simplicity and happiness, away from the evils of industrialism. Negroes are superior to whites: "Better to be poor and black and contented with whatever God sends than to be vast-rich and restless." Since Negro school-children will come into their legacy of "ancient earthly wisdom" it is no tragedy that Negro schools are open only from harvest to planting time. Poverty, ignorance, disease and exploitation are lightly touched upon or omitted.

> Plantation days may be hard sometimes if *the moon gets contrary.* . . . Their stories and songs teach the children to look for victory from the disadvantages *to which life has sentenced them,* when death takes their souls to heaven. (Italics mine.)

The Negro's fear of the chain-gang is airily waved away: "Courtesy and kindliness are the law of the land." It does Mrs. Peterkin disservice to consider her *the* interpreter of *the Negro.* She is, instead, a plantation mistress who sees with sympathy and intimacy a few characters in a restricted segment of South Carolina, from a highly specialized point of view.

The recorder of another section of South Carolina, not so far off, has a different tale to tell. A slim volume called *Congaree Sketches* (1927) was immediately recognized as one of the most faithful representations of Negro folk life. The author, E. C. L. Adams, a physician of Columbia, S. C., kept out of the scene, and allowed his Negro characters to speak

122

for themselves. The result was neither sentimentality nor clowning. In a poetic dialect, Tad and Scipio and other spokesmen built up a most convincing picture of Negro life and character "down in de big swamps, down in de land of mosquito, down on de Congaree." There are folk-tales, sermons and prayers, but chiefly stories in dialogue dealing with dances, hot suppers, wakes, bootlegging, church services, farming, and the chain gang. The tone varies from rich comedy, such as that of the Hopkins Negro who throws heaven into an uproar, and of Ole Sister who does the same for hell, down to the restrained but powerful satires of southern justice:

> "Atter while ole man Hall walk up to Noah an' bus' him over de head wid er axe halve and beat him up . . . an' Jedge Foolbird axe ole man Hall what de nigger do . . . an' ole man Hall say 'He ain't do nuthin', but he look like he goin' say sumpin,' and Jedge Foolbird fined Noah one hunnerd dollars."
> Voice: "What did he do wid ole man Hall?"
> Perk: "He fine him fi' dollars. . . ."

Dr. Adams' second book, *Nigger to Nigger,* is fuller and even more forceful. The title suggests the method. Here Negroes are assumed to be talking to themselves, without any eavesdroppers, although the author reveals that he has listened closely, and has been privileged with confidences. As a result the humor is true folk humor, and the bitterness at social injustice is undiluted. There is fine laughter in "The Telephone Call," but most of the tales are tragic. "Fifteen Years" is the Negroes' brooding summary of the "Ben Bess Case" where a Negro, envied by white neighbors, was framed on a rape charge. "A Damn Nigger" is one of the harshest stories to come out of the new realism.

> Jake was a nigger. De judge were a kind judge—a good man —wuh ain' b'lieve in too severe punishment for white folks when a nigger is kilt, ain' matter wha' kind er white folks—And de solicitor wha' prosecute an' see dat de criminal git he full jues is a merciful man. An' he got great ideas er bein' light in punishment of dem white mens.

123

Some of the sketches deal with slavery, in a manner far removed from the plantation tradition. The unusual chorus of Tad and Scipio and their fellows reveals that though they may be unlettered, they are cynical realists, and are certainly not being fooled. When Reverend Hickman urges Christian forbearance he is met with taunts:

> Dere ain' no use. De courts er dis land is not for niggers. Ain' nothin' but for 'em but a gun an' a knife in a white man's hand, an' den de grave, an' sorrow an' tear for he people. De Bible say, "De Lord watcheth de fall of every sparrow," an' I says: "Why ain't He take He eye off sparrow an' luh 'em rest some time on bigger game?"

Nigger to Nigger gets more of the true picture of Negro life in the South than do most other books combined. And the picture, for all of Dr. Adams' mastering of humor, is not a pleasant one to linger over.

Acquainted with Gullah Negroes and dialect from their earliest days, Samuel Gaillard Stoney and Gertrude Mathews Shelby have retold in *Black Genesis* (1930) the charming fables of guileful Br' Rabbit and foiled Br' Wolf, short-tempered Br' Wasp, Br' Alligator, Br' Frog, Br' Partridge and Sis' Nanny Goat, together with free biblical reinterpretations of the creation of the world, of Adam, Eve, Cain and Abel, and the beginning of the race problem. In one of the best stories, Br' Rabbit pesters God for a longer tail; God assigns him difficult tasks to get rid of him. Smart and cocky, Br' Rabbit turns up again with his tasks completed, surprising and throwing God out of patience:

> 'Bout dat time, God in de Big House look out de window to see how dat t'under an' lightnin' he send fix dat bowdacious Br' Rabbit, so he won't be pesterin' roun' no mo'. An' he see a little somet'ing jis' a-skeedaddlin' down de Abenue . . . He lean out de window, an' he put he two hands to he mout', an he holler: "Ah-hah! Ah-hah!! AH-HAH!! You so *drat* smart! Well, GIT A LONG TAIL YO'SELF!"

124

Folk of the Deep South. R. Emmet Kennedy speaks of the Louisiana Negroes he knows so well as "unlettered folk who have not lost the gracious charm of being natural: wonderfully gifted and fairly tingling with poetic tendencies." His enthusiasm accounts for good essays upon their music and their patois. But *Black Cameos* (1924), Kennedy's first book, is more marked by picturesque dialect and songs than by penetration into character. *Mellows,* a collection of folk "melodies" includes charming vignettes of life along the dusty roads of the delta.

In *Gritny People* (1927) Kennedy goes deeper. His aim is to portray a community opposite New Orleans. The plan is an old one: people of different types gather at old Aunt Susan Smiley's cook-shop, and tell their stories, or are told about. A cross section of rural life results: there is tragedy as well as comedy, and the life-story of Gussie is especially moving. *Red Bean Row* (1929) is an episodic novel; Kennedy's abilities, like those of earlier local colorists, seem best fitted for the short story. The narrative is partly a satire of a philandering elder, and a traditional story of old Gramma Veenia's devotion to a weakling white man of "quality." Kennedy faithfully conveys a way of life. Here and there he shows the injustices of the section; the fire company is indifferent to the burning Negro shanty, and one woman speaks almost like Dr. Adams' Tad: "But white folks has a seecut way of handlin' the law to suit their own mind, and a poor simple nigger has to take just what comes along." All in all, however, *Red Bean Row* does not match *Gritny People.*

With a Negro for a nurse and Negroes for playmates, having paid devoted attention to Negroes in the fields, in the levee camps, on the river, in church, at picnics and funerals, Roark Bradford is, as his

125

publishers state, amply qualified to write about the Negro. Their further assertion (duplicate of her publishers' claim for Mrs. Peterkin) "that Roark Bradford is perhaps better fitted to write of the southern Negro than anyone in the United States" is hardly attested by his work. In a foreword to *"Ol' Man Adam An' His Chillun"* (1928) Bradford repeats the platitudes about Negro character that have been used to sanction injustice since proslavery days. There is no indication from later books that Bradford has changed: his Negroes are nothing but easy-come, easy-go children, creatures of laughter and of song. What other observers have recorded, Bradford, for all his wide experience, has not yet seen.

Ol' Man Adam An' His Chillun is rip-roaring burlesque, a book of tall tales told by an imaginative humorist in the fine tradition of Mark Twain. A mythical preacher of the old school brings Biblical stories down from heaven to the realistic setting of the delta:

> Well, a long time ago things was diffrunt. Hit wa'nt nothin' on de yearth 'cause hit wa'nt no yearth. And hit wa'nt nothin' nowheres and ev'day was Sunday. Wid de Lawd r'ared back preachin' all day long ev'y day. 'Ceptin' on Sadday, and den ev'ybody went to de fish fry. . . . So one day ev'ybody was out to de fish fry, eatin' fish and biled custard and carryin' on, to all at once de Lawd swallowed some biled custard which didn't suit his tase. . . .

For all the truth to idiom, this is obviously not Negro religion. The difference between the personified God in the spirituals, and God with a fedora upon his head and a ten-cent segar in his mouth should be apparent to anyone in the least familiar with Negro believers and their dread of sacrilege. *The Green Pastures,* suggested by *Ol' Man Adam An' His Chillun,* did something toward getting reverence and awe back into the material, but here it is pure farce. *King David*

126

and the Philistine Boys (1930) repeats this formula, with flagging powers.

This Side of Jordan (1929) is naturalistic local color. Elder Videll, muddy-colored like the river (Bradford does not like mulattoes), is a lustful villain. He is killed by Scrap in a scene that sheds more light on Bradford than on Negro character: "The blade of a razor flashed through the air. . . . *Her Negro blood sent it unerringly between two ribs. Her Indian blood sent it back for an unnecessary second and third slash."* One surmises that her refusal to be chilled with horror might be attributed to her Esquimo blood. *John Henry* (1932), for all of its amusing folk-speech and lore, belittles the hero. He is changed, not for the better, from a steel driving railroad man to a cotton-toting roustabout, from a great working class hero to a woman's fool. Bradford has taken undue liberties with folk stuff of dignity and power. The best of Bradford's many short stories have been collected in *Let the Band Play Dixie* (1935). Some, like "Child of God" have ingenuity and tenderness, others are first-rate folklore and mule-lore, and some show exotics in honkey-tonks going native with a vengeance. The characterization is conventional; for all of his comic genius, Bradford too often merely brings the plantation tradition up to date.

In 1928, Howard Odum, one of America's leading sociologists, turned to fiction. Dr. Odum had already interpreted the Negro in his collaboration with Guy Johnson on *The Negro and His Songs* and *Negro Workaday Songs. Rainbow Round My Shoulder* is an attempt to render fiction sociological. The hero, Left Wing Gordon, is a garrulous roustabout, rambling from job to job, and from one teasing brown to another. Left Wing Gordon tells us of his boyhood, his work-life, his love-life, his "jamborees." Vividly

127

written passages interpret the experiences. There is no gainsaying the thorough grasp of the material, nor the picaresque fascination of its handling. The book is so crammed with folk-sayings and blues, however, that it seems "made-up," and both story and hero get lost. Nevertheless, *Rainbow Round My Shoulder* is a valuable case study, done without flattery or concern for delicate feelings, white or black, humorous without being minstrel, tragic without being sentimentalized. And Left Wing Gordon is one of the best folk-characters of recent realism.

Wings On My Feet (1929) takes Left Wing overseas in the World War. It is told in the same racy idiom, as authentic as thorough investigation can make it. One of the few treatments of the Negro in the war, it is valuable for what it shows of a stevedore's reaction to Armageddon. It is a compound of humor, pathos, and tragedy.

> Me an' war same thing. Want me to fight; I been doing it all my life. . . . White buddies mighty funny, too, sometimes. Sometimes we sorry for 'em, sometimes we jes' have to laugh at 'em. Sometimes we don't keer if some white boys, meaner'n devil, have hard time, Lawd, we don't keer, Lawd we don't keer. Been treatin' us wrong, been hard on colored soldiers. White men been fightin' colored man. Now fightin' selves. . . . Boys laugh at 'em cause didn't want salute officers. Colored soldiers salutin' all time. . . . Maybe war got him, didn't get me. He's big captain an' I'm high private in rear rank, but I gets there just the same. . . . Buddy so worried in mind. Germans got him, blowed him clean to pieces. Wa'n't necessary for him to go but nobody couldn't tell him nothin'. He wus gonna save little child. And so he gave his life for little French child. Made me sad an' I kept hollerin', "Say, Buddy, is you hurt, is you killed?" Knowed he wus but jes' kept hollerin to him. . . .

Cold Blue Moon (1931) is the last and least of this trilogy dealing with Left Wing Gordon. In this book the hero is among the stable boys in a shed, telling ghost stories. When his turn comes, he launches, great tale-teller that he is, into a series of legends on the Old South. Some of them dispute the plantation tradition, but in the main they run true to what Odum has called the Grandeur that Was, and the Glory that Was Not. Left Wing is not at his best in these: he is too far from the center of the picture.

One of the best twentieth century examples of the Uncle Remus tradition is John B. Sales' *The Tree Named John* (1929), a collection of Mississippi folklore in authentic dialect. Aunt Betsey plants an elm tree—a quick budder, a fast grower and tough—as a name tree for the grandchild of Ole Miss. Then she presides over his upbringing, giving him lessons in folk-cures, nature study and in "spe'ence" ("whut you gits w'en you won't larn by lis'enin to whut de old folks tells you"). She and Aunt Polly and Uncle Alvord tell him tales of animals of old days. One story, "Ghos'es," is a bitter story of a master who was kind until he got drunk, when he became vicious. But *The Tree Named John* stresses the affection between the white family and its servants, and "the better and gentler side of the Negro . . . a phase of Negro life which is fast being swallowed up in the 'Harlem movement.' "

In his *Juneteenth* (1932), J. Mason Brewer is likewise concerned "about how unrepresentative of his people in the South and Southwest the loudly-heralded Negro literature of Harlem is—how false both in psychology and language." It is not clear why one should expect the treatment of Harlem to be representative of Brazos Bottom. One of the first collections of old-time tales by a Negro, *Juneteenth* is generally amusing. In a few tales the tables are turned on old "Massa," but there are none so harsh as Sales' "Ghos'es" or the memories of slavery found in E. C. L. Adams. A few good additions to the Brer Rabbit cycle, and some interesting folk-tales called "White Man's Nigger: I," "White Man's Nigger: II," "The Tale of the Stud Nigger" and "Railroad Bill" are

129

included in Carl Carmer's *Stars Fell on Alabama* (1934) which, true to its title, concentrates upon the strange and mysterious. Vincent McHugh's *Caleb Catlum's America* (1937) brings Uncle Remus and John Henry together with American folk-heroes in a fine yarn.

Summary. Whether sociological realism or folklore or partaking of both, the books considered in this chapter have been marked by a close and often sympathetic study of the Negro. Even in the case of Bradford's comics and Julia Peterkin's exotics, authenticity has been carefully sought. This regard for realism, even when incomplete, has meant the discarding of traditional estimates. Occasionally as in Wood and Heyward, and especially in Adams, concern for complete truth has resulted in the recording of tragedies which no Negro folk group, however isolated, has been so fortunate as to escape. With new information and insight these authors have brought the Negro into the mainstream of American realism.

DISCUSSION QUESTIONS

1. Trace the growing criticism of the South in this chapter. What is significant about this?

2. How does the place of the Negro in the picture in this chapter, differ from his place in the work of Kennedy, Page, Harris, Cable and Twain?

3. Compare Harris and Adams in their treatment of the folk.

4. Which authors seem closest to the plantation tradition?

5. Read Bradford's "Foreword" to *Ol' Man Adam and His Chillun* and relate to Thomas Nelson Page.

6. Compare the authors of folk-realism with the apologists of the preceding chapter.

CHAPTER IX

THE URBAN SCENE

The Harlem School.—Before 1925 there was
little in American fiction about Negro life in northern
cities. But when "the peasant moved cityward" in
the great sweeps of migration, books about the urban
Negro multiplied. The numbers of Negroes in northern cities grew by leaps and bounds from 1916 on.
Although various cities beckoned—Pittsburgh with
its steelmills, Chicago with its stockyards, Detroit
with its automobile factories—it was Harlem that
became the Mecca for the southern Negro, the West
Indian, and the African. One historian of Harlem
states that it contains more Negroes to the square
mile than any other spot on earth. Harlem became
a Mecca likewise for white pleasure seekers from
downtown and abroad, who, hunting the new thrill
with the desperate eagerness of the post-war generation, rushed to what they considered a place of primitive abandon, of unfailing "joy of life." Cabarets
sprang up like mushrooms; putting on a big time became a major industry. In revolt against Victorian
prudishness and repression, and machine-age stand-
ardization, writers and artists escaped to dark Harlem
for vicarious joy, and discovered an "exotic, savage
world," only a nickel's subway ride from the heart of
an over-civilized city. The Harlem Boom was useful
to Negro writers, who were influenced by the growing
race-consciousness of the "greatest Negro city in the
world." Some accepted the downtown version of
pagan Harlem as gospel, others put in disclaimers, but
all made eager contact with the literary world.

131

Carl Van Vechten's *Nigger Heaven* (1925) was the first novel to exploit this newly discovered territory, and has remained the most influential. The author, already known for sophisticated fiction, was attracted by the high spirits and piquant contrasts of Harlem. Running through the descriptions of cabarets, wild parties, and sensational orgies is the story of Byron, an "intellectual" wastrel. He is loved by Mary, a girl superior to the fast set, but he cannot resist the wiles of Lasca, "a gorgeous brown Messalina of Seventh Avenue." Byron's character cracks under the strain of fast living. His last gesture is one of typical futility: in a fit of jealous and drunken rage, he empties his gun into the body of his rival, who was already dead, while the police approach.

Nigger Heaven presented a setting and type of life that were little known to American fiction except for *The Autobiography of An Ex-Colored Man*. The gin-mills and cabarets, the kept men and loose ladies of Harlem's bohemian fringe, have surface accuracy and the appeal of the unfamiliar. Van Vechten in a short space of time observed closely. But like a discoverer, he was partial to exotic singularities. That these exist does not validate the claim of the publishers that "Herein is caught the fascination and tortured ecstasies of Harlem. . . . The author tells the story of modern Negro life." Modern Negro life is not in *Nigger Heaven;* certain selected scenes to prove Negro primitivism are.

Claude McKay's *Home To Harlem* (1926) has for its setting the speak-easies, buffet flats and "tonsorial parlors" of a pagan Harlem. The characters are longshoremen, dining car cooks and waiters, and members of sporting circles. Casual love affairs are their main pursuits. Jake, an ex-soldier, recently returned from the World War, meets and loses a marvelous brown charmer on his first night in Harlem. His picaresque adventures and those of his cronies take up the rest of the book, until he finds the long-lost beauty at the end. Working conditions on the railroad are described with some grimness, but *Home To Harlem* lacks McKay's sharpest protest. McKay's nearest approach to his poetry is in the ecstatic worship with which Jake looks upon the abandon of the gay Mecca.

McKay's *Banjo* (1929) is related to the Harlem school of fiction, describing the life of stevedores, tramps, sailors and panhandlers in the "Ditch" at Marseilles. Ray, a vagabond intellectual from *Home To Harlem,* does much of the talking; savoring color, joy and beauty wherever he finds it, he is attracted to the primitive and violent longshoremen.

> Educated Negroes ashamed of their race's intuitive love of color . . . ashamed of Congo-sounding laughter, ashamed of their complexion (bleaching out), ashamed of their strong appetites. No being ashamed for Ray. Rather than lose his soul, let intellect go to hell and live instinct!

To Ray, "A black man, even though educated, was in closer biological kinship to the swell of primitive earth life." Anti-bourgeois and anti-imperialist, seeing the "civilized world" from the bottom, Ray is nevertheless a racialist, not a radical. And such, in *Banjo,* is the author's position. He has been praised for dealing with the proletariat, but the beachcombers here can hardly be so considered. It is hard to see how reliance upon instinct will improve the lot of the submerged and the defeated.

The Harlem stories in *Gingertown* (1932) return us to blues singers, "sweet backs," entertainers, longshoremen, railroad men, barbers, chambermaids, bellhops, waiters and beautiful "brownskins." All of these are called by McKay the "joy-lovers" of the belt, but their stories do not reveal great joy. In "Brownskin Blues" and "Mattie and Her Sweetman" McKay

133

bitterly scores color prejudice among Negroes themselves; in "Highball" he scores prejudice among the whites. "Near-White" tells conventionally of the unhappy "passer." In "Truant," a dining car waiter, married to a social climber, throws up his menial job like a Sherwood Anderson hero. The stories are done with unabashed realism, but they do not cover a wide range.

McKay's stories of his native Jamaica in *Gingertown* and his third novel *Banana Bottom* (1933), though realistic, have a pastoral quality. A setting and way of life are skillfully and affectionately conveyed in both books and we are spared preachments on "the problem." In *Banana Bottom* especially, character development is uppermost. The story of Bita Plant, educated in England, is simple and winning. Minor characters. like Squire Gensir, Jubban, Anty Nommy and Crazy Bow are memorable, not idealized, but emerging with dignity and warm flesh-and-blood humanity.

Although these are perhaps McKay's best fiction, the greater part of his work deals with American Negroes, particularly in Harlem. McKay has denied that he was influenced by Van Vechten, stating that *Home To Harlem* was about completed before *Nigger Heaven* was published. There are points of agreement, however; McKay, like Van Vechten, believes in "the inexpressible exuberance and legendary vitality of the black race," and therefore seeks in the main the colorful aspects of "the joy-belt." There are differences as well. Having worked as dining car waiter, porter and longshoreman, McKay knew the unskilled Negro worker at first hand, not from an outside view. "I created my Negro characters without sandpaper and varnish." Because of this, his people are not the quaint, artless innocents endeared

134

to so many authors and readers. They live hard lives, and are consequently hardened: they may be ignorant, but they are not naïve. In dealing with the urban worker, McKay opened a new field. But the Harlem he portrayed still seems too close to the Harlem of a popular literary fashion. And the "inner lives" he knows so well have not yet been shown with the depth of understanding that one might expect of Claude McKay.

Rudolph Fisher portrays Harlem with a jaunty realism. *The Walls of Jericho* deals with types as different as piano-movers and "race-leaders." The antics of Jinx and Bubber are first-rate slapstick, and though traces of Octavus Roy Cohen appear, most of the comedy is close to Harlem side-walks. Fisher is likewise master of irony. Miss Cramp, the philanthropist, who believes that mulattoes are the result of the American climate, is caricatured, but the picture of the Annual Costume Ball of the G.I.A. (General Improvement Association) is rich comedy of manners. He deftly ridicules the thrill-seekers from downtown who find everything in Harlem "simply marvelous." Satiric toward professional uplifters, *The Walls of Jericho* still has the New Negro militancy. Merrit is an embittered "New Negro"; he believes that the Negro should let the Nordic do the serious things, and spend his time in "tropic nonchalance, developing nothing but his capacity for enjoyment," and then take complete possession through force of numbers. Fisher likewise shows the spirit of racial unity between the "dicties" and the masses—"Fays don' see no difference 'tween dicky shines and any other kind o' shines. One jig in danger is ev'y jig in danger." It is significant, however, that the wrecking of a Negro's house in a white neighborhood is the work of a disgruntled Negro, the villain of the book.

But Fisher was less interested in the "problem" than in the life and language of Harlem's poolrooms, cafes, and barber shops. *The Conjure Man Dies* (1932), the first detective novel by a Negro, brings Jinx and Bubber back to the scene to help solve one of Harlem's grisliest murders. A high-brow detective, an efficient Negro police sergeant and an erudite doctor of voodoo are interesting new characters. The novel is above the average in its popular field and was followed by a Harlem tenement murder mystery solved by the same detective.

Before his untimely death, Fisher became one of the best short story writers of the New Negro movement. "The City of Refuge," containing a good description of the southern migrant's happy amazement at Harlem, and "Blades of Steel" are first-rate local color of the barber shops, dance-halls and cafes. "Vestiges" and "Miss Cynthie," for all of their light touch, have an unusual tenderness and fidelity to middle class experience. Fisher was an observer with a quick eye and a keen ear, and a witty commentator. At times his plots are too neat, with something of O. Henry's trickery. His Harlem is less bitter than McKay's, but it exists; and his realism, as far as it goes, is as definite as that of any of the numerous writers who took Harlem for their province.

In Countee Cullen's *One Way To Heaven* (1932), Sam Lucas, a one-armed gambler and vagabond, practices a racket around the churches, pretending to be saved at revivals and thereby collecting money. His testimony in a Harlem church converts Mattie, who falls in love with him. Alternately vicious and sentimental, Sam makes Mattie's life miserable until his pretended death-bed vision of salvation brings happiness to the religious girl. Mattie's working for Constancia Brown, an upper-class Negro, serves as an excuse to bring in the artistic-bohemian Harlem. Cullen's pictures of this set are almost cartoons. He lampoons the back-to-Africa movement, the philistines who form Book-Lovers' Societies, the public reciters and the extreme New Negro racialists. But Constancia, who refuses to "pass," speaks the New Negro creed:

> Enjoyment isn't across the line. Money is there, and privilege, and the sort of power which comes with numbers but as for enjoyment, they don't know what it is. . . . I have seen two Negroes turn more than one dull party, where I was longing for home and Harlem, into a revel which Puck himself would find it hard to duplicate.

The best part of the novel is the portrayal of the Negro church. This is fresher material, presented with understanding.

Purpose Novels. More realistic than his earlier fiction, *Dark Princess* (1928) by W. E. B. DuBois, is still part fantasy, and part mordant social criticism. As editor of the *Crisis,* DuBois had urged a union of the darker races of the world. *Dark Princess* is an allegory driving home the same message. In its last chapter Matthew Towns, the Negro hero, flies to his homeplace in rural Virginia where his wife, Kautilya, Her Royal Highness of Bwodpur, India, has just given birth to a son, Matthew or Madhu. The son is acclaimed "King of the Snows of Gaurisaukar, Grand Mughal of Utter India, Messenger and Messiah to all the Darker Worlds!" Kautilya explains:

> There had to be a Maharajah in Bwodpur of the blood royal; else brown reaction and white intrigue had made of it a footstool of England. If I had not borne your son . . . Bwodpur and Sindrabad, India, and all the Darker World [would have been lost.]

Less fantastic are the sections dealing with America, in which Matthew Towns meets with galling insults, lack of opportunity on every hand, and the smooth chicanery of Negro politicians. Two interesting characters are Perigua, a Negro anarchist, and Sara, a striving Negro woman, who plays the political game. There are plots and counterplots in the manner of E. Phillips Oppenheim. DuBois speaks of the novel as "rich and colored gossamer of a dream which the Queen of Faerie lent to me for a season." But the fusion of dream and social realism is not achieved; the novel falls between the two.

A prominent figure in the National Association for the Advancement of Colored People, Walter White has made use of the novel for social protest. *The Fire In The Flint* (1925) tells the tragedy of a better-class, aspiring Negro family in a Georgia town. Bob Harper kills two white men who raped his sister. Tracked down by a lynching mob, he shoots himself with his last bullet. His brother Kenneth, a promising young physician, is lynched in the ensuing hysteria for "assaulting a white woman" whom he had been called in to attend. *The Fire In The Flint* contains sardonic comment upon the backwardness of the South. The millhands of Factoryville have only "one strong conviction—the inherent and carefully nurtured hatred of the 'nigger'." Like the earlier apologists, White makes use of well educated heroes, avoids dialect in the main, concentrates the injustices of the South into fairly small compass, and has bitter contempt for the "cracker" and the Klan. But *The Fire In The Flint* has more of an impact than the earlier books on lynching.

Although Walter White's *Flight* (1926) describes the Atlanta riot, it is principally a novel about "passing." Mimi Daquin, a New Orleans octoroon of distinguished lineage, has an unfortunate love affair with an upper class Negro in Atlanta, and goes to the North. Seeking security for her child she marries a

138

white broker, but remains essentially unhappy. Her husband has no love for Negroes. Even as a child, Mimi had believed that Creoles of Negro blood had something "tangible, yet intangible . . . a warmth, a delicate humanness" that white Creoles did not have. As a woman, she believes that Negroes alone "can laugh and . . . enjoy the benefits of the machine without being crushed by it." A furtive trip to Harlem makes her wonder if her somber cynical white companions, "whose unhappiness shone through all they did or said," were worth the price she was paying. When she hears a great Negro artist singing spirituals, she is set free, and returns to her own.

Bourgeois Realism.—Continuing the earlier apologist tradition, with propaganda a little less direct, certain novelists have set out to prove the presence of a Negro upper-class, and to deplore the injustices of its lot. Their standards are bourgeois; they respect characters in ratio to their color, breeding, gentility, wealth and prestige. "Realism" is perhaps a misnomer, if these novels are judged by their plots, which are seldom very life-like; the realism is chiefly in the settings.

Gertrude Sanborn's *Veiled Aristocrats* (1923) reveals the type. The "aristocrats under the veil" are mulatto descendants of southern aristocrats—"the souls of worthy men and women caught by a mad fate in a prison of prejudice!" A sentimental white youth is brought into contact with these fine people, especially with Carr McClellan, a World War hero, and a great sculptor. Carr is beloved by the beautiful daughter of a white financier. At the right time she is revealed to be colored too, another "veiled aristocrat," so everything ends happily. There are many incredible coincidences. Though well-meaning, the author is still condescending. Her protest concludes lamely:

139

"Fact of the matter, most of us are not giving our colored brothers a square deal."

Zona Gale, introducing Jessie Fauset's third novel, states inaccurately: "Wherever the American Negro has appeared in fiction, only the uneducated Negro has been pictured." She is on surer ground when she writes that Negroes of education and substance "merit the awareness of their fellow countrymen." In her own foreword, Jessie Fauset reveals her bent to "the colored American who is not pressed too hard by the Furies of Prejudice, Ignorance, and Economic Injustice," and who has his own caste lines.

> As naturally as his white compatriot he speaks of his "old Boston families," "old Philadelphians," "old Charlestonians." And he has a wholesome respect for family and education and labor and the fruits of labor . . . sufficiently conservative to lay a slightly greater stress on the first two of these four.

There Is Confusion (1924) has as central characters Joanna Marshall, an ambitious dancer, whose "success and fame were instant," and Peter Bye, a brilliant, sensitive medical student. The home-life of middle-class Philadelphia receives some attention, but the love story receives far more. The "problem" is never far off. In a pageant, Joanna represents America. Forced by great applause to unmask, she speaks:

> I hardly need tell you that there is no one in the audience more American than I am. My great grandfather fought in the Revolution, my uncle fought in the Civil War, and my brother is 'over there' now.

Joanna refuses to marry a Negro whom she found "charming and sympathetic . . . [but] too white. She did not want a marriage which would keep the difficulties of color more than ever before her eyes." *Plum Bun* (1929) is greatly concerned with "passing." Believing that "the great rewards of life— riches, glamour, pleasure—are for white-skinned people only," Angela goes "over the line." After a disillusioning liaison with a rich white man, "which left no trace on her moral nature," she falls in love with Anthony Cross, and fears to reveal her secret. But love will find a way: he reveals that he too is of Negro parentage, "passing" because his father was lynched by a mob. So now they can marry, as in *Veiled Aristocrats*. The beautiful brown sister, for whom life has been evenly pleasant, likewise marries happily at the book's end.

The Chinaberry Tree (1931) is again concerned less with the unspectacular drama of the Negro middle class, than with the melodrama of the octoroon. The two heroines are illegitimate. Laurentine is the daughter of Aunt Sal and Colonel Halloway, who loved Sal devotedly but could not marry her. In contrast to Laurentine's love affair, there is a great deal of confusion in the life of Melissa, who is saved only in the nick of time from marrying her half-brother. There are valuable glimpses of Negro community life in Red Brook, the characters ranging from Mrs. Ismay, a Bostonian of "innate gentility," to young pool-room sports. But the complications springing from the "mystery of birth" make what could have been realism into old-fashioned romance. Olivia Cary, who dominates *Comedy, American Style* (1933) is obsessed by the need to be white, not out of shame for her blood, but because of the things which the white world possesses. She persecutes her husband and drives her daughter into a loveless marriage and her son to suicide. The bitter comedy of race-prejudice is ultimately blamed. With random flashes of power, *Comedy, American Style* is without satiric drive, and manages to be sentimental instead of tragic.

Jessie Fauset has been called by one critic the American woman most worthy "to wear the mantle of Jane

Austen's genius." This comparison is not apt: Jane Austen's satiric approach to her people and setting and her neatly logical plots are not evident in Miss Fauset's four novels. Miss Fauset is sentimental, and regardless of her disclaimers, is an apologist. She records a class in order to praise a race. Favorite characters are chauvinists, condemning "the dastardly American whites," believing that Negro blood is "the leaven that will purify this Nordic people of their cruelty and their savage lust of power." Having courageously set herself to chart the class of Negroes she knows, Jessie Fauset, at her best, succeeds in a realism of the sort sponsored by Willian Dean Howells. Too often, however, instead of typical Negro middle class experience we get the more spectacular "passing," and exceptional Negro artists and cosmopolitans. Miss Fauset has written:

> To be a Negro in America posits a dramatic situation. The elements of the play fall together involuntarily; they are just waiting for Fate the producer to quicken them into movement,— for Chance the Prompter to interpret them with fidelity.

But her novels rely too much upon Fate and Chance.

The Tragic Mulatto Passes For White. Nella Larsen's *Quicksand* (1928) covers a great deal of ground, from Georgia to Chicago, Harlem, Copenhagen, and finally a small southern town. Upper class Negroes are her main characters, and their snobbishness is revealed (both consciously and unconsciously). Helga Crane is buffeted about, but does not attain tragic stature. The attempt to reveal a self-centred, harassed personality is commendable, but is not helped by scenes like the one in which the sophisticated heroine attends a church meeting, and there, overwhelmed by the frenzy, begins to yell like one insane, and to weep torrents of tears. She felt "a supreme aspiration toward the regaining of simple happiness

142

. . . unburdened by the complexities of the lives she had known." In *Passing* (1930) Mrs. Larsen is anxious to set before us the refinement and good taste of wealthier Negroes. Clare, who "passes," is unhappy, and frequently visits Harlem. "You don't realize, you can't realize how I want to see Negroes, to be with them again, to talk with them, to hear them laugh." Says the author's spokesman, "they always come back." Discovered in Harlem by her Negro-hating husband, Clare falls from a sixth story window—death solves her problems. Her friend, Irene, who would not "pass," lives in contrast a happy, respectable life.

White novelists rushed into print with a different version. Vara Caspary's *The White Girl* (1929) and Geoffrey Barnes' *Dark Lustre* (1932) are so alike in essentials that they should be considered together. Both of the heroines are repelled by Negro life and Negro suitors. Both because of their exotic beauty become artistic models, and both have tragic love affairs with white men. In *The White Girl,* Solaria's secret is revealed by the coincidental appearance of her brown-skinned brother. Desperate, and believing that she is growing darker, she drinks poison. In *Dark Lustre* Aline's dilemma is solved by having her die in childbirth, but her whiter baby lives to continue "a cycle of pain." Both books advance the old superstitions. Solaria at a wild party is thus explained: "It was the colored blood in her, the heritage from some forgotten ancestor, that released these warm wild winds of passion." Aline is thus explained: "There was too much nigger in her to follow a line of reasoning when the black cloud of her emotions settled over it." It is all so sad.

Hallie Dickerman's *Stephen Kent* (1935), on the other hand, takes up the cudgel for her mulatto hero's superiority, but he is made too superior, winning prizes

143

and acting nobly at every turn. There is much mystery about "tainted blood," about the reappearance of colored blood "unto the third and fourth generations." A sympathetic plea for justice, *Stephen Kent* is still hard to credit. *Imitation of Life* (1933) by Fannie Hurst was well meaning, perhaps, but it, too, perpetuated old stereotypes. Peola longs to be white: "I won't be a nigger! I won't be a nigger!" Her black mother is philosophical about it: "It may be mixed up wid plenty of white blood . . . but thin out chicken gravy wid water an' it remains chicken gravy, only not so good." When Peola meets with problems:

> Lord git de white horses drove out of her blood. Kill de curse —shame de curse her light-colored pap lef' for his baby. Chase it, rabbit's foot. Chase de wild white horses trampin' on my chile's happiness. . . . It's de white horses dat's wild, a-swimmin' in de blood of mah chile. . . .

It is no wonder that, longing to be stable, Peola "passes" and marries on the other side. Delilah, with a "rambunctious capacity for devotion," is the old contented slave, brought up to date, worshipful of her white Miss Honey Bea, to whom her drudgery has brought wealth. The statement is clear: black Negroes, contented with serving and worshipping whites; mixed Negroes, discontented, aspiring, and therefore tragic. Alas, the poor mulatto!

We have thus seen that the mulatto who "passes" has been a victim of opposing interpretations. Negro novelists urge his unhappiness, until he is summoned back to his people by the spirituals, or their full-throated laughter, or their simple sweet ways. One of Wallace Thurman's characters says:

> My dear, you've been reading novels. Thousands of Negroes cross the line and I assure you that few, if any, feel that fictional urge to rejoin their own kind. . . . Negroes who can and do pass are so glad to get away they probably join the K.K.K. to uphold white supremacy.

144

But this is heresy: a mystical bond must be shown, the cutting of which produces grief, since the white world is "pallid and to be pitied."

White novelists insist upon the mulatto's unhappiness for other reasons. To them he is the anguished victim of a divided inheritance. Mathematically they work it out that his intellectual strivings and self-control come from his white blood, and his emotional urgings, indolence and potential savagery come from his Negro blood. Their favorite character, the octoroon, wretched because of the "single drop of midnight in her veins," desires a white lover above all else, and must therefore go down to a tragic end. The white version is nearly a century old; the Negro version sprang up recently. Both are examples of race flattery. Divided between conflicting attitudes, the poor mulatto finds added unhappiness in his interpreters.

In Opposition. But the idealism seen in the apologistic, the bourgeois, and the "passing" novels found a gleeful critic in George Schuyler, of the H. L. Mencken school of satirists. *Black No More* (1931) tells how Dr. Crookman discovers a drug that will turn Negroes white. Negroes rush to use it, even the chauvinists who had preached pride of race. Schuyler lampoons both sides, the professional "race-men" who were tremendous gainers from the "problem," and the spokesman of the Knights of Nordica who, though totally ignorant, discussed over the radio "anthropology, psychology, miscegenation, cooperation with Christ, getting right with God, and curbing Bolshevism. . . ." Telling blows are landed on statisticians, rhetorical windbags, pretentious strivers and hat-in-hand Negroes, but *Black No More* is farce rather than satire, in the last analysis—provoking more mirth than thought. It was, however, refreshingly different. *Slaves Today* (1932) is an attack upon the mistreatment of the natives in Liberia by the upper-class America-Liberians. Schuyler's narrative sketches in such magazines as *The American Mercury* are told with terseness and point.

Wallace Thurman is likewise the "devil's advocate" in his two novels. Emma Lou in *The Blacker The Berry* (1929) is another defeated heroine, not because she is an octoroon, however, but for precisely the opposite reason. Well-educated, she is unable to get suitable positions and social life because she is black. She goes around for a time with the "New Negro intellectuals," but is ill at ease with them. Scorned and rejected, she sinks deeper and deeper into drabness. Thurman thus puts his finger upon one of the sorest points of the Negro bourgeoisie, its color snobbishness, "its blue vein circle," "aspiring to be whiter and whiter every generation." His descriptions of Harlem rent parties and the like are of Van Vechten's school, but the theme of his novel deserves attention. Unfortunately the writing is slipshod, and the steady decline of his central character is less tragic than depressing. His heroine is as morbidly sensitive about color as any tragic octoroon, and shows as little fight.

The Infants of The Spring (1932) shows Thurman taking less seriously his coterie of Harlem artists. Young in years and achievement, they flatter themselves as "a lost generation," and like Van Vechten's Byron, seek escape in dissipation. One cynical character speaks:

> Being a Negro writer in these days is a racket and I'm going to make the most of it while it lasts. I find queer places for whites to go in Harlem . . . out-of-the-way primitive churches, side street speakeasies and they fall for it. About twice a year I manage to sell a story. . . . I am a genius in the making. Thank God for this Negro Literary Renaissance! Long may it flourish!

Debunking the Bohemian futility of the intellectuals, Thurman is just as severe on the bourgeois idealists

146

and the various race-messiahs. *Infants of The Spring* is at times peevish, at times angry, crudely written, and not always well thought out. But like Thurman's first novel, it had something to say.

Black Sadie (1928) by T. Bowyer Campbell is an irritated southerner's attempt to debunk the Harlem that lured jaded Bohemians. From "corn-field nigger" Sadie rises to be model for the New Negro exaltation of *Africa victrix,* and the toast of artistic New York. Even in her affluence, however, Sadie is a kleptomaniac. After causing a murder, she returns to happy Virginia. "Easy come, easy go, niggers" are Campbell's closing words. Campbell's satire has point, but he is too vexed to get it across. It is obvious, also, that the stereotype he prefers is that of the comic menial.

Dark Surrender by Ronald Kirkbride (1933), after describing South Carolina plantation life in the manner of Julia Peterkin, delivers an attack upon the "New Negro." Having deserted a wife on the plantation, who promptly becomes a Scarlet Sister Mary, Tom goes to the North, graduates from Harvard with athletic and scholastic honors, visits Europe, and becomes a great poet. But he gives it all up as "imitation of the accomplishments of the white man," and returns to the soil. To the white owner of the plantation he states that Negroes

> who have aspirations and yearn to be great . . . are fools in the sense that they are not true negroes. . . . To live from day to day in simple enjoyment, with no cares nor worries, with no great attempts to be something which you are not . . . that is life, the true life. . . . The negro has his place in the present, in the simple life, with no desires but of the body, with no yearnings for the future nor for the past. . . .

Maxwell Bodenheim, with a naturalist's approach, could not see in Harlem only a place of joy-filled Negroes. In *Naked On Roller Skates* (1931) he shows the harsher, truculent aspects of Harlem dives. In *Ninth Avenue* (1926) he shows the seamy aspects

147

of Manhattan. His white heroine in this book marries a Negro, a better man than any of the Ninth Avenue set. Contrary to O'Neill's *All God's Chillun Got Wings* this intermarriage is not doomed to failure. In *Deep River* (1934) Clement Wood does not have the regret, disdain, or anxiety with which most southern novelists look upon Harlem and the "New Negro." This chronicle of the marriage of a noted Negro singer to a white woman is frankly done, exploiting a subject generally taboo. But it is hardly worthy to stand alongside Wood's earlier novel *Nigger*.

Summary. The fiction of urban realism was valuable for introducing new characters in a new milieu. Whether created by Negro or white authors, the characters are race-conscious, and at times militant. But the old stereotypes by no means disappeared. Carl Van Vechten has a noted magazine editor comment on the possibilities of Negro literature:

> Nobody has yet written a good gambling story; nobody has gone into the curious subject of the divers tribes of the region. . . . Nobody has ever done the Negro servant-girl, who refuses to live in. Washing dishes in the day-time, she returns at night to Harlem where she smacks her daddy in the jaw or else dances and makes love. On the whole I should say she has the best time of any domestic servant in the world. . . . The Negro fast set does everything the Long Island fast set does . . . but it is vastly more amusing . . . for the simple reason that it is *amused*.

Most authors took this to heart. What resulted was a search for the exotic and an insistence that Negroes were peculiarly marked by a "joy of living." Dance-halls, rent-parties, gambling, sprees, casual love-affairs crowded out more serious realism. The cabin was exchanged for the cabaret, but Negroes were still described as "creatures of joy." Even Negro propagandists urged this, seeking to find some superior "racial gift." To look for the true life of a Negro community in cabarets, most often run by white managers for white thrill-seekers, is like looking for the

148

truth about slavery in the off-time banjo-plunking and capers before the big house. Focusing upon carefree abandon, the Harlem school, like the plantation tradition, neglected the servitude. Except for brief glimpses, the drama of the workaday life, the struggles, the conflicts, are missing. And such definite features of Harlem as the lines of the unemployed, the over-crowded schools, the delinquent children headed straight to petty crime, the surly resentment—all of these seeds that bore such bitter fruit in the Harlem riot—are conspicuously absent.

Bourgeois realists did "apprise white humanity of the better classes among Negro humanity," but this is a value apart from the values of fiction. Their upper-class characters too often seem to serve as window-display. "Passing for white" is made a much more acute and frequent problem that it is in ordinary Negro middle class experience. With discerning satire, Martha Gruening sums up the argument of Negro bourgeois realism:

> I am writing this book because most white people still believe that all Colored People are cooks called Mandy or Pullman porters called George—but they aren't. They think we all live in cotton field cabins or in city slums, but actually some of us live on Edgecomb Avenue or Chestnut Street. We don't all shout at Camp Meeting or even all belong to the Baptist or Methodist church. Some of us are *Episcopalians.* If you were privileged to visit our homes (which you aren't, for we are just as exclusive as you are) you would find bathtubs, sets of the best authors and etchings! That's how refined we are. We have class distinctions, too. . . . The daughters of our upper classes are beautiful and virtuous and look like illustrations in *Vogue* . . . far more attractive than white girls of the same class, for they come in assorted shades. . . . Joy isn't on your side of the line, nor song, nor laughter.

There is certainly place in American fiction for treatment of the Negro middle-class. The precarious situation of this small group could well attract a realist of vision, not only to satirize its pretense, but also to record its dogged struggling. But to approve

149

it in proportion to its resembling white middle-class life, is not the way of important realism.

DISCUSSION QUESTIONS

1. What earlier fiction dealt with the Negro in northern cities?

2. How is the Van Vechten tradition similar to the plantation tradition?

3. List the authors who consider the Negro to be a "creature of joy."

4. Why have the novels of "bourgeois realism" been called "prospectuses to sell the white world the idea of a Negro middle class?"

5. Why are the opposing attitudes to "passing" examples of race flattery?

6. What northern cities with large Negro populations are as yet untreated by novelists?

7. What is race-chauvinism? Point out examples in the fiction discussed.

CHAPTER X

SOUTHERN REALISM

Mystics and Poets. In his *Notebook* (1926) Sherwood Anderson tells of a Mississippian who showed the ear of a lynched Negro as a symbol of "white superiority." Anderson seldom mentions such gruesome facts of Negro experience; like Van Vechten and Julia Peterkin he is attracted to the Negro's elemental exoticism. In "I Want To Know Why," the white hero is drawn to Negro jockeys, cooks and stable boys; in *Dark Laughter* (1925) Anderson himself is fascinated by the Negro's superiority to dull, standardized whites.

> Niggers on the docks, niggers in the city streets, niggers laughing. A slow dance is going on. . . . A brown woman having thirteen children—a different man for every child—going to church too, singing, dancing, broad shoulders, broad hips, soft eyes, a soft laughing voice. . . . Negroes singing had sometimes a way of getting at the ultimate truth of things.

This chorus of happy sensualists mocking repressed whites may explain "ultimate truth" to Anderson, but a great deal of truth about their lives escapes his penetrating interest. Harassed by Puritanism and industrialism, Anderson has found elements that bring him peace, rather than interpretation of a people.

Waldo Frank looks upon *Holiday* (1923) as his story of "one of the greatest of American dramas—the struggle in the South between the white race and the black . . . *each of which . . . needs what the other possesses."* Like his fellow mystic Anderson, Frank sees Niggertown to be full of warm song and happy, ironic laughter, free from the strain of money-making, repressed White-town. But he likewise sees insult,

151

exploitation and struggle. "Chokin' is de black man's life," says one old woman, who knows the South too well. The passive cruelty of White Nazareth is introduced when a Negro deckhand drowns and no one makes an effort to save him. We see the active cruelty when John Cloud, ambitious and manly young Negro, and Virginia, "weary of her whiteness," of being incessantly sheltered, step out from the pattern. In a spell of drought and revivals, John and Virginia meet by accident in the woods above Nazareth. Though "boss-girl" and "servant-man," they have been drawn from mutual respect into desire. When Virginia returns to Nazareth, the meeting is misunderstood, and the men, already whipped up by religious hysteria, quickly form a mob. Shocked from her dream of escape, Virginia sinks back into southern conventionality and half-remorseful inertia, and does not speak. At dusk, John is burned in the Square of Nazareth.

Frank sees that White-town, assuring itself that the "nigger will stay in his place," is still forever suspicious of "the muttering, the stirring." More boldly than others, Frank reveals what he considers the deepest cause of much of the fear:

> 'Good mo'nin . . . I have been walkin' by yo' side all of this street. An' yo' didn't see me.' He gives these words with a prophetic dryness. John feels the ominous threat. . . . *'I've watched you, nigger,'* they say, *'I've watched you lookin' at my daughter. How dare you look at my daughter? Nigger, that look in yo' eyes means murder in our land. How dare you nigger, look so hard at my daughter that you forget to salute the white man at yo' side?'*

When Virginia, who knows how free her brother is with Negro women, laughs at the "fanatical obsessions" of her men-folk, she adds flame to the tinder. Symbolic and difficult, *Holiday* is still a true, powerful and different version of race relations in the South. In *The Death and Birth of David Markand* (1933), however, the brief treatment of the Negro falls below the penetration of *Holiday*.

Deriving in part from Anderson and Waldo Frank, Jean Toomer's *Cane* (1923) has much greater intimacy with Negro life, dealing equally well with the black belt of Georgia and bourgeois Washington. Toomer is master of fluid, evocative prose; some of his stories are prose-poems.

> The sun is hammered to a band of gold. Pine-needles, like mazda, are brilliantly aglow. No rain has come to take the rustle from the falling sweet-gum leaves. Over in the forest, across the swamp, a sawmill blows its closing whistle. Smoke curls up. . . . Curls up and spreads itself pine-high above the branch, a single silver band along the eastern valley. A black boy . . . you are the most sleepiest man I ever seed, Sleeping Beauty . . . cradled on a gray mule, guided by the hollow sound of cowbells, heads for them through a rusty cotton field.

His faithfully portrayed Georgia landscape Toomer has peopled with faithfully drawn characters, such as Fern, the shiftless, ignorant beauty of the Georgia Pike, and Becky, a white outcast, who bears two Negro children. "Blood Burning Moon" tells of the rivalry between a Negro and a white man for a Negro girl, that ends in a murder and a lynching. Not propaganda in the manner of the apologists, it is tragic realism at its best.

Neither debunking Negro society nor glorifying it, Toomer pictures Washington with the thoroughness of one who knew it from the inside. The futile, and in the story of "Avey," the drably tragic revolt against the smugness of a rising middle-class, are brilliantly set before us. Toomer was sharply criticized by Negroes for his "betrayal"; his insight and tenderness seemed to escape them. "Kabnis" is a long, occasionally obscure story of a northern Negro teaching school in Georgia. No one has done so well as Toomer the hypocritical school principal, a petty, puritanical tyrant who truckles to the whites. Laymon, a preacher-

153

teacher who "knows more than would be good for anyone other than a silent man"; Halsey, a self-assured, courageous artisan; and Kabnis, a weakling idealist driven to cynicism and dissipation until he discovers, mystically, the strength of his people, are similarly well drawn. Toomer reveals in "Kabnis" an insight that makes his failure to write a novel about Negro life one of the undoubted losses of contemporary literature.

In another brilliant first book, *Tropic Death* (1926), Eric Walrond is as conversant with his native West Indian life as Toomer was with that of Georgia. Like Toomer he stressed the tragedy and pain in his milieu rather than the joy-of-living stressed by the Harlem school. Gifted with a power of description, Walrond gives us, for the first time, a vivid sense of Negro life in the tropics below the Gulf stream.

All of the stories deal with death, which to these peasants, sailors and workers does not come easily, but violently, often horribly. One child, in the droughts, eats marl; her stomach distended like "a wind-filling balloon." Another dies, poisoned by *obeah*. Two "wharf rats" who dive for the coins flung by bored tourists are killed by a shark. The approach is unapologetically naturalistic; life in the tropics is not pleasant to Walrond, and he has not idealized it. He seems completely familiar with the divers West Indian dialects and with his characters' ways of life, whether they are underpaid workers on the Big Ditch, or truck gardeners in Barbadoes, or waiters and cooks on the old vessels that plow the Spanish Main. "Subjection" tells of the murder of a Negro laborer by a marine, for interference when the marine was beating a sick worker on a road-gang. With the exception of this story, Walrond writes little of social protest. He

154

is sardonically aware of the way imperialism is made to work, but his chief purpose is to make the reader "see," to give him sense impression of a unique, interesting world. The prose of *Tropic Death* is sometimes overwritten, sometimes too oblique for clarity. But it revealed uncommon powers that, regrettably, Walrond has not used further.

Langston Hughes' first novel, *Not Without Laughter* (1930), one of the best by a Negro author, is set in a small Kansas town, a transplanted bit of the South. Sandy's mother, Annjee, works in the white-folks' kitchen and his grandmother, Aunt Hager, takes in washing so that Sandy shall have his chance, in spite of his irresponsible father, Jimboy. A life poor in the world's goods is shown to be "not without laughter": there are great colored tent meetings, carnivals, barbecues, dances, and guitar concerts by the beloved vagabond Jimboy. At their best, however, these enjoyments are poor reliefs from the day's hard work for the white-folks. Prejudice lies all around Sandy; going to the carnival on Children's Day, he is ordered away with "I told you little darkies this wasn't your party." For Sandy's pretty, joyful Aunt Harriet, there was nothing in Stanton after awhile but street-walking to the great grief of old, tired Aunt Hager. Excepting Aunt Tempy, who is sharply satirized as a hightoned striver, all of the characters are treated with sympathy. Here, done with poetic realism, is a good novel of boyhood.

God Sends Sunday (1931), the first novel of another Negro poet, Arna Bontemps, deals with sporting life at the turn of the century. Born on a Red River plantation, little Augie, a lover of horses, becomes a famous jockey in such racing towns as San Antonio, New Orleans, Louisville, and St. Louis. At the height of his fame he was "a treat to casual eyes."

"I'se gonna git me a two-gallon high-roller hat dat won't do.
Gonna git me a box-back coat an' a milk white ves' wid red
roses painted on it." . . . His high-roller had twenty naked women
worked in the eyelets in the crown. His shirts had two-inch
candy stripes of purple, pink, green or orange. . . . His shoes had
mirrors in the toes and dove-colored uppers with large pearl
buttons. . . .

Women flocked to him, especially Della and Florence,
whom he loved "worse than a horse loves corn." But
his luck turns, and Lil Augie says:

I ain't nobody. I ain't nuthin. I's jes a po picked sparrow.
I ain't big as a dime, an' I don't worth a nickel.

With all his bravado and vanity, Lil Augie is courageous as a bantam, always ready "to try anybody one
barrel." *God Sends Sunday* is not pretentious, but it
is a well-done portrait of a winning character.

Against Southern Charm. Three of the most intelligent women of the southern literary renaissance have
had their say about the South's vaunted charm. In
Elizabeth Madox Roberts' *My Heart and My Flesh*
(1927) the heroine discovers that she is half-sister
to Stiggins, a Negro stable boy, who is the half-witted
butt of the town, and to two Negro women. Frustrated and desperate, she turns more and more to
furtive companionship with her sullen half-sisters. The
incidental Negroes who work in boarding house
kitchens, or take in washing, or do the heavy manual
labor of the Kentucky town are far from the quaintly
funny folk of Irvin Cobb and Ruth McEnery Stuart.

A roughly similar situation appears in Isa Glenn's
A Short History of Julia (1928), an incisive attack
upon the upper caste South. While Julia is being
brought up as a hot-house plant, her servant Cynthia
has a full and loose love-life. Both end up unhappily,
with nothing to look forward to. Patty, one of the
most believable mammies in fiction, brings up her white
charges most decorously, but neglects her attractive and

156

rebellious daughter. Chivalry is summed up by Negro characters as "white women jes' lying and lying to theirselves." The aristocratic men-folk, old topers, who, untrue to one "southern tradition," often get drunk, declaim that "a pure and virtuous lady is the finest work of the Almighty." But they keep Negro mistresses, and, in their dotage, unlike the earlier gentlemen, "forget to cover up."

Emily Clark's *Stuffed Peacocks* (1927) is affectionately ironic toward the F. F. V's. In "Chocolate Sponge," a servant calmly states that she is a lady, because her grandfather was Colonel Ashton Wycherly. Since Negroes did not usually mention such facts, she is "frightfully uncomfortable to have around." In spite of the mask of servility, which the cleverest house-servants "are careful never to let slip," there are others who produce discomfort. Mammy Sally

> had been separated, as a young woman, from her first husband, whom she loved, and transplanted in another country. . . . Her ancient eyes were inscrutable and not altogether pleasant when she was questioned about it.

Similarly aloof, unconventional and forbidding are two other mammies, who disdain both Negro hilarity and white sentimentality. In "Fast Color," a Negro butler, almost a "stage darky," kept his thoughts carefully guarded. Knowing Negro servants in "their dining-room work, the most gracious form of labor," Miss Clark likewise knows that "their swiftest and simplest ways to impromptu gratuities" are not their only ways.

Regionalism. Less ambitious than the mystics and less probing than the critics of southern caste, a number of regionalists have followed the lead of DuBose Heyward, Howard Odum and Julia Peterkin. Nearly a decade ago a southern critic wrote that "the southerner has had to turn to the Negro when he wanted to paint life as it is"; and although less pertinent today, this partly explains the rush to describe the Negro. Many had new stories to tell, and they told them honestly and sincerely; many others offered twice-told tales. Their coverage of the South is widespread, and to follow them from Virginia to Louisiana is as good a plan as any.

Pernet Patterson's *The Road to Canaan* (1931), a collection of eight stories, deals with Negro life in Richmond and the nearby country. Some are farcical, as the story where a visiting anthropologist, seeking to measure heads, spreads terror; some are pathetic. "Conjur" is a good tale of black magic; "Shoofly," one the best, re-creates life in a tobacco factory; and "Buttin' Blood" tells convincingly of the friendship of white and Negro boys. With no social protest and more than a trace of condescension, often engineered to end happily, Patterson's stories still show understanding.

Paul Green's few sketches of Negroes in *Wide Fields* (1928) do not have the power of his plays of Negro life, but they are sympathetic and true. There is bitterness in the stories of Arthur Loring, humble and hardworking "synonym for what the white folks thought Negroes ought to be," and of Lalie Fowler, the mother of a child by a white farmer. Hardworking tenant farmers, "flash" sports and bad men are convincingly shown in this book as well as in Green's novel *The Body of This Earth* (1935). It is significant that Green made over a story of poor-whites into a Negro farce, *The Man Who Died At Twelve O'clock,* with hardly any changes in idiom, characterization, and incident. A different Carolina locale and type of life are in R. H. Harriss' *The Foxes* (1936), a good hunting novel which includes well described Negro stable-boys, dog trainers, and old servants.

South Carolina. A new locale of South Carolina and a new type of people are discovered in *Po' Buckra* (1930) by Gertrude Shelby and Samuel Stoney, the authors of *Black Genesis.* In a community of quality white folks, "crackers," Negroes and "Brass-Ankles," Barty attempts to rise out of the last despised group, a mixture of Portuguese-Indian-Negro and American white stocks. But suspicion and gossip dog him about, and he becomes a drunkard and murderer. Minor Negro characters are well handled.

But where the authors of *Po' Buckra* stand on their own feet, Mrs. L. M. Alexander in *Candy* (1934) seems to lean heavily upon Julia Peterkin. Trouble visits only rarely the love-free, carefree pagans of Mimosa Hill Plantation, and then it is such trouble as jealousy. *Candy* won a ten thousand dollar prize. *Don't You Weep, Don't You Moan* (1935) did not win a literary prize, but it did win for its author, Richard Coleman, the distinction (bandied about by so many publishers) of being one who in a single book presented "the true Southern Negro." Needless to say Coleman approves the old dogmas such as "A nigger . . . like de cotton fiel' bettuh den any othuh place in de worl'. . ." and omits from his novel of exotic primitives any mention of insult and injustice.

Florida. Unlike Mrs. Alexander and Coleman, Zora Neale Hurston has no need to rely upon either DuBose Heyward or Julia Peterkin. Her short stories "Drenched With Light," "Spunk" and "The Gilded Six Bits" showed a command of folklore and idiom excelled by no earlier Negro novelist. *Jonah's Gourd Vine* (1934) recounts the rise of handsome, stalwart John Buddy from plowboy to moderator of the Baptists of Florida. But his flair for preaching and

159

praying is exceeded by his weakness for women; even when he is married to the devoted Lucy who is "pretty as a speckled pup," he still cannot hold his straying feet. His fall is as abrupt as his rise. Loosely constructed, the novel presents authentic scenes of timber camps, railroad gangs with the "hammer-muscling men, the liars, fighters, bluffers and lovers," and the all-colored towns of Florida. The folk-speech is richly, almost too consistently, poetic. The characters are less developed than the setting; and the life they live is self-contained and untroubled. Nevertheless, *Jonah's Gourd Vine* contains the stuff of life, well observed and rendered.

A trained anthropologist as well as a native of Florida, Zora Neale Hurston has made in *Mules and Men* (1935) the first substantial collection of folktales by a Negro scholar. Zestful towards her material, and completely unashamed of it, she ingratiated herself with the tellers of tall tales in turpentine camps, or on store porches, and with the preachers of tall sermons in backwoods churches. Whether of the folk hero John, or of Brer Dog, Brer Snail, and Brer Gator, or of more contemporary people and activity, Miss Hurston's "big old lies" are a delight to read. Miss Hurston writes:

> The Negro, in spite of his open-faced laughter, his seeming acquiescence, is particularly evasive. You see we are a polite people and do not say to our questioner: 'Get out of here!' We smile and tell him or her something that satisfies the white person, because, caring so little about us, he doesn't know what he is missing. . . . 'He can read my writing but he sho' can't read my mind.'

Unfortunately, *Mules and Men* does not uncover so much that white collectors have been unable to get. The tales ring genuine, but there seem to be omissions. The picture is too pastoral, with only a bit of grumbling about hard work, or a few slave anecdotes

160

that turn the tables on old marster. The bitterness that E. C. L. Adams recorded in *Nigger to Nigger* is not to be found in *Mules and Men*.

Miss Hurston's second novel, *Their Eyes Were Watching God* (1937) is informed and sympathetic. After unfortunate marriages—the first husband, a grubbing farmer, looked like "some old skull-head in de graveyard," and the second was intent only upon being the "big voice" in Eatonville—Janie Sparks is whirled into an idyllic marriage with high-spirited Tea Cake. There are good sketches of the all-colored town where comic-serious debates and tall tales are told on the mayor's store porch. But the love story and the poetic folk-speech are the chief interests. The people, "ugly from ignorance and broken from being poor," who swarm upon the "muck" for short-time jobs, do not get much attention. Life in the all-colored town is fairly easy, with enough money and work to go around. Here and there social protest is evident: in the aftermath of the hurricane the conscripted grave-diggers are ordered to make sure of the race of the victims, since the whites are to get pine coffins, and the Negroes, quick lime.

> They's mighty particular how dese dead folks goes tuh judg-ment. Look lak they think God don't know nothin' 'bout de Jim Crow law.

The pine barrens and the swamps of Florida are the setting of Edwin Granberry's *Strangers and Lovers* (1928) in which the mutual hostility of the Negroes and "crackers," the brutality and the violence are skillfully detailed. In Theodore Pratt's *Big Blow* (1936) a poor white girl who lives by herself in the waste-land is protected by Clay, a giant Negro. When a "cracker" forces his attention upon her, Clay saves the girl, apologetically but firmly. "The "cracker" is astounded that Clay has "put hand to a white man."

161

Clay is strung up by a mob, and it is only by the greatest luck that he is saved.

Georgia. In *Glory* (1932), Nan Bagby Stephens, dealing with Negro life in a small southern Georgia town, is as intimate as Julia Peterkin with Negro speech and folkways. But her people, not the unmoral pagans of Blue Brook plantation, are earnest, self-reliant workers, in whose lives the church plays a very important part. The new minister, though not an Elmer Gantry, brings grief to the community by seducing Leah, one of the finest girls of his congregation. Roseanne, her sister, in a melodramatic scene confronts him with news of the girl's death, and revenge is swift. Although the seduction scenes are unconvincing, the setting and characters are well drawn. Roseanne, shrewd about human nature until hypnotized by the preacher, is like Heyward's Mamba and Hughes' Aunt Hager, laboring and sacrificing so that the young will have a chance. Other characters are interesting: the railroad men, the charcoal peddler, the hair-dresser who says, "I puts 'em in and I takes 'em out," meaning that she marcels on one side of the railroad tracks and straightens hair on the other. And the Ladies Aid Society, pathetically caring for their little church and worshipful of the preacher, is much more representative of Negro religion than the usual scenes of revival frenzy.

Death Is A Little Man (1936) by Minnie Hite Moody likewise deals with a hard-working, sacrificial heroine of strict morality who, living in the Atlanta Bottoms, has more than her share of trials and tribulations. The overfrequent violence becomes melodramatic, much that affects the life of the Bottoms is left out, and Fate is blamed too often. But the insight into character, the true local color and the skillful prose, entirely in the cadence and idiom of southern

162

Negro speech, bear witness to an informed and sympethetic observer.

The Black Belt. Earth Born by Howard Snyder (1929) records the superstitions, songs, dances and church services of tenant farmers in the cotton belt. Parson Robinson, the Negro plantation owner, the wanton Malindy, her lover Big Jim Mississippi, and the violence and loose love making of an isolated community, are in the tradition of Julia Peterkin. So is *Ollie Miss* (1935) by George Wylie Henderson, the first Negro novelist to deal with sharecroppers. But the heroine, whether working her crop like a man, or restlessly hankering after the old days with her lover, or planning a farm for herself and her child, is well drawn, and the novel is a work of faithful realism.

Reuben Davis' *Butcher Bird* (1936), another story of Negro sharecroppers, likewise centers attention upon a woman, "a butcher bird . . . one of these here womens that gobbles up all the mens she can, then sticks the rest of them around on thorn trees and barb wire till she gets hongry again." This wanton brings trouble to the hard-working hero until his quiet dependability makes a new woman of her and she sacrifices her life for his. Written out of considerable knowledge of folk-life, *Butcher Bird* excels local color like *Earth Born* by its sympathetic characterization.

George Lee's *River George* (1936) is less concerned with free love affairs that end in violence, and more with the troubles of sharecropping life disclosed by recent studies. In the first part, as good a picture of sharecropping as any Negro author has achieved, George is a good worker, but since he is educated, knows when he is cheated, and teaches organization, he is a "bad Negro." He becomes worse when the Negro paramour of a white man falls in love with him. Forced to run away to Memphis after shooting

163

the white man, he becomes the legendary man of the river, told of in the author's earlier *Beale Street*. Unreasonably, he returns to his native section and is lynched upon arrival. The second part of the book contains too much, but the first is truthful and therefore bitter. Its grimness stands in no need of the final less credible lynching.

The Delta. Evans Wall writes in *The No-Nation Girl* (1929) of Précieuse, the daughter of a white swamp-dweller and a Negro woman. It is the conventional story of the mulatto, who "had no right to be born," falling in love with a white "outsider" and when abandoned, drowning herself in Suicide Basin, convenient for "no-nation girls." The primitive goings-on are often halted for dogmas about the mulatto. Whenever she is decent, it is because of the inheritance from her father, who was a degraded outcast. But in moments of passion, her mother's inheritance rules:

> The girl's half-heritage of savagery rose in a flood that washed away all trace of her father's people except the supersensitiveness imparted by her taut nerves. She must dance or scream to relieve the rising torrent of response to the wild, monotonous rhythm.

In *Love Fetish* (1933) Wall deals with a "no-nation boy" in similar fashion.

Gulf Stream (1930) by Marie Stanley has more sympathy for the Creole heroine, but drives home the same thesis—that you "can't hide from God and Affaca." Adele, with "cream-ivory, magnolia petal skin" is easily seduced by a white man to whose home she delivers laundry. When her child is born, she refuses to look at it, fearing it will be black. Years later when she discovers that her daughter is miky-white, she becomes a devoted mother. The daughter, broadened by education, becomes engaged to a dark Negro. Adele cannot endure this, and walks into the

164

bay to commit suicide, but love for her daughter makes her renounce the usual gesture of the tragic octoroon. Mille Fleurs Island, below Mobile, the home of mulatto Creoles of wealth and culture, is new to fiction, as is Adele's final tirade against the father of her child. But there is also much of the usual trite generalizing about the tragedy of mixed blood.

Louisiana. Barry Benefield's *Short Turns* (1926) includes two stories of Negro life. In "Ole Mistis" Old Jeff, one of the many "slaves of legal documents and ruthless legal machinery," loses his crops and farm, and would have lost his horse, "Ole Mistis," but for a landlord's last-minute kindheartedness. "Sugar Pie" tells of the terror in a northern Louisiana town when Negroes are burned out, tarred and feathered, and hanged upon telegraph poles. Sugar Pie leaves the hate-ridden town, carrying the corpse of her nearly white baby. *Green Margins* by E. P. O'Donnell (1936) is a poetic book of the life in the delta below New Orleans, the melting pot of Slavonian, Filipino, French, Italian, Cajan and Negro fishermen, trappers and smugglers. Outstanding among the strange characters are the mulatto girl, Unga January, and Bonus, a mad Negro murderer. O'Donnell's short stories about Negro life such as "Jesus Knew" are informed, bitter realism.

Elma Godchaux' *Stubborn Roots* (1936) has a weird Negro character in Zero, who, although he insists upon wearing woman's clothing, is the dynamic foreman on a sugar cane plantation. The respect and liking between Zero and the planter is persuasively conveyed. Other Negroes are convincingly shown at their work of planting and grinding cane and repairing the Mississippi levees. The same fidelity is in Miss Godchaux' "The Horn That Called Bambine" and "Chains," which contain sympathetic characterizations of Negro life along the river, with recognition of the brutality.

Lyle Saxon has brought to his novel *Children of Strangers* (1937) the skill and authority of his studies of New Orleans. Contrary to the usual procedure, the Negroes are treated with seriousness, and the patronizing whites who see Negroes "as the happiest people in the world" are ridiculed. Famie, the beautiful descendant of the free mulattoes who once, cultured and wealthy, owned vast plantations on Cane River, is the tragic heroine. After a traditional love affair with a white outlaw, Famie devotes herself to her child. Poverty-stricken, she sells some of the ancient heirlooms, then she becomes a servant for whites. These are violations of the caste-tabus, whereas having a child by a white man was not. When, in her loneliness, she turns to black people, and finally accepts the attention of Henry Tyler, she cuts the last family tie. *Children of Strangers* reveals a little known locale and people, the last of a

> delicate race of Latins which had lived too near the sun. . . . The very old were curiously erect, their shoulders back, their chins up. They were sad, but they had dignity. . . . The boys and girls were handsome, their skins cream-colored or light tan. . . .

Almost as interesting as Famie is Henry Tyler, a "shut mouth nigger—studying to himself all the time, wanting to learn to read letters." The only socially conscious character in the book says to Henry:

> It has always been like this in the South . . . white men leaning on black men . . . from the beginning. We made slaves of you. . . . You made us rich. . . . In rising, we pushed you further away from us. . . . Black men began to think, to move about, to go away. . . . That is why I couldn't get you out of my mind as I watched you sweating in the field working for something that can never be yours because I have taken it from you.

Short story writers have industriously added to this new regionalism, in such numbers that even mention of their names is impracticable. Wilbur Daniel Steele, however, should be mentioned for his grasp of folk-

166

lore and types apparent in such stories as "Sooth" and "Conjure." Other stories of distinction are James Boyd's "Bloodhound," Vernon Sherwin's "Nigger-Lover," from the many good stories of Negro life published in *Story Magazine,* and Louis Paul's "No More Trouble For Jedwick." The liberal and radical magazines are publishing informed and sincere fiction of Negro life. *The Crisis* and *Opportunity,* Negro magazines, have published many good interpretations "from the inside." Skill and penetration mark such stories as "Symphonesque" by Arthur Huff Fauset, "The Flyer" by Cecil Blue, "Swamp Moccasin" and "Fog" by John F. Matheus, and the work of Henry Jones.

An admittedly inadequate word might be included here on children's books. In a long line from *Little Black Sambo* to the newest *Ezekiel* by Elvira Garner (1937) Negro children have generally been written of in the same terms as their mothers and fathers, as quaint, living jokes, designed to make white children laugh. Against this tradition of comic condescension, Eva Knox Evans, in *Araminta* (1935) and *Jerome Anthony* (1936), has written with sincere and informed sympathy. The same qualities are in the children's stories of Arna Bontemps, one of the most versatile Negro authors, who collaborated with Langston Hughes on *Popo and Fifina* (1933) a story of Haitian children, and has written *You Can't Pet A Possum* (1936) and *Sad Faced Boy* (1937).

DISCUSSION QUESTIONS

1. How does Sherwood Anderson resemble Julia Peterkin and Van Vechten?

2. Account for the growing revolt on the part of southern women against the tradition of "southern charm."

3. What is regionalism? How does it differ from local color?

4. What states seem to be as yet uncovered by regionalists?

5. Compare the work of the regionalists with the plantation tradition.

6. What authors include pictures of southern injustice?

7. In what respects are *The No-Nation Girl, Gulf Stream* and *Children of Strangers* similar?

CHAPTER XI

NEW ROADS

The Pattern of Violence. Although we have seen that such authors as Wood, Heyward, Adams and Frank revealed southern injustice to the Negro, it has remained for a later group of writers to register the fullest social protest. They know the land of the jasmines and myrtles; but they know a great deal more about it than those gentle symbols. Aware that one southern tradition—that of violence—is as long-standing as any, they have added darker color to the picture of the regionalists and folk-lorists, who often in their search for the peculiar and amusing, overlooked harsh and socially significant facts. They record what, according to the formula of taboos and restrictions, should be unmentioned. In spite of the chorus of comfortable and ostrich-like people who insist that in their state "the problem has been solved," they reveal a widespread pattern of violence.

Sweet Man (1930) by Gilmore Millen tells of John Henry, the son of a white plantation agent who could not let Negro women alone. John Henry launches out as a "sweet man," attractive to women on the plantations and in Memphis, and finally becomes the paramour of a wealthy white woman in California. When, unbalanced by jealousy, she tries to frame him for rape, he kills her, then himself. The early chapters give a good, naturalistic picture of plantation life; the last chapters, even though sensational, are convincing.

Amber Satyr by Roy Flannagan (1932) is similar in some respects. Luther, strong and handsome, of

169

Negro-Indian stock, has caution enough to resist the open advances of the love-sick farm wife for whom he works. But through her brazenness, the affair is discovered, and Luther is killed by her two brothers-in-law. The newspaper report is the usual one: Luther was killed by an unknown mob. In ironic contrast, one of Luther's murderers is the father of a child by Luther's daughter, and at the time of the tragedy a special session of the Virginia legislature is considering the "racial-integrity" bill. *Amber Satyr* is shot through with sardonic humor, but its chief impact is tragic.

Less spectacular, Welbourn Kelley's *Inchin' Along* (1932) deals with Dink Britt, whose enterprise and endurance make him a dangerous example to the croppers, white and black, who must be kept brow-beaten and shiftless. A marked man, he narrowly escapes being lynched. *Inchin' Along* has some traditional and silly comments about racial characteristics, but the sympathy for the plugging hero and the picture of the hard lot of the tenant farmer, show Kelly to be clear-eyed and courageous.

Robert Rylee is well informed about life in delta Mississippi, and deeply concerned with its injustice. In *Deep Dark River* (1935) Mose Southwick, a share-cropper, protests against his wife's carryings-on with the plantation manager. In self defense Mose kills a bad Negro, hired to kill him. When Mose is captured and framed, a liberal white woman lawyer takes his case, but cannot defeat the concerted line-up. Mose is dependable, sober, self-contained, with grim, double-edged humor, and burdened by the miseries of his people even more than by his own. So Mose must be put out of the way. *Deep Dark River* is unconvincing where Rylee makes his hero a symbol of Christian resignation and attachment to the soil, and is conventional in such statements as "Mose had the mystic singing and intuitiveness of the black race and the intelligence of the white race." The white characters here are less intelligent than stupid and vicious. Although humane, Rylee does not idealize the Negro; he includes sketches of Negro highjackers, bootleggers, easy women, and toadies for white folks. His second novel *St. George of Weldon* (1937) is a character study of a sensitive southern youth, and the harsh treatment of the Negro is an important element in his education.

In *Death in The Deep South* (1936) by Ward Greene, a novel of southern injustice, the use of the third degree to exact confessions from Negroes is powerfully depicted. Theodore Strauss' *Night At Hogwallow* (1937) is a hair-raising narrative. A Negro laborer is falsely accused of rape. This results in a battle between a northern road crew and the aroused southern townsmen, a beating by the Klan, the burning of the Negro section, and a gruesome lynching. It is a dark melodrama, as life in towns like Hogwallow too often is.

Jim Tully's *Circus Parade* (1927) tells the story of "Whiteface," a Negro who rose from stake-driver to clown, and who was burned at the stake by a mob on the rampage because a Negro had stepped in front of a white woman in the ticket line. "A Negro Girl" is likewise grim naturalism; the girl, caught sneaking into the circus, is assaulted by the circus roughnecks. In *Violence, A Story of Today's South* by Marcet and Emanuel Haldeman-Julius (1928) a Negro boy, in terror of exposure after a love affair, kills a white girl. He is saved from a lynching mob, but is electrocuted. In contrast, a philandering white minister who commits murder is freed.

171

Exceptional Negroes. Sinclair Lewis was one of the first to break with the preconceptions of the Negro held by Main Street. In *Arrowsmith* (1925) he includes a capable Negro scientist who, though a minor character, stands out from the ruck of the petty, grasping victims of Lewis' satire. In *Work of Art* (1934) the attractive, intelligent and bookish Tansy Quill illustrates the "common tragedy of the superior Negro . . . laden with all the complexities of twentieth century America heaped upon the dark burden lugged up from old Africa's abyss." Her suicide is conventional, but it gives Lewis a chance to satirize authors who, from a casual acquaintance with a hotel maid, build up masterpieces about Negro psychology and the voodoo of the swamps.

Come In At The Door (1934) by William March is merciless in its exposure of certain elements of southern life, and original in its treatment of Negro characters. A Negro woman, Mitty, bears six children to the "aristocrat" Robert Hurry, who, gone to seed, is now going with the wind in the waste land of the delta country. Mitty is wily but superstitious, loyal but self-centered, kindhearted but capable of fierce hate. The traditional Aunt Hatty and Jim are well observed. Most striking of the Negro characters is Baptiste, an educated Creole, a vagabond philosopher, whose tragedy is to haunt forever the southern boy whom he tutored.

The portrait of Baptiste indicates that as southern realists look more closely at life, they too become aware of exceptional Negroes. T. S. Stribling has complained that "White educated Southerners are completely cut off from black educated Southerners by the inherited attitudes of master and slave, and the one really does not know the other exists." Lack of contact and ignorance still handicap honest realists,

172

but their attempt at a complete cast of characters is noteworthy.

To James Saxon Childers, "White men and black men have long ago walked out of their color and are only men." *A Novel About A White Man and A Black Man In The Deep South* (1936) deals with Gordon Nicholson, a white man, and Dave Parker, a Negro, educated at the same northern school. When Dave, a talented musician, visits his friend, the southern town is alarmed, since Gordon has a sister Anne. Dave is accused of a crime for which there is not a shred of evidence. He is acquitted, but Anne's end is tragic, merely because Dave visits her brother. Irritated by northern interference as much as by southern injustice, Childers believes that the "problem" will gradually be solved by men of good will. His Negro characters, like most of the educated Negroes in propaganda novels, are nearly faultless. The novel is unusual in its sympathy, but it is jumbled, coincidental and not always plausible.

One of the South's most promising novelists, Hamilton Basso included recognizable Negro characters in *Relics and Angels* (1929). *Cinnamon Seed* (1934) shows deeper understanding of Negroes, both in slavery and in the present; Horace, the old family servant; Sam, ambitious, resentful and therefore doomed, and Lance who rises to be a world famous "trombone player in a band" are especially well done. In *Courthouse Square* (1936) which deals mainly with the plight of a justice-loving liberal in a southern town, Basso's pictures of Negro life are even more authentic and sympathetic. Of Niggertown, which the Negroes called High Rent, he writes:

> Poverty ran through the section like a plague, hunger was a frequent visitor or permanent boarder in almost every house, but the inhabitants of High Rent, merging a simple philosophy with the terrible patience of the poor, complained but little and trusted

173

in the humanity of a singularly inhumane and white-faced God for eventual succor and release.

An unusual character is Alcide Fauget, who is "like the reverend and respected head of a tribe: banker, counsellor, physician, friend." So fair that he had attended a white southern medical school, he serves the darker half of his people. Neither obsequious nor arrogant, he goes his own way. But when he wishes to buy an old house, falling to rack and ruin, for a much-needed Negro hospital, he has stepped over his bounds, and is driven away by a mob of his inferiors. An intelligent, humane realist, Basso has unobtrusively but memorably conveyed the tragedy of Negro life in the South.

The "Multiple" Novel : Many writers have attempted to give cross-sections of the life of southern towns by using many characters on all levels. Margaret Sperry's *Portrait of Eden* (1934) shows a Florida town which, after the boom, sinks back into lethargy and intolerance. The Negroes are generally shown as exotic primitives, especially at their shouting services in "The Church of Jesus Colored." But the picture has social understanding as well:

> Aunt Melissie danced, tangling her feet in a bitter tune against all the days she'd spent serving white folks, walking their ways, and all her children born to do bidding to white men. She danced and fell reeling at last, her shoes flung to the darkness. . . .

Outstanding is the educated Negro, John Marquis, a native of the section, who, hated by whites and double-crossed by Negroes, wants to start a school for Negro children. He is lynched, and a white liberal, his best friend, is murdered. *Portrait of Eden* has some exaggeration, but what it records is not too spectacular in a state where the Klan still rides.

Less directly intent upon revealing intolerance and injustice than Basso and Miss Sperry, other novelists still include these since they wish truthful pictures.

174

Siesta, by Berry Fleming (1935), is one of the finest examples. Cotton brokers, cotton farmers, plaintively wasting "aristocrats," society folk and crackers, in "Georgetown," Alabama, in the long drought of summer, are unforgettably set before us. Negro characters, an important part of the town's life, are as authentically handled. Laney Shields, ambitious and decent, is trapped in a sordid love affair with the young white doctor for whom she is office girl. A little boy's going after the laundry becomes a dangerous odyssey in the bullying town. Mattie Small, the "obsteprician"; a famed faith-healing Bishop and his blind stooge, are similarly well drawn. In *Siesta* the best talkers refer to the Negro's tragic mask, and say that southern whites can know of the Negro only what he wants them to know. This is wise: Fleming's recognition of the tragic mask helps him to get beneath it.

South, by Frederick Wight (1935) attempts a panoramic view of a South Carolina city. Negro characters are only slightly sketched domestics or levee workers. Mob terror threatens the Negro section at one point, but is averted when the victim is discovered to be a light-colored Negro woman. The manufacturing town of "Tuttle," North Carolina, comes to life in *Where the Weak Grow Strong* by Eugene Armfield (1936). Negro characters are drawn with attention to truth more than to tradition. A servant asking for her six weeks back pay of twelve dollars, is called an "ungrateful nigger" and is ordered from the house.

> Miss Evelyn, you ain't got no call to talk to me like that. I only ast you for what I worked for. I may be a nigger like you says. The Lord made me the color I is. But I ain't never done nobody out of the money that's coming to them.

A white mother resents the reserving of the carnival merry-go-round for Negroes, during the supper

175

hour for the whites: "They ought not let them do it."
A love affair between a Negro man and a white
woman is told with quiet, tragic realism.

Incidental Characters, But Real. In George Milburn's sharply observed *Oklahoma Town* (1930),
"The Nigger-Lover" tells of a lawyer who earned
his nickname by urging Negroes to vote, who violated
taboos such as handing a Negro boy a glass of water
from a soda fountain, and who is among the first
victims in a race riot. In "The Nigger Doctor" the
educated physician makes the town uneasy by his
quietly defiant manner and his scientific skill. *No
More Trumpets* (1933) contains a story "white
Meat" in which a boarding house keeper gets her
greatest delight in baiting Negroes and describing a
lynching she saw as a girl. Deserted by her resentful
daughters, she reveals that their father had Negro
blood. In Milburn's novel *Catalogue,* the lynching
of a Negro is shown to be one of the holiday excitements for Oklahoma yokels.

James T. Farrell, in his trilogy *Studs Lonigan*
(1935), has old man Lonigan commenting on Amos
and Andy:

> You would have laughed yourself sick at them. They're so
> much like darkies. Not the fresh northern niggers, but the genuine real southern darkies, the good niggers . . . . with long
> names and honors, just like in real life . . . Golly, Bill, they sure
> are a card.

In bitter contrast, however, Farrell shows the anger
of the Chicago Irish to the encroaching black belt.
Studs Lonigan believes that "they ought to hang every
nigger in the city to telephone poles." Fellow victims
of poverty, the Negroes and Irish have fierce street
fights of which the riot of 1919 was a natural climax,
although Farrell describes the present as similarly
explosive. Except in a few stories, Farrell does not
present individual Negroes, but he has given powerful

176

and grimly true pictures of northern prejudice, which seems to be little different from the lynch-spirit of the South.   ..

William Faulkner's *Sartoris* (1929) has many minor but ably individualized Negro characters. Uncle Simon's dismaying first automobile ride, and his difficulties as treasurer of the church board—"he jes put de money out, sort of,"— are well described. Simon rebukes his son Caspy, who, home from the World War is bragging too much: "What us niggers want ter be free fer, anyhow. Ain't we got ez many white folks now ez we kin suppo't?" The servants of the tragic family in Faulkner's *The Sound and The Fury* (1920)—Aunt Dilsey, hobbling about her kitchen, impudent and bullying, with her temper worn short by the bickering and turmoil, Uncle Job, and Luster, who is guardian to Benjy, the idiot of the family—are likewise convincing. The Negroes are generally described from the point of view of their harassed white folks:

> Like I say the only place for them is in the field, where they'd have to work from sunup to sundown. . . . They got so they can outguess you about work before your very eyes. . . . Shirking and giving you a little more lip and a little more lip until some day you have to lay them out with a scantling or something. . . .

The Negroes themselves are an unflattering chorus in this drama of the fall of a family. One of them expresses their surliness: "I works to suit de man whut pays me Sat'day night. When I does dat, it don't leave me a whole lot of time to please other folks." Insolent just up to the breaking point, contradicting their white-folks without apologies, these servants are miles away from the plantation tradition menials. If familiarity has not bred contempt, it has at least bred rough irony in place of worship.

These Thirteen (1931) contains "That Evening Sun," one of the best of Negro stories. A Negro woman is shown waiting in dread suspense, certain that her husband is going to kill her. Nancy is truculent and cynical about humanity whether white or black. Her husband is likewise desperate:

> I can't hang around white man's kitchen. But white man can hang around mine. White man can come in my house, but I can't stop him. When white man wants to come in my house, I ain't got no house. I can't stop him, but he can't kick me outen it. He can't do that.

"Dry September" is a powerful lynching story, but the stress is less upon the victim than upon the psychology of the mob, especially of the leader. No one knows whether the assault happened or was imagined, but the mob gets its man.

In *Sanctuary* (1929) the incidental picture of a jailed Negro murderer is striking:

> He would lean in the window in the evening and sing. After supper a few Negroes gathered along the fence below—natty, shoddy suits and sweat-stained overalls shoulder to shoulder— and in chorus with the murderer, they sang . . . "Fo days mo! Den dey ghy 'stroy de bes' ba'ytone singer in Nawth Mississippi!"

Light in August (1932) has as its most interesting character Joe Christmas. A foundling, the son of a white mother and a Negro father, he is raised by his fanatical grandfather. Taken for white until the mystery of his birth is cleared up, he is silent, friendless and proud. After he murders a sex-obsessed Yankee woman, a relic of Reconstruction, he is pursued and killed. Although one character imputes his tragedy to the warfare in him of white and black, there is sufficient reason to see him as a victim of a hostile environment. He is more complex than Faulkner's other Negroes, fully characterized, and one of Faulkner's most memorable creations.

Faulkner is a naturalist, and sees humanity in a harsh light. Like the weak, mean, and degenerate white characters whom he has set before us, his Negro characters are shown unflatteringly. House-servants

178

and farmers, loose women and murderers; whether in rocking ecstasy in church, or getting the third degree from a sheriff, or fearing to help out in an accident— "White folks be sayin' we done it"—they are all equally convincing. Faulkner records Negro speech with complete accuracy, but more important, he gets into character with the uncanny penetration that makes him one of the most significant of the new novelists. His Negroes are a long way from happy-go-lucky comics. If they agree in anything, it is in their surly understanding of the bitter life that they are doomed to live in a backward, hate-ridden South. He does not write social protest, but he is fiercely intent upon the truth, and the truth that he sees is tragic.

In *Tobacco Road,* after a Negro has been run down by the crazy-driving of a poor-white, Jeeter philosophizes: "Wal, niggers will get kilt." The same callousness is depicted in Caldwell's first book, *American Earth* (1931). "Saturday Afternoon" tells of a mob's filling a Negro "so full of lead that his body sagged from his neck where the trace-chain held him up." The Negro was too smart a farmer. "Savannah River Payday" is even more gruesome. A Negro sawmill hand, killed in an accident, is being carried to the town's undertaker. The drunk "crackers" driving the car hammer out his gold teeth and fight over them. Arriving in town, they go into a pool room and forget all about the corpse. *We Are The Living* (1933) contains Negro cotton-pickers, and servants whose attractiveness is a household problem. The stories are frequently humorous but the laughter of the Negroe is ironic at perplexed and inept "superiors."

"Candy Man Beechum" in *Kneel To The Rising Sun* (1935) is about a travelling boy with flapping feet, who, on his way to see his gal, is shot down for nothing by a white policeman. "Blue Boy" is the ugly anecdote of a Negro idiot whose grotesque tricks entertain a group of satiated "high class ladies and gentlemen." "Kneel To The Rising Sun", probably Caldwell's greatest short story, portrays the misery of short-rationed sharecroppers, the sadism of ignorant, bored landlords, the crushing force of an unjust system. Lonnie, a white man, made a whining coward by years of share-cropping slavery, betrays Clem, who has befriended him, to their mutual enemy the landlord, and his mob of lynchers. Clem is a doggedly courageous Negro, willing to take only so much before rebelling.

> All Arch asked . . . was for Clem Henry to overstep his place just one little half inch, or to talk back to him with just one little short word, and he would do the rest. Everybody knew what Arch meant by that, especially if Clem did not turn and run. And Clem had not been known to run from anybody, after fifteen years in the country.

Caldwell is convinced that "much of the matter about the southern Negro and the southern white man has been a garbled mixture of romance and mis-statement," and the authoritative fiction he writes about his native sharecropping country bears this out.

Proletarian Realism. Caldwell's "Kneel To The Rising Sun" represents one of the most important trends in contemporary fiction. The Negro is at last being discovered as part of the working class. Radical novelists now stress the exploitation of the Negro masses, and urge that it is only by the solidarity of all workers that a new social order can be achieved. In spite of the overstress of propaganda, these writers contribute a great deal to realism. Seeing many of the so-called Negro characteristics as class disabilities, aware of much that is common in the lives of the poor, they have been able to get close to their characters, without condescension and without idealizing. They start from the basic beliefs that the Negro has

180

been a great factor in building up America, that he has been miserably underpaid, that he is growing steadily more conscious of, and restive under exploitation, and that he can get nowhere without the white worker, nor the white worker without him. These are all truths that have long needed to be told. By themselves, they do not guarantee good fiction, but they cannot be neglected without falsity to Negro experience, and the contemporary American scene.

Scott Nearing's *Free-Born* (1932), "unpublishable by any commercial concern," is as well documented as his *Black America,* a sociological exposé of exploitation and persecution. The title is ironic: the "freeborn" Negroes are landless sharecroppers, kept from "jumping contracts" by a patrol system. One southern judge threatens to adjourn court and "attend to the matter himself" if there are not enough "he-Americans" to do a job of lynching. Jim, the hero, sees the burning of the Rosenwald school and the lynching of his mother and father (one of the most gruesome ever recorded in fiction and taken from actuality). His sweetheart is raped and murdered. In Chicago he is caught up in the race-riot. Embittered and desperate, he is taught by a communist that "t'aint cause you'se black that you'se exploited," and that only by fighting shoulder to shoulder with white workers will there ever be a "free world under working class control." Rebuffed by labor leaders, Jim nevertheless sticks to his new-found cause. Jailed for leading a strike, he dedicates himself to black and white slaves "who never were freed . . . who keep your high and mighty world a-goin'." *Free Born* crowds too much upon the shoulders of its young hero, and is unconvincing in such details as Jim's continued dialect after he has read Upton Sinclair, Marx and Lenin. But it is significant as the first revolutionary novel of Negro life.

Georgia Nigger (1932) is another exposure, attacking the convict-lease system and the chain-gang, with thorough documentation based upon visits, prison records and photographs. Spivak describes such devices of punishment as the iron collar, spikes, double-shackles, the stocks, the whipping post, the Georgia rack, where convicts are tortured by stretching, and the "sweat-box, a coffin of thick wood standing upright." The convicts who rot their lives away in the filthy cages may be robbers and killers, or they may just as often be like David, a mere lad, picked up on petty charges to do the county's hard work. Arrested in a round-up because Mr. Deering, in cahoots with the sheriff, has a lot of cotton to be picked, David is "redeemed" by the planter. Escaping from Deering's armed camp, where Negroes who die from overwork are weighted and buried in the swamp, David is rearrested as a vagrant, and this time chooses the chain gang in preference to peonage, exchanging hell for hell. Throughout *Georgia Nigger* the Negro is shown to be a catspaw; vicious and murderous guards, landlords and sheriffs nullify the half-hearted interference of the better-disposed whites. But it contains more than the shocking; the heartbreaking struggle of David's family against poverty is conveyed with deep feeling.

In Myra Page's *Gathering Storm* (1932) the hill-people who have become underpaid, hungry "lint-heads," doomed to shameful living, and the Negroes whose wretchedness is even greater, come together because of common suffering. Marge, a child of hill people, reaches out to Negro workers "across the miles", denounces the old way of hatred and bitterness, and urges the new way of solidarity. She and a Negro organizer are forerunners of the "gathering storm." Like *Free-Born* in many respects, covering too much ground, *Gathering Storm* is even more of a thesis

182

novel. But Miss Page's sympathy with her Negro characters goes deep.

Dealing with a similar setting, *Call Home The Heart* contains but few scenes involving Negroes. Ishma, a mountain woman, saves a Negro organizer from a lynch mob but is revolted by close contact with Negroes: "Mountain people are always white." A matured radical, recognizing the strength of her long-bred prejudice, patiently tries to persuade her that unless the workers of both races stand together, they will continue to be clubbed, driven and starved. Miss Burke's *A Stone Came Rolling* (1935) contains more about the Negro. The "kindliness" of the past is satirized in an excellent description of a slave-trading. The present is desperate: a Negro woman says: "I ain't had what you could call work in six months—not a tap at a snake." An educated Negro, brought in as a safe speaker at a political rally, waits until white hearers have left, and then attacks the conservative speechmakers and urges Negroes to organize. Unemployed whites and Negroes march together, singing militant words to hymn tunes. In such a crisis, the city fathers, churchmen, and sheriff must have a victim. Stomp Nelson, a tireless, fearless, Negro organizer is selected, but by a ruse, his white comrades of the Unemployed Council save him from the mob. Negro characters are not major actors, but the Negro is shown as an important participant in the stirring of southern labor. The use of race prejudice by the overlords to prevent workers' solidarity is clearly indicated.

In *Now In November* (1934) and *Winter Orchard* (1935) Josephine Johnson occasionally describes the harshness of Negro life. Her *Jordanstown* (1937) records a fight for better living conditions for the jobless and the underpaid in a small midwestern town. Anna Mosely, "a tall, mammoth Negress . . . too

183

articulate and brooding for her own people, too proud to be popular with employers . . . alien in the bitter gifts of intelligence and race" is an interesting person, whether in her married life with Ham, or talking in meetings, or writing the song for the disinherited, or leading the march, or lying unconquered in jail, or inspiring the young white leaders: "Not till we do something all together . . . we won't change mo' than a stitch in the world."

The bitterness and understanding of Grace Lumpkin's "White Man" (1927), the story of a Negro girl seduced by her employer, reappears with added power in *A Sign For Cain* (1935). A small southern community is well realized: the well meaning but weak liberals, resenting any interference with their "contented nigras"; the respectable judge (bought and paid for); the bootlegging and pandering leader of the American Legion who is the defender of law and order; the white men with their Negro women; the high-school boys ripe for violence; and the sheriff who keeps the Negroes "scared to raise their voices too high." Nevertheless, when Denis, a young organizer returns home, he finds allies ready to join his struggle for justice. Denis is slowly but surely bringing about the union of underpaid white and black workers, when a few leaflets are lost, and traitors sell him out. Framed for the murder of a wealthy white woman, Denis is shot by the real murderer, who fears investigation by the northern lawyers. Denis is quiet but strong, humble only before the great work he has set himself to do; in jail, attacked by the deputies, he cries out "I've got no rights as a citizen. Then I stand on my rights as a man." Other Negroes are well done: Mum Nancy, whose long years of meekness bring a sorry inheritance; Selah, the bound-out slavey, awaking to courage and hatred; Brother Shadrack Morton

184

whose sermon on submissiveness in lynch-time is drowned out by groans, and Ficents, easy-going, but insisting "I got some fight in me yet; if there's something to fight for." Most interesting after Denis is old Ed Clarke, whose memory of his lynched father is still burning, a hard worker, unlearned but manly, leaving one master because he could do with "less kindness and more cash," and contemptuous of "white-folks' niggers." The old plantation record furnishes ironic asides: one entry reads, "Sold Negro $1,200. Beautiful day"; another reads, "Candies for little Negroes . . . 25 cents worth."

Negro Novelists On New Roads. Except for a few cartoons, such as *Two Black Crows in the A.E.F.,* the Negro in the World War has been scarcely mentioned. Victor Daly's *Not Only War* (1932) "dedicated to the army of disillusioned," attempts to do justice to the record of Negro troops. There is less about warfare, however, than about the workings of race prejudice. A southern white officer, who has carried on a flirtation with a Negro girl in the states, "breaks" a Negro non-commissioned officer for visiting a French girl. In a big drive the white officer is wounded; the Negro soldier tries to save his life. They are found the next morning, "face downward, their arms about each other." Coincidences are too much relied upon, and the novel follows the apologist pattern, but the aim to deal seriously with what has been caricatured is noteworthy. *Greater Need Below* (1936) by O'Wendell Shaw deals with the life of a southern Negro college, but the characters are too idealized, and the plot is forced. The subject deserves a better novel.

Langston Hughes, in *The Ways of White Folks* (1934), his first collection of short stories, shows far superior artistry. All of the stories deal with manifestations of white prejudice. Hughes states that by white folks he really means "some white folks," but the stories which turn the tables of caricature and contempt often seem inclusive. "Slave On the Block" and "The Blues I'm Playing" satirize the people "who went in for Negroes—a race that was too charming and naive and lovely for words." "A Good Job Gone" shows the break-up of a wealthy white man who, fascinated by a golden-brown wanton, is jilted for a Negro elevator boy. "Rejuvenation Through Joy" farcically tells of a colony of effete whites who listen to lectures by a Negro, passing for white, who preaches the occult value of primitive rhythm. "Cora," one of the most successful stories, attacks small town puritanism. In "Home" a world renowned artist returns home to be lynched as an "uppity nigger." In "Father and Son," from which the play *Mulatto* was taken, the son of Colonel Norwood and his house-keeper, determined not to be "a white folks' nigger," chokes his father to death after a quarrel and is lynched. In this not always convincing story, Hughes looks forward to the time when

> the cotton will blaze and the cabins will burn and the chains will be broken, and men, all of a sudden, will shake hands, black men and white men, like steel meeting steel.

Hughes does not often strike this radical note in *The Ways of White Folks;* most of his stories protest jim-crow insults and injustice. In "Professor," one of his latest stories, he attacks the compromising race "leader." Hughes' stories exist largely for the theses, but they are skillfully done, realistic in detail and bitingly ironic.

One of the most promising explorations of a new road is Richard Wright's "Big Boy Leaves Home," which appeared in *The New Caravan* (1936). The portrait of the gang of Negro boys in the South is done

186

with robust understanding. Swimming in a pool posted "No Trespassing," which meant "No dogs and niggers allowed," the boys are caught by a white man. In a fight after one of the boys has been shot, Big Boy gets possession of the man's rifle, and when the white man lunges for it, Big Boy shoots him. His pal, Bobo, is caught and lynched. The terror of the community before Big Boy is spirited away is graphically conveyed. "Big Boy Leaves Home" is well informed realism, rendered with power and originality.

Without the distinction of Wright's technique, Waters Edward Turpin's *These Low Grounds* (1937) is still extremely promising. For the first time a Negro novelist tells the story of four generations of Negroes. Thoroughly conversant with the life of the farmers and crabbers and oyster shuckers of the Eastern Shore, Turpin has had the courage to handle this life without idealization, without shame, but with full sympathy. The story has its bitterness and sharp protest. Poverty is omnipresent, and oppression. The town of Shrewsbury is really Salisbury, ill-famed because of a recent lynching, and Turpin describes this tragedy. His characters, for all of their illiteracy and squalor, have dogged courage. Less successful in his hasty sketches of the life of better off Negroes in the big cities, Turpin's novel still belongs with the best novels by Negro authors.

Summary. If many of the foregoing books have contained lynchings, this may partly be explained as a natural reaction to books that have stressed the contented, comical or quaintly picturesque Negro in a sunny South which "understands him." It is important that American novelists are revealing the tragic in Negro experience. This has been present from the earliest, and honest observers know that it has been met with fortitude and struggle. Some novelists have

187

recorded the brutality and shame as part of a tragic America; others show the Negro resisting heroically; and still others, hoping for social justice, are urging solidarity of all of the oppressed. They indicate a new and momentous trend in modern literature. It is a trend that makes the way easier for Negro novelists who, coming of age in technique and understanding, will find an audience ready for the important stories that still must be told.

DISCUSSION QUESTIONS

1. What subjects tabooed in the South are treated in the novels of this chapter?

2. Why is it natural to expect that many southern novels would stress violence?

3. What is the advantage of the "multiple novel" in setting forth a community's life?

4. List the "exceptional" negroes in the books of this chapter.

5. What differentiates the radical novelists from the realists who show the pattern of violence?

6. Compare the newer realists among Negroes with the apologist and the Harlem school.

CHAPTER XII

HISTORICAL FICTION

The present vogue of historical fiction has given new impetus to the long-standing interest in the Old South and the Negro. The African slave-trade, the antebellum and the reconstruction South are popular hunting grounds. Some novelists continue the plantation tradition, some, the antislavery tradition, and many others, in the spirit of regionalism, seek the truth of their sectional pasts, without apology and without indictment.

The Slave Trade. The ghastly middle passage, the shackled mobs below the hatches, the lack of water, the plagues, are background for novels like Mary Johnston's *The Slave Ship* (1924), and George King's *The Last Slaver* (1936). Deeper pity and understanding inform *The Trader's Wife* (1930) by Jean Kenyon McKenzie. A sheltered Newport girl confronted by the traffic—"Wretched blacks at sea, packed in trays like dead fish, stinking like fish, some of them to die . . . and to be cast in the sea"—is broken in Africa by the misery of the barracoon. As her last gesture before she dies she sets free a contingent of slaves.

> With the dawn there came a wailing on the river—as the canoes multiplied at the landing—the high desolate wailing that is the voice of the sorrows of Africa. . . . It was the slaves come down the river into the barracoon.

Hervey Allen's *Anthony Adverse* (1933) describes the barracoons through which "Africa was poured into America," the serpent-like line

> composed of hundreds of naked, human bodies rubbed slimy for their approaching sale with palm oil and rancid butter. . . .

189

> Bamboo withes stretched from one tight neck-fork to another.
> . . . Hovering about it, and along its flanks were white-robed
> Arabs with rhinoceros-hide whips.

The bartering, with slaves coquettish, or compliant, or
sullen, or tiger-like, the inspections and the packing on
the slave-ships are fully pictured, obviously after a
great deal of research. But it strikes one as historical
pageantry rather than tragedy.

In *Babouk* (1934), Guy Endore concentrates upon
the shocking features of the slave-trade: the captives
"lying shoulder to shoulder, feet pointing toward the
center, not only chained in pairs, but each pair attached
to a great chain—a gigantic necklace of blacks"; the
separated tribesmen forced to sing and dance—"a
centipede dancing, chains clanking"; opthalmy and
other epidemics ravaging the hold. "Nigger-tasters,"
telling the slaves' condition by their sweat, and other
connoisseurs of black flesh winnowed out the drugged,
the doctored; only the finest were fit to be slaves. After
horrible life on San Domingo plantations the slaves
revolt. Based upon considerable research, convincing
in its descriptions of the slave-trade, of African tales
and customs, and of West Indian plantations, *Babouk*
is still more than a historical romance. It is a revolutionary novel, bitterly opposed to imperialism and the
contemporary slavery of any race.

The Plantation Tradition. But Endore is unusual;
Joseph Hergesheimer is much more typical. In *Quiet
Cities* (1927) he yearns for the return of the past,
based on slavery—for which "I'd be happy to pay—
with everything, everything the wasted present holds."
In his picture slaves do little other than raise soft
staves of song, or play quoits, or fiddle, or sleep. The
only ugly feature is an ill-smelling slave-den, for which
a transplanted northerner is responsible. Emancipation was a failure since "a free Negro is more often

190

wretched than not." Reconstruction was ignominious: Negro legislators dared to utter shouts of laughter, with "incredible feet elevated on the desks" in southern state capitols. Mingo Harth, a vicious Negro politician worthy of Thomas Dixon, is called a "symbol of Union, a black seal on the fate of South Carolina."

Most of the historical romances repeat these patterns with little variation. Dealing with the times of George Washington, *Princess Malah* (1933), by a Negro author, John H. Hill, subscribes in the main to the plantation tradition of humaneness, mutual affection and lavishness. Frances Griswold's *"The Tides of Malvern* (1930) and Caroline Gordon's *Penhally* (1931) recount the long history of southern families with Negro characters in the background, where they stay correctly. A few step out of the picture after Sherman's march, but the majority will not be moved. In Mary Johnston's *Miss Delicia Allen* (1933) both Negro slaves and white owners are conventionally drawn.

Somewhat similar to Cable's *Madame Delphine* is E. Laroque Tinker's *Toucoutou* (1928). After being married to a white man, Toucoutou is proved in court to be partly Negro. In bitter envy, Negroes satirize her in street-songs; whites condemn her because her marriage means that "a black flood will rush through the crevasse that will sully white purity and retard our civilization a thousand years." The picture of New Orleans is not idyllic; the yellow fever epidemic, the exotic *bamboula, calinda* and *counjaille* danced in the *Place Congo,* and other customs of New Orleans are vividly described. With some sympathy for his heroine, Tinker yields at times to the doubtful traditions about the mulatto. *Old New Orleans* (1931) by E. Laroque Tinker and Frances Tinker presents minor and familiar Negro characters. Life on the

191

lower Mississippi, in a later period is in Edna Ferber's *Show-Boat* (1926), which has a few Negroes singing the plaintive songs of their "wronged race," and a melodramatic scene involving an octoroon.

Look Back to Glory (1933) by Herbert Ravenel Sass is worshipful of the duelling cavaliers and glamorous women of low-country South Carolina, "a paradise . . . the proud, the knightly South." Slavery is called a godsend to elevate the Negro from barbarism. The subtle poison of slavery was the "inevitable" miscegenation, "invited nine-tenths of the time" by Negro girls, and guaranteeing "the purity of the southern women of education and family." Best characterized of the Negroes is Vienna, a beautiful quadroon, to whom "curtsying did not come easy." The others are conventional, grateful for the godsend.

The Civil War has long been a favorite subject for historical novelists, but earlier novels like Winston Churchill's *The Crisis* (1901), Upton Sinclair's *Manassas* (1904) and Mary Johnston's *The Long Roll* (1911) and *Cease Firing* (1912) are little concerned with deepening the characterization of the Negro. *The Battleground* (1902) by Ellen Glasgow, has many of the standbys of the plantation tradition— the noble hero who deplores slavery, the wretched free Negro and the giant slave who rescues his master (one of the most familiar battle activities from "Marse Chan" to *So Red The Rose.*) Recent Civil War novels like Caroline Gordon's *None Shall Look Back* (1936) and Clifford Dowdey's *Bugles Blow No More* (1936) are skillfully written and based upon research, but the latter does not particularly extend to Negro characters.

The slaves in *Old Miss* (1929) by T. Bowyer Campbell are "like children, trusting, expecting, receiving everything as a matter of course from their mas-

192

ters." The hero is proslavery, only because of altruism: "What would the poor things do without us to care for them, and see that they pass peaceful, useful lives?" When Aunt Christian is told that she is free, she angrily hits her informant with a stick, like the ancient tyrants upon hearing bad news. Roark Bradford's *Kingdom Coming* (1933) likewise carries the thesis that freedom was a mistake. Aunt Free buys her freedom and then does not want it; Telegram is set free by a Yankee firing squad; free Negroes die like flies in concentration camps. There is an interesting account of the "blind Underground" which held out false hopes of freedom that ended in murder. That the freed Negro is little better off than the slave is true in sections that Bradford should know very well, but it hardly seems a defense of slavery. Promising "the true story of slavery and the true story of freedom," *Kingdom Coming* merely gives some good local color of plantation life and voodoo, to support the century-old beliefs advanced in *Swallow Barn*.

Stark Young has shown a knowledge of certain types of Negroes in sketches like "The Poorhouse Goes to The Circus" (1929) and *Heaven Trees* (1926). His best seller, *So Red The Rose* (1934), is a melancholy recital of the folk-tales that southerners heard in their youth. The war blown along by northern and southern windbags destroys "a gracious system of living that has seldom seen its equal." Negroes, in spite of "fetid . . . old maid idealism" had their best place in that system. A typical old faithful, William Veal, seeks his dead master on the battlefield at night; he felt the hair of the corpses until he found him: "he knew him by his hair; you know how fine it was." In contrast are the Negro soldiers—grog-filled burners and looters —and the ingrates who run off to the Yankees and are stricken with plagues. Written in skillful, disarming prose, *So Red The Rose* nevertheless remains a thrice-told tale.

Elliot Crayton McCants in *White Oak Farm* (1928) gives the traditional picture of Reconstruction, though with less rancor than Page and Dixon. *Bottom Rail On Top* (1935) by H. J. Eckenrode is a less orthodox novel, not in the "bloody-shirt" tradition. Negroes scatter after emancipation and learn fast in reconstruction. The hero is often shown siding with the Negroes and radicals in the brawling.

Not fooled by all of the hallowed creeds of the South, Margaret Mitchell in the best-selling *Gone With The Wind* (1937) accepts whole-heartedly the traditional estimate of the Negro. "Slaves were neither miserable nor unfortunate. . . . There never had been a slave sold from Tara and only one whipping." Mammy, Dilcey, Toby and the other house-servants, proud of their quality white-folks, disdainful of field hands, "free issues" and poor whites, have been with us time and time again. Slaves who were different were "mean." The "least energetic, trustworthy and intelligent and most vicious and brutal" were the ones who left the plantation to enjoy a long "carnival of idleness and theft and insolence" interrupted only by plagues in crowded Atlanta. Negro insults range from "looking impudent" and being "uppity to a lady" to assuming Anglo-Saxon prerogatives:

> In the legislature . . . they spent most of their time eating goobers and easing their unaccustomed feet into and out of new shoes. They frolicked . . . .

But the intelligent house-servants, the highest caste, spoke the correct, heart-warming lines:

> Ah done had nuff freedom. Ah wants somebody to feed me good vittles reglar an' tell me what ter do an' what not ter do, an' look affer me when Ah gets sick.

194

Needless to say, the Klan is as knightly here as in *The Authentic History of the Ku Klux Klan,* an authentic hymn of praise.

Summary. DuBose Heyward has written: "This relationship [between master and slave] has been sentimentalized and utilized *ad nauseam* in writing of the slave period." The plots of the foregoing books are uninventive, and the characters and situations are repeated over and over. Aristocrats and house-servants still monopolize attention, as if the many "yeoman" farmers and field-hands had not existed. With the hindsight of the present, secession is admitted to have been bad, but although most of the aristocrats detested slavery (in principle), the intelligent Negroes detested freedom (in principle and practise) and the romancers agree with the Negroes. The very infrequent floggings are the work of uncouth overseers, who are knocked down by blooded cavaliers. Fugitive slaves have been spirited away from these books. Faithful servants bring back dead heroes from battlefields, bury the silver, despise the Yankees and prefer to work for their ex-masters without wages. Unfaithful slaves, corrupted from their childish virtue, run away to die in concentration camps, or loot, insult and rape. Negroes who bought land, rushed to schools and proved freedom to be no mistake, are non-existent, in spite of the record. An unpartisan historian writes:

> These Reconstruction governments erected public school systems; democratized local and county units, created public social services, and sought to distribute tax burdens equitably.

But in these books the legislatures are composed of a few depraved Northerners, and a mob of Negroes who did little else but put their feet upon desks and "eat peanuts by the peck." The Freedmen's Bureau is villainous, the Klan reproachless, organized to preserve chastity, not for political and economic control.

195

It is wrong to assume that these books are merely pageants of a departed past; they definitely further attitudes that justify the worst kind of contemporary reaction. Their popularity is a dangerous sign. Based on the principle that the many must be kept "in their place" for the good of the few, they encourage slavery in a world where slaves are still too numerous.

The Anti-Slavery Tradition. But there is a party of opposition which, like Emerson, has cried "fiddle-faddle to the Old South." In the tradition of Harriet Beecher Stowe and Albion Tourgée. some twentieth century authors have described the tragedy of slavery, and have dealt with heroes and heroines who would not buckle under.

Rowland E. Robinson, in *Out of Bondage and Other Stories* (collected posthumously in 1936) records the heroism and drama of the Underground Railroad in Vermont where slaves on their way to Canada were hidden in loaded sleighs and wagons, or stowed away in attics or barnlofts or deserted sugar-houses. John E. Paynter's *Fugitives of the Pearl* (1930) one of the few historic romances by Negro authors, deals with the escape of seventy-seven Negroes from Washington aboard the *Pearl,* whose captain was an abolitionist. A Negro informer gave away their plot, and they were captured down the Potomac. Of the old school in technique, *Fugitives of the Pearl* is more fictionalized history than a re-creation of characters and settings. But the precarious life of Negroes in antebellum Washington, "the seat and center of the slave trade" is truthfully presented.

The Railroad to Freedom (1932) by Hildegarde Swift is the fictionalized biography of Harriet Tubman, the most famous agent of the Underground Railroad, and a nurse and scout with the Union troops. Supposed to be a story for children, *The Railroad to*

196

Freedom is still one of the best records of an important movement and a fascinating heroine of American history. One of America's finest historical novels, *God's Angry Man* (1933) by Leonard Ehrlich re-creates the life and times of John Brown. There is unusual sympathy in the treatment of the Negro characters. These are Frederick Douglass, who is willing to use violence against slavers but not against a government arsenal, realizing bitterly that too many Negroes, broken by slavery, wanted only "hot yams and a roof and not to be beaten"; "Emperor" Green, who, in spite of Douglass' logic, says the historic "I b'lieve I go wid de ole man"; Harriet Tubman, the splendid, wanted "dead or alive, and ten thousand dollars would be paid for the body"; William Still, who knew more about the "underground" than any man in the land, saying to Brown "You free them, I'll lead them out"; John Copeland, mulatto student at Oberlin, who left his garret lamp of learning for an even finer light, and Dangerfield Newby, killed in action, with a wife in the far South who was never to be redeemed. All of these are brought to life in a moving book.

Black Thunder (1936) by Arna Bontemps likewise bears witness to a staunch desire to be free—a fact of the Negro's past that most of the historical romancers have not cared to record. *Black Thunder* deals with Gabriel's Rebellion in the Virginia of 1800. Gabriel, the strongest slave of Henrico county, is courageous as well:

> I been studying about freedom a heap, me. I heard a plenty folks talk and I listened a heap. . . . Something keep telling me that anything what's equal to a gray squirrel wants to be free.

Stimulated by the example of Touissant in Haiti and by the propaganda of the *Amis des Noirs* and exasperated by an act of cruelty, Gabriel leads eleven hundred slaves upon Richmond. A storm postpones the

197

attack, and the treachery of Pharaoh and Ben does the rest. The leaders are hanged, Gabriel's sweetheart Juba is sold to the deep South, and Ben goes on driving the cariole for the aristocrats. In addition to Gabriel, other Negroes are excellently characterized: Ben, the docile, gray-headed house-boy; Melody, the quadroon darling of rich planters' sons; Juba, handsome and spirited, sole woman on the march; Mingo, whose personal freedom is not enough; and Bundy, who "kept drinking up all that rum because he couldn't get up enough nerve to make his get-away." *Black Thunder* does not have the urgent passion of *God's Angry Man;* it is elegy rather than a tocsin of revolt, but it is a fine American historical novel.

Realism. In *Look Homeward, Angel* Thomas Wolfe's autobiographical hero decries

> The romantic halo . . . the whole fantastic distortion of that period where people were said to live in mansions and slavery was a benevolent institution, conducted to a constant banjo-strumming, the strewn largesses of the colonel and the shuffle-dance of his happy dependents, where all women were pure, gentle, beautiful, all men chivalrous and brave, and the Rebel horde a company of swagger, death-mocking cavaliers. Years later, when he could no longer think of the barren spiritual wilderness . . . when their cheap mythology, their legend of the charm of their manners, the aristocratic culture . . . made him writhe . . . so great was his fear of the legend, his fear of their antagonism, that he still pretended the most fantastic devotion to them.

Many other southerners of Wolfe's generation, as seen in the previous chapter, have recognized the barren spiritual wilderness; others have repudiated or at least humanized the legend.

John Peale Bishop, although not so outspoken a Wolfe and Faulkner, approaches the legend realistically in *Many Thousands Gone* (1930), stories of the Civil War and postwar years. Just as the southerners are not marvels of gallantry and beauty, the Negroes, while certainly not flattered, are recognizable products of slavery. One old woman while her mistress lies

198

dead is more worried about her promised freedom than grief-stricken; a sullen girl blazes forth her hatred of her carping mistress, and leaves to cook for the Yankees, for whose love-making she has been prepared by her experiences with southern gentlemen. In one symbolic story, Bones, a marvelous cook, gives two old Virginia ladies a feeling of security; in reality a lunatic, he is submissive and devoted, and they are willing to live in terror as long as they can live in the tradition, their dear "obsession."

Christopher Ward's *Jonathan Drew, A Rolling Stone* (1932), and *A Yankee Rover* (1932) carry the Yankee hero all over early nineteenth century America. One dramatic section shows Drew saving two slaves from border ruffians who were running a "blind underground" and fomenting a slave insurrection in order to plunder the countryside. *A Yankee Rover* deals more fully with slavery; one of the episodes involves Tommy, the little "white nigger," whose aristocratic father does not leave him free.

> What d'ye say to a nigger that ain't no color at all cause he's white . . . as white as any on ye an' whiter than most . . . with straight silky hair, no kinks at all, an yaller hair at that, golden yaller, an' blue eyes? Ef that ain't jest a natural curiosity . . . Pass up lot 56, Mr. Barnes.

As we have seen the "blind underground" intrigues both the realists and the defenders of the Old South, who traditionally isolate criminals as the agents of the underground railroad. The "blind underground" did exist as a profitable enterprise for such gangs as Murrell's, but this hardly explains the neglect of the genuine underground that carried thousands of slaves to the North. The workings of this system appear incidentally in MacKinlay Kantor's *Arouse and Beware* (1936). In this impartial and accurate narrative we have most interesting descriptions of the "Right Sort of People," "The Sons of America," both whites and

Negroes, who with their grips and passwords and secret hiding places enable three fugitives to get to the Union lines. One slave woman, in a low tone, gives them valuable information, and then, to fool her curious children, curses them. The narrator says:

> There was a canniness about these slaves which I had never imagined before. I had thought them barbaric or stupid or lazy . . . and doubtless many of them were. And many others, too, were loyal to their masters and the Confederacy; but somehow I cannot hear jubilee singers chanting of Moses, and bondage and their freedom from it, without thinking of this thin, brown-faced wench, with her high shoulders and long straight arms . . .

Andrew Lytle's "Mister McGregor" (1936) is a first-rate story of slavery. Rhears, "no common field-hand, but proud, black and spoiled" had "fretted and sulled" over McGregor's whipping his wife Bella, and rather than run away, he decides to have it out with his owner. In one of the best fights of "frontier" realism, Rhears is stabbed by his master. The teller says of Rhears

> I never seen such guts in nobody, nigger or white man . . . Rhears spoke so low you could hardly hear him: "Marster, if you hadn't got me, I'd a got you."

In Lytle's *The Long Night* (1936) Negroes are only incidental, but the organized stealing of slaves by a band of frontier criminals is important to the plot.

A young southerner muses disgustedly in Evelyn Scott's *Migrations* (1927): "How close we come to the niggers without knowing anything about them." Being aware that merely "coming close" is not knowledge, Mrs. Scott presents convincing Negro characters. Silas is filled with hatred for the white father of his sweetheart Fanny's baby. But conditioned to respect his master, as Fanny had done to her sorrow, he persuades himself that the overseer was responsible. His sullen disobedience causes him to be lashed and he takes to the woods. Bosh is a less successful runaway; a half-wit, he frightens a white girl and is caught by a mob and burned to death. Of a very different type is Eugenia De Negre Blair, a brilliant and handsome adventuress, who has a trace of Negro blood. Without the emphasis of the abolitionists, Mrs. Scott still records the uneasy and tragic aspects of slavery.

In *The Wave* (1929), a series of chronicles of the Civil War, the stories of Eugenia and Silas are continued. One of the best sections shows the Negroes swarming to Sherman's army; Aunt Nancy, to whom the army means food but who has given too much strength to slavery to live to see the promised land of freedom; Dilsy, who hopes that life-long drudgery is over; Lou, apologetic because her religious master had influenced her; Anna, bold and ready; and Uncle Vic, who has been sold to one "mean piece uv trash after another." When the Federals, realizing that the horde of fugitives is more than they bargained for, tear up the pontoon bridges, they discover that the horde still presses on to freedom. "Gawd, you gotta shoot 'em to stop 'em." There is symbolism in both the despairing cry of the Negroes left on the bank: "My home is ovah Jawdon," and the callousness of the Yankee who thinks: "If we could only let them drown. Dam 'em, they get over their Jordan, but we have to carry 'em."

In *A Calendar of Sin* (1931), Mrs. Scott re-creates the Reconstruction: the Klan, determined to return the Negro to slavery—where was the tobacco to come from?—flogging Negroes, destroying schools, hounding Yankees; and the carpet-baggers, more intent on wealth and politics than on helping the impoverished, ignorant and often shiftless Negroes—both pretending high idealism to cover up lurking meanness. Good comedy is in the episode of the old Auntie, who sus-

201

picious of Yankees anyway, leaves the new school in high dudgeon because, instead of learning to read the Bible right-off, she is started on the alphabet. There is a powerful narrative about a mulatto lynched for assault. Some Negroes, taught by "the raw-hide whip on their naked backs" betray the Union League and deny that they want the vote and book-learning. Others show a grasp of the developing folk-belief that everything mean and bad in the South "comes to us fru de Yankees." Although the narratives are called "American Melodramas," Mrs. Scott portrays neither villains nor heroes but sensitively understood human beings. And that is why, for truth to an era and a section, her work is immeasurably superior to such real melodramas as *Gone With the Wind*.

T. S. Stribling's earlier *Birthright* is excelled by his trilogy of a southern family: *The Forge* (1931), *The Store* (1933) and *Unfinished Cathedral* (1934). In *The Forge*, the pictures of slave life and character are among the most convincing in American fiction. The plantation tradition gets short shrift. Old man Vaiden runs a one-horse, two-mule farm, but calls himself a "gentleman" since he owns five Negroes. A hard-fisted, hard drinking, bull-headed, irascible Primitive Baptist, blustering in north Alabama dialect instead of in cultured phrases, he wins some liking, and, more important, is a credible human being. To Vaiden, as to so many farmers "on the make," slavery meant "working the daylight out of slaves." The slaves' food is little more than corn-dodgers and bacon, and the boasted medical care is what "would be given a sick calf." Attached to the family and farm by lifelong ties, the slaves still want freedom. While George is being praised as devoted, he is nursing hatred against his master.

202

Gracie Vaiden stands out. Although friendly with her white half-sisters, she broods over slavery. She feels that the flogging of her husband

transformed her from a kind of tentative wife of Solomon into a brood mare . . . changed Solomon into a stud; and her child, if she and Solomon had a child, into a little animal.

She reasons correctly; she is ravished by Miltiades Vaiden who does not know that he is her half-brother. On the eve of secession she would have been sold to clear up her father's debts if she had not escaped to the Yankee lines. Stribling's pictures of the Reconstruction, especially of the Klan, are likewise unorthodox and authentic.

In *The Store* Gracie Vaiden, who has been the mistress first of the Yankee lieutenant who becomes govenor of Alabama, and then of a white merchant, a pillar of the church, works so that her octoroon son can escape the shame she has met with as a Negro. From the start, however, we see that Touissaint is doomed. "The most despisable nigger in Florence,' he will not run from bullying white boys, hates shining shoes, and insists upon honest dealing in the store, standing up for a whole pound when "everybody knows a nigger pound is about twelve ounces." Come of age, he tries to vote, but his blue eyes and blond hair do not prove that his grandfather was free; and he fights a "cracker" who insults his mother. Just as his mother was put on the block because her white half-sisters and brothers ran up bills at the store, so Touissaint loses all of his year's work because his landlord (and father) messes up a business deal. As an end to his rebellious career he is lynched. While Gracie is cutting down his body, "A dozen drunken voices in the mob broke into laughter at the downfall of the Negro mother and her dead son." His father furnishes the mules and wagon to carry him away. Other Negro characters are surly, cunning and aware of what is being done to them: "If dey shawt weight you too much, wras'le wid de Lawd about hit in prayah" . . . "If a white man di'n fly into uh niggah tull he done somepin to him, all us niggahs be settin' in easy chairs." Stribling presents with fine sympathy the Negro urchin who announced the miracle: "I can write my name . . ." Lucy, Touissaint's wife, prefers farming to domestic service. She thereby astounds the ex-planters to whom these "uppish" Negroes who want independence and education are "unnatural, highly affected and utterly absurd . . . the new uncomfortable colored people."

In *Unfinished Cathedral* the Negro characters are shown to be more and more progressive and educated, but still subjected to indecency from both upper-class and hoodlum whites. Militant Negroes are now in the picture; even beneath their grotesque robes, the lodge brothers carry guns. There is a frame-up very similar to the Scottsboro case; the bankers, realtors, sheriffs, judges, and even clergy are shown to be closely related to lynching mobs. One of the boys hustled off a train is Gracie's great-grandson. To Miltiades Vaiden, now eminently respectable, Gracie cries out:

> What colored relations? I was born to my mother, old Hannah, long after Old Pap sold off her husband Jericho! I'm not white for nothing! Aunt Creasy told me long ago that my father was Old Pap, the same as yours! Toussaint, the son I had by you, was nothing but a Vaiden on both sides. The child Lucy had by Toussaint, the son you hanged, I named Marcia; and Marcia's boy you're holding in jail this minute. Who would my grandchild come back to see except white people, Miltiades?

To these words the old Colonel replies: "Shame on you, Gracie . . . talking disrespectfully like this." In spite of some faults, such as the stretched coincidences, this trilogy is remarkable for the honesty, courage and sympathy with which a southern author has faced the past.

William Faulkner's "The Raid" (1934) describes the blowing up of the bridges to destroy the Negroes following Sherman's army, a scene relished by southerners as symbolic, but the slave boy Ringo and the doggedly marching contrabands are excellently done. Thoroughly conversant with the old South, Faulkner has created in *Absalom, Absalom!* (1936) a credible and powerful, if at times fantastic novel out of "a few old mouth-to-mouth tales" and old letters. From the bleak hills of western Virginia where the cabins were "boiling with children," Thomas Sutpen comes to frontier Mississippi, "a country of lawless opportunity." Naked, plastered over with muck against mosquitoes, he and his "wild Negroes tore a plantation out of the wilderness . . . dragged a house and garden out of the virgin swamp." But the Sutpen line is doomed. Charles Bon, Sutpen's son by a woman in Haiti, who was discarded because she had a "spot of Negro blood," is murdered to keep him from marrying Sutpen's daughter (the incest was less abhorred than the miscegenation). The Sutpen fortunes decline, until at the last we see Jim Bond, Charles Bon's mulattto grandson, lurking around the ashes of the destroyed mansion. A Mississippi "Fall of the House of Usher," *Absalom, Absalom!* seems in part an allegory of slavery. Negro characters, whether the savages so like their wild master, or Clytie, Sutpen's mulatto daughter, who could be neither tamed nor freed, or Charles Bon, most elegant cavalier and yet of Negro blood; or Charles' son, who in self-laceration turns completely to Negroes, are original and convincing, "living creatures, living flesh to feel pain and writhe and cry out."

205

Conclusion. A northerner in *Absalom, Absalom!* ironical at the tyranny of the southern legends, says:

> What is it? Something you live and breathe in like air? . . . A kind of entailed birthright . . . of never forgiving General Sherman, so that forevermore as long as your children's children produce children you won't be anything but a descendant of a long line of colonels killed in Pickett's charge at Manassas?

Faulkner himself has felt the fascination of the plantation birthright, but he determined to be honest in spite of tradition. Of a different order of genius, he still belongs with his fellow southerners Stribling and Evelyn Scott, who are trying above all else to give a truthful reinterpretation of the old South, and therefore of the Negro. Their work is by no means completely adequate, but together with the work of other honest, sympathetic writers, northern and southern, Negro and white, historical novelists or recorders o contemporary America, it gives promise that the Negro character in fiction may meet with the justice that has been so long deferred.

DISCUSSION QUESTIONS

1. Since slavery has been abolished, what social policy is served by the continued defense of the plantation tradition?

2. List similar characters and incidents in the plantation tradition novels of this chapter.

3. Describe the antislavery heroes mentioned as the plantation tradition would characterize them.

4. Why are so many southern aristocrats in these books shown as opponents of slavery?

5. Account for the best-selling qualities of *So Red the Rose* and *Gone With The Wind*.

6. Defend, attack, or qualify: "Since these historical romances are based on research, they must be truthful about Negro life and character."

206

7. What are the contributions of Stribling and Evelyn Scott to the southern historical novel?

SELECTED READING LIST

Books

1. Barton, Rebecca Chalmers: *Race Consciousness and The American Negro*—Arnold Busck, Copenhagen—1934.
2. Boynton, Percy H.: *Literature and American Life*—Ginn & Co., New York—1936.
3. Brawley, Benjamin Griffith: *The Negro in Literature and Art*—Duffield and Co., New York—1929, revised and enlarged to *The Negro Genius*—Dodd, Mead & Co., New York—1937.
4. Calverton, V. F.: *The Liberation of American Literature*—Chas. Scribner's Sons, New York—1932.
5. DuBois, W. E. B.: *The Gift of Black Folk*—The Stratford Co., Boston—1924.
6. Edgar, Pelham: *The Art of the Novel*—The Macmillan Co., New York—1933.
7. Ford, Nick Aaron: *The Contemporary Negro Novel*—Meador Co., Boston—1936.
8. Gaines, Francis Pendleton: *The Southern Plantation*—Columbia University Press, New York—1925.
9. Green, Elizabeth Lay: *The Negro in Contemporary American Literature*—The University of North Carolina Press, Chapel Hill —1928.
10. Hartwick, Harry: *The Foreground of American Fiction*—American Book Co., New York—1934.
11. Hatcher, Harlan: *Creating The Modern American Novel*—Farrar and Rinehart, New York—1935.
12. Hicks, Granville: *The Great Tradition*—The Macmillan Co., New York—1933.
13. Lewissohn, Ludwig: *Expression In America*—Harper & Bros., New York—1932.
14. Linn, James Weber, and Taylor, Houghton Wells: *A Foreword to Fiction*—D. Appleton-Century Co., New York—1935.
15. Locke, Alain: *The New Negro*—A. & C. Boni, New York—1925.
16. Loggins, Vernon: *The Negro Author*—Columbia University Press, New York—1931.
17. Loggins, Vernon: *I Hear America*—Thomas Y. Crowell Co., New York—1937.
18. Nelson, John Herbert: *The Negro Character In American Literature*—University of Kansas, Lawrence—1926.
19. Parrington, V. F.: *Main Currents in American Thought*—Harcourt, Brace & Co., New York—1930.
20. Pattee, Fred Lewis: *The Development of the American Short Story* —Harper & Bros., New York—1923.
21. Pattee, Fred Lewis: *The First Century of American Literature, 1770-1870*—D. Appleton, Century Co., New York—1935.
22. Pattee, Fred Lewis: *A History of American Literature Since 1870* —The Century Co., New York—1915.

23. Quinn, Arthur Hobson: *American Fiction*—D. Appleton, Century Co., New York—1936.
24. Turner, Lorenzo Dow: *Anti-slavery Sentiment in American Literature Prior to 1865*—The Association for the Study of Negro Life and History, Inc., Washington—1929.
25. Van Doren, Carl: *The American Novel*—The Macmillan Co., New York—1931.

Articles

1. Braithwaite, William Stanley: "The Negro In American Literature" in *The New Negro*, edited by Alain Locke—A. & C. Boni, New York—1925.
2. Brawley, Benjamin Griffith: "The Negro In American Fiction" in *Anthology of American Negro Literature*, edited by V. F. Calverton—The Modern Library, New York—1929.
3. Brown, Sterling A.: "Negro Characters As Seen By White Authors" in *Journal of Negro Education* (April, 1933),—Howard University, Washington, D. C.
4. Brown, Sterling A.: "Our Literary Audience" in *Opportunity, a Journal of Negro Life*, February, 1930.
5. Brown, Sterling A.: "The Literary Scene: Chronicle and Comment" in *Opportunity, a Journal of Negro Life* from 1930–36.
6. Burke, Kenneth: "The Negro's Pattern of Life" in *The Saturday Review of Literature*, July 29, 1933.
7. Chamberlain, John: "The Negro As Writer" in *The Bookman*, Vol. LXX, February, 1930.
8. Clay, Eugene: "The Negro In Recent American Literature" in *American Writers' Congress*, edited by Henry Hart—International Publishers, Inc., New York—1935.
9. Davidson, Donald: "The Trend of Literature" in *Culture In The South*, edited by W. T. Couch—University of North Carolina Press, Chapel Hill—1935.
10. Davis, Allison: "Our Negro Intellectuals" in *The Crisis*, August, 1928.
11. Farrell, James T.: "The Short Story" in *American Writers' Congress*, edited by Henry Hart—International Publishers, Inc., New York—1935.
12. Gordon, Eugene: "Social and Political Problems of the Negro Writer" in *American Writers' Congress*, edited by Henry Hart—International Publishers, Inc., New York—1935.
13. Gruening, Martha: "The Negro Renaissance" in *Hound and Horn*, April-June, 1932.
14. Johnson, Guy: "Folk Values in Recent Literature on the Negro" in *Folk-Say*, edited by B. A. Botkin—University of Oklahoma Press, Norman—1930.
15. Locke, Alain: "The Negro's Contribution to American Art and Literature" in *The Annals of the American Academy of Political and Social Science*, Vol. CXXXX, November, 1928.
16. Locke, Alain: "Negro Youth Speaks" in *The New Negro*, edited by Alain Locke—A. & C. Boni, New York—1925.
17. Locke, Alain: "Retrospective Reviews" (annual surveys of books in *Opportunity, a Journal of Negro Life*, from 1929 to date.)

208

18. T. K. Whipple: "The Negro and Modern Literature" in *Creative Reading*, Vol. III, No. 11, Institute of Current Literature, Cambridge, Mass.—1929.
19. White, Walter: "Negro Literature" in *American Writers On American Literature*, edited by John Macy—Horace Liveright, Inc., New York—1931.
20. Woodson, Carter G.: "The Negro and American Literature" in *The African Background Outlined* by Carter G. Woodson—The Association For The Study of Negro Life and History, Washington, D. C.—1936.
21. Wright, Richard: "Blueprint for Negro Writing" in *New Challenge*, Fall, 1937.

209

Atheneum Paperbacks

STUDIES IN AMERICAN NEGRO LIFE

Atheneum Paperbacks

HISTORY—AMERICAN—1900 TO THE PRESENT

Atheneum Paperbacks

HISTORY

HISTORY—ASIA

Atheneum Paperbacks

LAW AND GOVERNMENT

DIPLOMACY AND INTERNATIONAL RELATIONS

Atheneum Paperbacks

Atheneum Paperbacks

THE WORLDS OF NATURE AND MAN

LITERATURE AND THE ARTS